MW01630992

Photo by Lynn Gregg

Photo by Matt Howard

This is the authorized story of my career, written by biographer and sports historian Richard Bak. Michael and Del Reddy of Immortal Investments Publishing produced it along with Dr. Bob Suchyta.

Norbert Schemansky

World's Heavyweight Champion

MR. WEIGHTLIFTING

Norbert Schemansky

www.immortalinvestments.com

www.norbertschemansky.com

[illegible]

Michael and Del Reddy of Immortal Investments Publishing proudly present

MR. WEIGHTLIFTING

Norbert Schemansky

History's Greatest Olympic & World Champion Heavyweight Lifter

Richard Bak

Foreword by

Al Oerter

Immortal Investments Publishing
Wayne, Michigan
1-800-497-1035
www.immortalinvestments.com

Publishers, Michael and Del Reddy
Editors, Lynn Gregg and John Makar
Book Formatter, Deb Tremper, Six Penny Graphics
Photo Formatters, Deb Tremper and Warren Parker
Book Cover Design, Barb Gunia

Special thanks to Jean Schroeder of Sheridan Books,
Jennifer Moitozo of Immortal Investments Publishing,
Joe Puleo, and Dr. Bob Suchyta

Mr. Weightlifting Norbert Schemansky, History's Greatest Olympic and World Champion Heavyweight Lifter
is published by
Immortal Investments Publishing, LLC.
35122 W. Michigan Avenue, Wayne, Michigan 48184
1-800-497-1035

First Edition
February 2007
ISBN: 978-0-9723637-8-5

Publisher's Cataloging-In-Publication Data
(Prepared by The Donohue Group, Inc.)

Bak, Richard, 1954-
Mr. Weightlifting, Norbert Schemansky : history's greatest Olympic and world champion heavyweight lifter / by Richard Bak. -- 1st ed.

p. ; cm.

Includes bibliographical references and index.
ISBN: 978-0-9723637-8-5

1. Schemansky, Norbert. 2. Weight lifters--United States--Biography.
I. Title.

GV545.52.S34 B35 2007
796.41/092
2005938647

Contents

This book is dedicated

to the memory of

Bernice Schemansky,

"Olympic wife"

Norb and Bernice hold Norb's trophy after he was crowned the 1964 United States Heavyweight Champion.

Introduction

What Muhammad Ali and Joe Louis are to boxing, what John Grimek and Arnold Schwarzenegger mean to bodybuilding, and what Gordie Howe and Wayne Gretzky represent in hockey, Norbert Schemansky is to Olympic weightlifting. Like these champions, Norb never liked to lose. A good thing for him, then, that he rarely did.

In a career spanning nearly three decades, the quiet, bespectacled weightlifter from Detroit brought home more than 300 trophies and medals. He earned the respect and admiration from enthusiasts around the globe while bringing glory and honor to the United States of America. He won titles at numerous national and international tournaments, where the competition was the toughest, and along the way set an amazing 75 world, national and Olympic records. By the time he retired in 1968 Schemansky had been crowned world champion four times, U.S. champion nine times, and North American champion seven times. His most impressive feat was earning what was then an unprecedented four Olympic medals in four separate Olympic games. The last two came after weightlifting's "miracle man" had astounded doctors and other doubters by bouncing back from a pair of crippling back injuries. It remains one of the most sensational comebacks in sports history. Schemansky's final medal came at the 1964 Games in Tokyo when he was 40 years old—an achievement still recorded on the pages of the *Guinness Book of World Records*. During his prime the indomitable heavyweight was heralded as "the world's strongest man" and his chiseled physique was considered the finest to be found on any podium on the planet. Remarkably, he did it all without the aid of amphetamines or steroids, pharmaceutical crutches that many top lifters and bodybuilders secretly depended on. In 2005, Schemansky—along with a select few others—was named the best weightlifter of the past 100 years by the International Weightlifting Federation. This was just the most recent accolade honoring the career of one of the world's greatest, most inspirational—and at the same time, least known—athletes.

In *Mr. Weightlifting*, published by Michael and Del Reddy of Immortal Investments, biographer and sports historian Richard Bak delivers the first book-length narrative of Norb Schemansky's incredible amateur career, beginning with his first lifts inside a makeshift Detroit gym during the Great Depression and continuing through his status as the iconic linchpin of American weightlifting. Although the sport barely registers on the radar for most Americans, Olympic weightlifting has traditionally been considered *the* sport in many countries, especially in Russia and Eastern Europe. During Schemansky's time it consisted of the three so-called Olympic lifts—the press, the snatch, and the clean & jerk. Lifting hundreds of pounds of iron overhead puts a premium on strength, speed, and agility, all of which the uniquely gifted Schemansky, America's greatest strength athlete, possessed in abundance.

"Skee," as the third-generation Polish-American was called by friends, was a central figure in what has come to be known as the golden age of U.S. weightlifting. This era of the 1940s and 1950s coincided with the deepening freeze of the Cold War. Individual strength was the most widely admired virtue in Soviet Bloc countries, so for the first time lifting platforms in Helsinki, Stockholm, and Rome became surrogate battlefields for the world's two superpowers. In *Mr. Weightlifting*, Schemansky's dramatic rivalries with Soviet national heroes Grigori Novak and Yuri Vlasov are fully documented. The author describes how Schemansky's performances made him a household word throughout Europe and Russia, while back home in America the general public remained largely unaware of his astonishing accomplishments.

Drawing upon scores of archival sources and featuring interviews with contemporaries like Tommy Kono, Jim Bradford, Pete George, Ike Berger, and Frank Spellman, *Mr. Weightlifting* brings to life the obscure but compelling sport of Olympic lifting and many of its most storied legends and moments. Readers are introduced to Bob Hoffman, the fitness mogul and financial angel of U.S. lifting; John Davis, the chain-smoking heavyweight and first great African-American champion; and Paul Anderson, the ungainly country boy with superhuman strength. Readers are transported back in time to the scenes of Schemansky's greatest triumphs. They are there in Helsinki in 1952, when Schemansky broke the Russians' hearts by beating the "invincible" Grigori Novak for the Olympic gold medal. They are there in Paris in 1954, when

Schemansky hoisted the fabled Apollon bell—actually, a misshapen set of railroad wheels—with an ease that left spectators gasping in disbelief and, fifty years later, is recognized as one of the greatest lifts of all-time. And they are there in Budapest in 1962, when Yuri Vlasov's infamous "double-dip" robbed the aging warhorse of American lifting of one last world title.

Schemansky's life outside of competition is also fully fleshed out. His blue-collar upbringing…his three years of wartime service (he earned five battle stars as an "ack-ack" gunner in England, France, Germany, and Belgium during World War II)…his financial woes as he continually battled unsympathetic employers and inept officials of the Amateur Athletic Union, all of whom gloried in his victories while simultaneously depriving him of making a decent living…his unaffected manner and unexpected dry wit…and his loving relationship with Bernice, his unbelievably supportive wife of 49 years, and their four children, Pam, Paula, Larry, and Laura.

For nearly 30 years he mesmerized and astounded fans around the globe with his unconquerable spirit, his awe-inspiring athleticism, and his indefatigable grit and determination. *Mr. Weightlifting* is much more than a tale of cold iron plates and dank gyms. It's a story of the triumph of the human spirit, of a stubborn drive for excellence that propelled one man to the very top—where, in the eyes of weightlifting aficionados, he remains to this day.

Journalist and author Richard Bak grew up in Detroit and graduated from Eastern Michigan University. He has written more than 20 books, including biographies of Joe Louis, Ty Cobb, Charles Lindbergh, and Henry and Edsel Ford. Bak also wrote and co-produced *Stranded at the Corner*, the award-winning documentary about the fight to preserve Detroit's historic Tiger Stadium.

Immortal Investments Publishers Michael and Del Reddy are visionaries in the volatile world of book publishing. Shunning the traditional mode of selling books primarily through book stores, the innovative father-son team pioneered the method of distributing their book titles through special direct marketing channels. Via unique partnerships, they help maximize distribution and income for the authors and athletes while also assisting a number of charitable organizations. The books published by Immortal Investments are not distributed through book store chains, are highly inspirational and are genuine collector's items.

Foreword

by Al Oerter

This is a helluva way to start a foreword, but I never met Norbert Schemansky. I know he lived in Detroit, but I have no idea of where he trained, what motivated him, or anything about his personal life that led him to become a champion in every sense of the word. Nonetheless, he was and is a hero to many people around the globe—and that includes me.

I'm certain all of the lifting places around the world in the 1930s, '40s and '50s shared similar characteristics. These were not health spas, fitness centers or even gyms, but rather dungeons where humans worked at one thing: creating greater strength. These dungeons were dimly lit with an abundance of steel bars and cast iron plates and not much else. There were few if any mirrors, no air conditioning, no showers (clean or not), and no people wearing spandex. No one cared if you sweated on the bars and there were no personal trainers exhorting their clients to do one more rep or to add one more pound. There were no pin-select machines; if you wanted to add weight you had to lift the damn bar to slide on another 45 pounds. If there was a lifting platform, it normally consisted of a couple of one-inch slabs of plywood. All the same, these primitive facilities were like a slice of Heaven to strength athletes like Norb and me.

I first became aware of Norbert's capability through the many articles about him in *Strength & Health, Iron Man,* and other physical culture magazines. The photo of Norbert in that deep split after hauling an incredible weight to his shoulders was taped to the wall of my father's garage, where I first started trying to emulate Norbert. To rise with that weight and then jerk it seemed an impossibility, but "Skee" did it over and over again.

I don't know exactly how many world records Norb set, but it was a bunch, with most of them occurring at large international competitions. Don't forget these lifts were accomplished in the era before steroids, corporate support, and training centers where athletes were housed and fed with national coaches advising them. One article from back then immediately comes to mind. That one described Norbert playing with the Apollon railway wheels, a challenging 366-pound weight that he handled like a toy. He not only raised it overhead several times, he forced the Frenchmen who owned the device to retire it forever.

One of Norb's published statements was, "If you can't get it done in 45 minutes, you can't get it done." That pithy quote also was taped to the garage wall. It simply meant: "No looking in the mirrors, no gassing with other lifters, just put your hands on the bar and pull for all your worth." This is a lunch-pail work ethic and one that should be followed by every athlete today that seeks to improve strength levels.

Norbert, who overcame major back surgeries to compete and win at the highest international levels, was a hero to me as I battled through a serious car accident and several injuries en route to fulfilling my own Olympic dreams. In that sense he was more than a lifter; he was an inspiration. To three generations of strength athletes, Norbert Schemansky is "Mr. Weightlifting." To me that is a title above that of doctor, congressman or senator.

Al Oerter

Discus thrower Al Oerter grew up in New York and attended the University of Kansas. He was the first track and field athlete to win the gold medal in four consecutive Olympics (1956, 1960, 1964, and 1968). Today Al is an accomplished painter. He and his wife, Cathy, travel the world exhibiting his artwork in prominent galleries and museums. www.aloerter.com.

Tributes to Mr. Weightlifting Norbert Schemansky

Norb was the greatest competitor you could find. He was one of the best—if not the greatest—when it came to lifting at world championships. Norb wouldn't shy away from anybody. I've always felt that he should have had another world championship title if Yuri Vlasov's double dip for the jerk was not passed at the 1962 World Championships in Budapest. Norb had him scared after the press and snatch and that made Vlasov miscue on the jerk, but the referees passed it. It robbed Norb of the title.

Norb lived for weightlifting. He was a great lifter, a true amateur, and a terrific fighter who never minded being the underdog

Tommy Kono, Two-time Olympic Weightlifting Gold Medalist

He was the best there ever was in the split snatch. None better. His 1,200 total at the time truly was an amazing accomplishment.

Vic Seipke, Junior Mr. America 1955

He was amazing. Skee was really a phenomenon who was as great as the big-name athletes in other sports like Joe Montana and Johnny Unitas. He was as great an athlete as those guys—no doubt about it.

Sid Henry, 1963 U.S. National Weightlifting Champion

Norb could be the Apollo on the statue. He looked terrific physically and represented the country so well. He was a terrific tactician with great body structure. I witnessed some of his amazing world record lifts.

Clyde Emrich, Four-time U.S. National Weightlifting Champion

He is number one in everybody's book. I believe Norb could have been the world champion boxer if he took up the sport. Great determination, tremendous ability, remarkable dedication, and guts are all hallmarks of Norb. Simply, he is in a class by himself.

Joe Pitman, Ten-time U.S. National Weightlifting Champion, 1948 Olympic Team

I always admired Norb as a champion. He is one of my all-time favorites because I did some Olympic lifting early in my career. He truly is an inspiration to me and to many others.

Frank Zane, Mr. Universe, Mr. America, Mr. Olympia

Skee is the real deal in today's fraudulent sport's world. His dedication and longevity of excellence is unprecedented. Truly, he is weightlifting's ultimate superman. I have been an avid follower of sports for over six decades and I believe, that pound for pound, he is the strongest man who ever lived.

John Turner Reddy, Former gym owner, Canton, Michigan

Schemansky could have been the champion body builder of the world if he had chosen that path. He was Herculean with his physique of all muscle and no fat. Norb is one of my all-time idols.

Harry Johnson, Mr. America 1959

Schemansky is just incredible. He could be so funny with his deadpan delivery. He and Kono were American lifting.

Louis Riecke, 1964 U.S. Olympic Weightlifting Team

Schemansky is a fantastic weightlifting champion and a superb, awesome strength athlete. Norb is the Gordie Howe and Jim Brown of our sport. You talk to any weightlifting expert on the international level and he is right there at the top. He is as good as they get.

Jim Schmitz, 1980, 1988 U.S. Olympic Weightlifting Team Coach

Before I was born, Norb was lifting weights competitively. A quarter of a century later, he retired from competing, but during that span, he remained among the most interesting, colorful, and determined lifters that ever handled the trio of lifts popular in his day. He had no room for nonsense, or excuses, or whining—from himself or others. Get into the gym, lift the weights, and try to lift heavier than last week.

In those days, lifters and bodybuilders, with a few exceptions, had no use for each other, and certainly no desire to cross genres. Lifters saw no point in looking strong if you weren't strong, and bodybuilders saw no compelling benefit to being strong if you looked fat, or for that matter, looked frail. Norb looked strong, and in certain phases of his career had a substantially well-formed physique, which never included chiseled abs but did include the unmistakable aura of muscularity and power. He was a gentle giant, but one who should be left unprovoked.

Norb had the misfortune to be lifting in the early to mid-1950s when Paul Anderson's 300-plus pounds outweighed Norb by more than Norb outweighed the lightest man in any competition. That he could remain competitive, or even motivated, was amazing. No doubt, his realism would say "You play the hand you are dealt". Indeed, and in deed, he did.

Joe Roark, IFBB men's historian, Ironhistory.com

There are those who have argued that many of the greats of weightlifting history, like Norbert Schemansky, have been forgotten, along with the greats in many other sports and human endeavors. Many of today's young people may well have never heard of Aristotle, Lou Gehrig or Norb Schemansky. However, this book provides a remedy for those who have never heard the name "Schemansky". Once those young men and women have read his story, they will never forget it, nor will they ever cease to be uplifted by this story.

His story illustrates the human spirit at its finest, a spirit driven by a special intelligence, an unique devotion, an unrelenting focus and an unstoppable spirit.

Artie Drechsler, author, *The Weightlifting Encyclopedia*

The international press recognized Norbert Schemansky as America's greatest individual Olympic champion. He showed the world that individual human achievement is honorable in our society, even if not rewarded economically. At 40 years of age, he was the oldest Olympic medal winner at the 1964 Tokyo Olympics, competing against the strongest heavyweights in history, all youths in their 20s. He is the last of the rugged individualists who won the world and Olympic heavyweight championship by sheer guts alone and in spite of all the obstacles of poverty and lack of social and economic rewards. To honor him is to honor pure human achievement.

Jack Katchmar, American Scientific Technical Research, Inc.

Norbert Schemansky is a decorated World War II veteran, a generous and dedicated citizen, and a man of quiet dignity. His strengths are beyond world championships and Olympic medals. He is a pleasure to know and a beacon of hope in today's world.

Helen K. Mamalakis, Archives specialist and author,
Dearborn Historical Museum

Norb is likely the greatest champion we have ever had in our sport. He was a fierce competitor with extraordinary concentration. No doubt about it, he is one of my all time heroes.

Joe Dube, 1969 Senior World Weightlifting Champion

I'm ninety years old—the oldest living former Mr. America—and I have seen first hand the greats of the iron game ranging from John Grimek to Arnold Schwarzenegger. All of us at York Barbell admired him; this includes me, John Grimek, and Steve Stanko. Bob Hoffman thought he was just phenomenal. I was there from day one when Norb began his career. In many parts of the world, your strength and what you can lift overhead is what is admired most. Norb lifted more than anybody else. Without a doubt, Norb was the greatest lifter that I've ever seen in my life.

Jules Bacon, IFBB Hall of Fame, 1943 Mr. America

Norb was ahead of his time. I lifted with him at a number of meets and he was so impressive physically because of the thickness of his muscles; he was as solid as a rock.

Joe Abbenda, 1962 Mr. Universe, Olympic weightlifter

We have been privileged to publish outstanding biographies of sports legends Colleen and Gordie Howe, Otto Graham, Eddie Feigner and others. Of all these books, Norb's is the most compelling. "Skee" is surely one of the greatest athletes of all time. Equally impressive is that he remained a true amateur his entire career and that his greatest supporters were his late wife Bernice and their four children. We predict that Norb's story will become a major motion picture and that the incredible saga of Mr. Weightlifting will inspire people now and in future generations.

Michael and Del Reddy, Publishers, Immortal Investments Publishing

Norb's years of competition will never be forgotten. Few athletes in the history of sports had his will and determination. He lived with pain and trained with the guts few men possessed. Nobody would break Anderson's records—they claimed—and he did at almost forty years of age! He never got the recognition he deserved, but he is the greatest heavyweight lifter in USA history!

Herb Glossbrenner, Publisher, *International Olympic Lifter Magazine*

CHAPTER ONE

Iroquois Street

Remember I am of Polish descent. I am an American and proud of it. Everybody knows that a man with Polish blood in his veins never gives up without a battle and an American accepts all challenges no matter how big or small.

Norb Schemansky

Some of the old familiar houses on Iroquois Street in Detroit still stand, in the way that a badly beaten prizefighter struggles to stay erect after surviving to the final bell—in shambles, wobbly and hollow-eyed, gamely hanging on to the last remnants of dignity. The once-bustling eastside neighborhood, previously home to solid working-class families of Polish, Lithuanian, and Ukrainian descent, is now largely emptied of promise. On a still day the roar from the nearby Edsel Ford Freeway, one of several expressways that helped destroy the homogeneity of the city in the 1950s, hangs like a dirty whisper in the air. The General Motors Cadillac Assembly Plant—better known as "Poletown" in recognition of the predominantly Polish community the sprawling factory displaced when it was built in the 1980s—is a couple of miles to the west. Taken collectively, this part of town can be considered the quintessential Rust Belt urban landscape—bleak, blue collar, blah.

Today, many miles and years removed from his roots, Norb Schemansky doesn't remember the old neighborhood quite this way. He grew up in the years between the two world wars in a two-story frame house at 6469 Iroquois, near Harper and Gratiot. Back then the sidewalks and streets hummed with activity and every corner had a store, church or bar. His was a typical Polish-American household of the time, with three generations jammed under one roof: several kids, mom, dad, and grandma. The boys all slept upstairs in the attic bedroom, where a small pot-bellied stove provided warmth in winter and a little back porch offered some relief on stuffy summer nights. Nobody had air conditioning then, so heat waves would find the Schemanskys and others throughout Detroit sleeping on their lawns or in city parks. "Can you imagine people doing that today?" he said. "It was a whole different era then, a whole different city." It was the kind of city that acted like a magnet to generations of immigrants, including Norb's paternal grandfather, Charles Szymanski.

Charles emigrated to the United States as a child, part of the wave of two million Poles who came to America between 1870 and 1920. The family settled in Posen, Michigan, a village founded in the 1870s by immigrants from a district of German-controlled Poland of the same name. The community, located about fifteen miles southeast of Rogers City, is best known today for its annual potato festival. In the 1870s, though, timber still was the dominant industry. Charles was only seventeen when he married Mary Guenther, a fifteen-year-old Wisconsin native, in 1887. Large families were the norm then, especially among Polish Catholics, who tended to be more attentive to the church's prohibition of birth control methods of any kind. Mary had thirteen children, of which Joseph—born in 1890—was the third.

Joseph Szymanski grew into a sturdy young man who was good with his hands. Somewhere along the line he (or possibly an employer) Anglicized his name to its phonetic spelling, Schemansky. In an era ripe with anti-Polish sentiment, a couple of Joseph's younger brothers went even further, changing their surname from Syzmanski to something more "American": Sherman.

At some point in the years leading up to World War I, Joseph Schemansky traveled the nearly 300 miles from drowsy Posen to dynamic Detroit. After all this time nobody can say for sure what compelled Joseph. He may have come on his own, a young man lured by the prospect of Henry Ford's "five-dollar day," an unheard-of sum for manual labor. Or his father, Charles, may have moved the family when the children were small, figuring the city was a welcome alternative to the limited opportunities of Posen, where the lumber was played out and the rocky limestone fields yielded a few potatoes, little money, and even less excitement. To a smitten young woman named Josephine Idalski, it really didn't matter why or when Joseph Schemansky came to Detroit, just that he did. They were married one day in early 1915 and immediately began raising a family.

Over the course of the next dozen or so years, Josephine gave birth to four boys and four girls. Eleanor, born in 1915, was the first. She was followed by Dennis (1916), Ralph (1919), Esther (1921), Lillian (1923), Norbert (1924), Jerome (1926), and Rita (1928). A ninth child, an unnamed boy, died shortly after birth. They grew up in the house on Iroquois Street, a dwelling that Joseph and his father built.

Norbert Schemansky came along on May 30, 1924—a good-sized baby, but nothing out of the ordinary. Certainly there was nothing to suggest one of history's greatest athletes had arrived. Indeed, Norb came into the world saddled with what proved a lifelong affliction: bad eyesight.

"My right eye was cock-eyed and weak," he explained. "They tried all these remedies from the old country—putting tea bags over it, or putting a patch over my eye with a pinhole through it."

Finally, when Norb was four years old, he got his first pair of glasses. He took one step back, decided he didn't like them, and threw them on the ground. The inevitable teasing and fights soon followed. Little Norb was called "Four Eyes" and "Cock-eyed."

Fighting didn't bother the bespectacled and vulnerable looking youngster. More often than not, he gave as good as he got. Scraps were part of growing up. "I remember once when I was about twelve or thirteen, this kid, Eddie, started picking on me in an alley," said Norb. "He was a year or two older than me. All of a sudden I saw my older brother, Ralph, coming our way, so I got brave. I started punching Eddie, figuring Ralph would see what was going on and save me."

This plan, as adolescent plans often do, went awry. "Ralph stopped, all right, but all he did was stand and watch." Left on his own, Norb gave a good accounting of himself before honorably disengaging. "Seems now like somebody was always chasing me," he said with a laugh.

Norb's father, Joseph Schemansky, was listed in city directories as a "builder," a catch-all term for a man who, like his own father, was basically a self-taught carpenter and a jack-of-all-trades. Certainly there was plenty of sawing and hammering going on in Detroit, a boom town thanks to the flourishing auto industry. In the quarter-century between 1899, the year Ransom Olds opened Detroit's first car factory, and 1924, when newborn Norb swelled the city's population by one, Detroit exploded in size and importance. During this period the emerging Motor City grew into the country's fourth largest city. Its million-plus citizens—three-quarters of whom were either immigrants or first-generation Americans—babbled in dozens of tongues as they built runabouts and flivvers during the day, jammed into boardinghouses and bungalows at night, and on their Sunday sojourns craned their necks to gaze with wonder at the latest skyscraper or church steeple climbing higher, ever higher, into the smudged sky draped over this industrial behemoth.

Joseph Schemansky always managed to find plenty of work, recalled Norb, even when times got tough in the dirty '30s.

"My dad was pretty strict," he said. "We hardly saw him around the house. He was always working. There was not too much of a connection. In fact, we hardly ever had a conversation. There was no time for discussion. He'd say something like 'We're going fishing at 4:30 tomorrow morning' and that was it. You just did it."

Mom was more approachable, if for no other reason than she was always home, trying her best to keep from being overwhelmed by the demands of a large family. Sophie Idalski, Norb's maternal *babcia* (grandmother), finally moved in to help out. "Seemed like my mom was always ironing and cooking," said Norb. "She was a hard worker. I can remember the clothes boiling away inside a copper kettle, and how she'd make *paczki*—you know, those Polish jelly doughnuts—by bobbing them in hot grease. When I was small, I'd stand on a chair in the kitchen and eat apple peelings while I watched her make apple pies."

Esther (Schemansky) Zoran, three years older than Norb, is his sole remaining sibling. At eighty-four, she is feisty and stubbornly independent, choosing to live alone in her suburban Detroit home despite being legally blind. According to Esther, mom could be as big a disciplinarian as dad. "At dinner we all had to sit at the table and be quiet. When food came around you took it because it was not going to come around again."

Although's Esther's memory has dimmed over the decades, she also recalled the time she, Norb, Ralph, and Lillian had their tonsils removed together. "We all had them taken out at the same time at Children's Hospital downtown," she said. "The four of us occupied a whole four-bed ward. Norb was the youngest; he was about five or six. I can still picture him sitting there on a stool, looking so pitiful."

Norb wouldn't describe his childhood as idyllic, but in retrospect it sure was less stressful than adulthood would prove to be. Between school and chores around the house there still was plenty of time to just be a kid. There were long walks to Belle Isle, river rides on the Bob-lo boat and cowboy movies for a nickel at the Crane Theatre on Harper. The Eastown Theatre at Van Dyke and Harper was a larger and nicer movie house to try to sneak into. Failing that, there were always pick-up baseball games. "You'd walk down the street, thumping your bat on the ground," he said. "By the time you got to the end of the block you had four to six kids." Occasionally they'd swipe some potatoes from the corner store. "We'd roast 'em in a ditch. One guy would get some salt...we'd think we're really doing something."

Norb's mother died one September day in 1933. Josephine Schemansky was only forty-one years old and worn out from a life of constant labor and multiple childbirths when she fell ill of liver dysfunction and succumbed to an infection. Norb was nine years old at the time. A big black wreath was hung on the outside of the house. As was customary, she was laid out at home, the coffin having to be tilted just so in order to get it through the narrow doorways. She was buried at Mount Olivet Cemetery.

Norb's grandparents died a few years later. "All the funerals in that house," he reflected. "Death appeared often back then."

Norb spent his first few years of school at St. Thomas the Apostle, where tuition cost 75 cents a month. Catholic nuns did their typically thorough job of teaching their uniformed pupils the basics. "They were tough," he said, "but they took care of you." The sisters, dressed in flowing dark blue habits with only their faces and hands showing, were an imposing presence. One small mystery was cleared up, however, the day Norb and a friend stayed after class to clean the chalkboard. Norb's classmate accidentally brushed up against the front of the nun's heavy wool habit and could barely contain his astonishment. "Norb!" the wide-eyed boy reported later. "Nuns have boobs!"

Norb rarely did any homework, but he still received good grades—much to the consternation of some nuns, who thought he surely must be cheating. One skeptical sister even put him in the back row all by himself. However, having empty desks as neighbors didn't prevent the bright youngster from continuing to pass his tests in fine style. But, he does admit today to passing small flat toothpicks to friends in class, where they'd discuss in excruciatingly small handwriting such pressing matters as where everybody would meet that day after school.

Norb made his First Holy Communion in the spring of 1933, just a few months before his mother's untimely death. A couple of years later he made his confirmation, choosing Joseph as his confirmation name. (Curiously, Norb wasn't given a middle name at birth.) His parochial education ended when he entered Burroughs Intermediate School, from which he graduated in June, 1939. That September he began tenth grade at Northeastern High School, just days after Poland had been invaded by Germany. The Nazi blitzkrieg of his ancestral homeland set off World War II, a conflict that would ultimately swallow up Norb, his brothers, and millions of others from their generation. For now, however, the fifteen-year-old boy gave fleeting thought to events unfolding far across the ocean. He had found an outlet for his energy, a casual pastime that would soon turn into a lifelong obsession.

Norb's oldest brother, Dennis, was a serious weightlifter on his way to winning the 1940 Junior Nationals title in the heavyweight division. Dennis was one of about twenty or thirty members of the Detroit Barbell Club. The club was housed inside a made-over garage on McClellan Street, near Gratiot Avenue, a few blocks from the Schemanskys' home. The gym offered weightlifters and bodybuilders the basics: mats, dumbbells, barbells, steel plates of various weights, some homemade racks, and a shower room. Dennis invited Norb to tag along one day. Neither knew it, but it was the start of something big.

"I'd watch the guys work out," recalled Norb, "and once they were in the showers and the gym was empty, I'd start fooling around with the weights myself. Within a few months I was lifting more than most of the guys who were working out regularly."

Although bodybuilders interested solely in sculpting their physique performed a variety of lifts and exercises, competitive weightlifters typically concentrated their workouts on what were known as the three "Olympic lifts": the two-hand military press, the two-hand snatch, and the two-hand clean and jerk. Norb soon learned the particulars of each exercise.

In the military press, the lifter was required to bring the barbell up to a chest position in a single movement, hold it there for two seconds while remaining motionless, and then upon the clap of a judge's hands "press" the barbell vertically until his arms were fully extended overhead. The two-part movement had to be continuous, not jerky or halting, and throughout the lifter had to keep his back as straight as possible. This was considered a "slow strength" exercise. It was more dependent on sheer brute strength than the other two Olympic lifts—commonly referred to as the "quick lifts"—which placed a premium on flexibility, timing, and explosiveness.

The first of the quick lifts, the snatch, required the lifter to pull the barbell up in one continuous movement that ended with his arms extended vertically overhead. The weight had to be held aloft with his feet in line until the referee signaled him to lower. No slowing of movement was permitted until the lifter's wrists turned over at a point higher than his head. No part of his body, except his feet, was allowed to touch the platform at any time.

In the other quick lift, the clean and jerk, the initial movement (the "clean") was similar to the military press. However, unlike the press, the exercise required greater force because more weight was being rammed overhead. The second phase (the "jerk") demanded an explosive upward extension of the arms.

Both quick lifts were executed with the same movement, the only difference being a wider grip on the snatch than on the clean and jerk. In order to accelerate the barbell sufficiently, both exercises required the lifter to briefly drop his body under the weight—thus establishing a base of power and stability—before returning to an upright position with his legs locked and his arms fully extended. Norb came to master the low split style of lifting: his front (left) leg in a full squat, his rear (right) leg nearly straight. In time most lifters would adopt the full squat style, believing it gave them better leverage, but Norb never saw any reason to change.

In each event the contestant was given three attempts to elevate the poundage he had selected over his head, with up to three minutes of rest allowed between attempts. A lifter could add weight after an attempt, but it had to be in increments of no less than ten pounds unless it was his final try, in which case it could be five pounds. In all lifts the contestant was required to hold the barbell overhead while remaining motionless for at least two seconds, whereupon the referee made a downward motion with his arm, indicating it was okay to drop the weight to the platform. To determine a lifter's final score, the best successful attempt in each of the three events was added up. Thus the scorecard for someone who lifted 200 pounds in the military press, 225 in the snatch, and 310 in the clean and jerk would read: 200 + 225 + 310 = 735 total pounds. The man with the highest total won. In the case of a tie, the lifter with the lowest body weight was declared the winner.

The rules Norb competed by throughout his career are basically the same today, although the military press was eliminated from competition after the 1972 Olympics. The extreme back bending needed to complete that particular lift had made it too hard to judge. Today, only the snatch and the clean and jerk are used to determine winners.

The Amateur Athletic Union of the United States, the governing body of numerous sports since its formation in 1888, began sanctioning nonprofessional lifting competitions in 1927. When Norb first began lifting, the three Olympic lifts were used in determining champions in a half-dozen body weight classifications: bantamweight (up to 123 pounds), featherweight (132), lightweight (148), middleweight (165), and light-heavyweight (181), with anyone weighing over 181 pounds considered a heavyweight. Since that time the number of classifications has grown to ten.

The designation of a 182-pounder as a "heavyweight" seems almost laughable by modern standards, but during the Great Depression oversize Americans were relatively rare. Poor nutrition, among other factors, saw to that. "Special diet?" said Schemansky, flashing back to the '30s. "Back then you were lucky to eat at all. You'd eat bread with lard. We didn't know any better, and it was cheaper than butter." When Norb was a kid, the Detroit Lions won the

National Football League championship one year with linemen whose average weight was just a little over 200 pounds.

Norb felt he was too small to play football in a large Class-A high school like Northeastern, where coaches had a pool of several hundred boys to draw from. As a fifteen-year-old sophomore he stood about 5-foot-9 and weighed 160 pounds. While his size wouldn't have cast an imposing shadow on the gridiron, he actually was a fairly solid specimen when compared to the many emaciated teenagers growing up in Depression-era Detroit. A more pressing consideration may have been his poor vision, which required him to wear glasses when competing in sports, even weightlifting. In any event, the bespectacled blonde youngster was far from the 97-pound weakling that Charles Atlas, the king of "mail order muscles," was making famous in his advertisements in popular magazines of the period. Within the dank confines of the Detroit Barbell Club he could clean and jerk 135 pounds, a respectable figure for a beginner. By the winter of 1940-41—the middle of his junior year—he was clean and jerking 195 pounds. In the spring of 1941 he upped that figure to 235 pounds.

Where did Norb's strength come from? Genetics certainly played a role, but so did hard labor inside and outside of the gym. Whenever the next shipment of coal arrived at the Schemanskys' house, Joseph Schemansky saved the fifty cents the delivery man charged customers to unload the wagon. "The boys will get it," he'd say. Norb and his brothers—Dennis, Ralph, and Jerome—all shoveled and lugged their share of coal while growing up. Norb got a regular upper-body workout from cleaning the basement furnace. He'd haul out the cinders in large buckets, lifting the thirty or forty pounds of ash up to an open cellar window and a waiting brother. As a wiry eleven-year-old he worked for a neighborhood grocery store, unloading 100-pound bags of potatoes.

Norb's introduction to formalized competition in "the iron game" was the 1941 Michigan A.A.U. Senior Weightlifting Championships, held in Detroit. The seventeen-year-old contestant, who tipped the scales at 182½ pounds that day, pressed 170, snatched 200, and clean-and-jerked 250. The 620 total pounds gave him second place in the heavyweight division. The bronze medal he received from the A.A.U. was unimpressive—at an inch high by a half-inch wide, it was smaller than a postage stamp—but this first taste of winning and official recognition among his peers proved addictive.

♦ ♦ ♦

In the fall of 1941, Norb should have been starting his final year of high school. Instead he was hundreds of miles north of his eastside Detroit neighborhood, in the pine-scented environs of Manistique in Michigan's rugged Upper Peninsula.

Norb was a somewhat reluctant member of the Civilian Conservation Corps, a quasi-military public works program that was one of the more successful initiatives of President Franklin Roosevelt's New Deal legislation. The idea was to take out-of-work young men off street corners and hardscrabble farms and transplant them to state parks and forests, where they would be paid to plant trees, build trails and bridges, stock lakes, and even occasionally fight fires. "It wasn't my decision to go," said Norb. "My dad said I was going to sign up, so I went. What are you going to do?"

CCC members lived army-style. They slept on cots, bunked in tents and barracks, wore uniforms, and woke up in the morning and turned in at night to the sound of a bugle. In many ways it was like an extended scouting trip. In the view of Donald Zettle, a former deputy director in the Department of Natural Resources, the CCC was indisputably a success for the nearly 100,000 idle young men between the ages of seventeen and twenty-eight who served in Michigan companies between 1933 and 1942.

"The CCC boys had been enrolled, moved many miles away from home, were clothed, fed, housed, given some spending money—and money was sent home to family. They really had nothing to worry about. They were now occupied and trained to work with their hands. Sure, it was hard work, but they were young, energetic, with warm clothes, good food, good sleeping and housing conditions, and time for relaxation…and they could see future dividends of their accomplishments. For many, the environment and living conditions were far better than anything they had experienced at home. Besides, there was just enough regimentation to keep them out of mischief, to keep them clean, healthy, fully occupied with the opportunity to improve both their mind and body."

Exchanging cement sidewalks for forest paths was a bit of a culture shock for a city kid like Norb, but he approached this new experience in his usual matter-of-fact way. He planted seedlings, he cleared rocks and brush, he took his turn at K.P., he did everything that was asked of him. There was plenty of free time for baseball, horseshoes, swimming, and general roughhousing, though Norb had no opportunity to raise a barbell in the woodsy environment. Each camp had an educational supervisor, with instructors offering boys courses ranging from building trades to basic English. CCC members were paid thirty dollars a month, of which twenty-five dollars was sent home to dependents. "Pretty good deal," he said. "I get five bucks a month and I'm doing all the work."

Norb also got three square meals each day, an unheard of luxury for many before enlisting in the CCC. According to a statistical survey, the typical enrollee grew a half-inch and packed on between twelve and twenty pounds during his average nine-month length of service. Some had it so good they continued to reenlist in the CCC every six months for years.

Norb's company was stationed in Gladstone on December 7, 1941, when news of the Japanese attack on Pearl Harbor interrupted a Sunday afternoon football game. "None of us knew where Pearl Harbor was," he recalled. "I know a bunch of the guys went out and volunteered the next day."

An undercurrent of household turmoil had factored into Norb's joining the CCC. His father had remarried, taking a widow named Katherine as his second wife. Katherine, who had children of her own, then had a baby girl, Jeannette, with Norb's father. Norb found himself with a half-sister and new stepsisters moving into the void left by siblings who had moved out of the house to get married. His stepmother could not come close to replacing his real mother. "I called her 'the old lady,'" he said. "We'd get along, on and off. She was miserly, strict. It just wasn't a good situation at home."

When his six-month CCC tour ended a couple weeks after Pearl Harbor, Norb returned home to an untenable situation. He'd been away for the first time in his young life, had grown up a bit, and he discovered that he enjoyed the freedom of being on his own. During the Depression, Detroit's unemployment rate had been as high as 40 percent. Boys regularly dropped out of school in the hope of somehow contributing their share to the family income; girls dropped out to get married once they reached child-bearing age. There was no shame attached to leaving school early. In fact, of the eight Schemansky children, only Esther, who graduated from Nativity High, went all the way through twelfth grade and got a diploma. The newfound prosperity of the "Arsenal of Democracy" made dropping out even more attractive. With the country gearing up for war with Japan and Germany and millions of men going into uniform, it was easy for a strong kid like Norb to find a job in a defense plant. He went to work grinding gauges at a machine shop near Woodward and Trowbridge.

"I made a buck an hour," he recalled. "I was going to give my stepmother half, but she said, 'I want it all.' I said to myself, 'Oh hell, time to get out.'" He moved in with his older sister, Lillian, and her husband, Fred Boza. The recently married couple lived on Jane Street, a few miles away.

Norb attended Northeastern that first wartime spring, but that was largely because he wanted to compete in track. "I wasn't applying myself in school," he admitted. He was one of the standout performers on Northeastern's track team, earning All-City honors as a shot putter under the guidance of coach Seymour Brown. Norb opened a few eyes at the city meet. "Some of the guys who were bigger than me wondered what I was doing there," he recalled. "I came in sixth and beat many of the bigger ones." Shot putting allowed Norb to showcase his emerging strength and agility, assets that paid big dividends in lifting. He earned a varsity letter in weightlifting and won the city meet as a heavyweight. But when the class of '42 graduated in June, Norb was still several credits shy of earning his degree.

By now his brother Dennis had given up serious competitive weightlifting, but Norb more than kept the Schemansky name alive in the iron game. He placed second as a heavyweight in the Tri-State Championships, held February 15, 1942 in Detroit, hoisting a total of 670 pounds. He traveled to Cincinnati in late May, just days before his eighteenth birthday, for the National Senior A.A.U. Weightlifting Championships. His original intention was to lift as a light-heavyweight, but he was late for the weigh-in. He wound up drinking several quarts of water to qualify as a heavyweight; somewhat bloated, he finished fourth. That November, however, he grabbed the crown at the Michigan A.A.U. Senior Weightlifting Championships as a true heavyweight. His scores had climbed since finishing runner-up at the same tournament a year earlier. He gained forty-five pounds in the press, forty in the snatch, and sixty in the clean and jerk, for an overall score of 765. His body weight was up to 191 pounds.

The lifting bug had bitten Norb. "I was getting a little better, a little better, and I kind of got hooked," is how he explained it many years later. He quit his job at the machine shop and spent more time in the gym. In a way, he was merely biding his time as the war dragged on. The neighborhood was becoming emptied of young men, as many enlisted and others waited for the inevitable draft notice to arrive in the mailbox. Gold stars signifying the death of a family member in uniform began appearing in windows, including the Stroheckers, who lived across the street from the Schemanskys on Iroquois. Alex Strohecker, the boy Norb knew as "Junior," was killed in Italy. He was one year older than Norb.

As 1942 gave way to 1943, Norb spent his time lifting, bowling, shooting pool, and hanging out with friends. In March, he finished second at the Central States Meet in Chicago, boosting 755 total pounds. It would turn out to be his last tournament for a long time. That spring, just as he was turning nineteen, Uncle Sam dropped him a line. "Greetings...," the letter began.

The barbells would gather dust for the next three years. Norb Schemansky was in the army now.

CHAPTER TWO

Private Hercules

It would be wrong to say that war is all grim; if it were, the human spirit could not survive two and three and four years of it....Our soldiers are still as roughly good-humored as they always were, and they laugh easily, although there isn't as much to laugh about as there used to be.

Ernie Pyle, Here Is Your War (1943)

For Private Norb Schemansky, World War II was a succession of eye-opening experiences, the first of which occurred during his draft physical in Detroit.

"We're all standing in line, waiting to get examined, and they tell this one guy to drop his pants," he recalled with a laugh. "The guy drops his pants—and he's got a wooden leg! 'How the hell did you get this far?' they ask him. 'I don't know,' the guy says. They sent him home."

Another fellow who managed to stay out of the fray was a considerably healthier specimen named Dennis Schemansky. "He missed his draft physical because he had the flu," Norb said of his older brother. "The draft board said, 'Okay, we'll call you.' They never called him and he didn't call them. He wound up spending the entire war working as a welder at a defense plant in Pontiac."

Norb's other brothers weren't as fortunate. Ralph was a sergeant in the tank corps in France and Germany while Jerome served as a Marine in China. All three Schemansky boys were destined to return safely to civilian life. One would reasonably expect that, over the years, the brothers shared stories of their war experiences—that is, until one remembers the Schemanskys' closemouthed ways. "No," said Norb. "Seems funny, I guess, but we never talked about it."

Even the Red Cross couldn't help. The organization once set up a reunion between Norb and Ralph when both were serving in Europe, but Ralph didn't make the scheduled meeting in Metz, Germany. However, while waiting for his brother, Norb ran into another familiar face from the neighborhood. "Some soldier called my name. I looked up and it's Joe McCloskey, a kid from across the street," he said. "Small world, huh?" Asked today why Ralph didn't show up, Norb shrugged. "I don't know. I never asked him and he never told me."

Norb first donned fatigues at Camp Stewart, where he was sent for basic training. According to Norb, the base outside Savannah, Georgia, was an inhospitable place of "swamps and snakes," but conditions were soon going to become even more uninviting. One October day in 1943, after spending several weeks in advanced weaponry training, he joined a couple of thousand other freshly minted GI's in trudging up the gangplank of the troopship *Mauritania*. The soldiers left Boston's harbor in a state of nervous excitement. The next stop was England—and the beginning of what would become twenty-seven straight months of overseas duty for Private Schemansky.

The *Mauritania* was a converted Cunard passenger liner, staffed with British personnel, but this was anything but a luxury cruise. The food was greasy, the sleeping accommodations (hammocks) were uncomfortable, and the decks were crowded with seasick men emptying their stomachs. The aging vessel's pedigree, had any of the soldiers known it, would certainly have been no boost to morale. The *Mauritania's* sister ship had been the ill-fated *Lusitania*, torpedoed by a German submarine in 1915 with great loss of life. Now, with the Allies at war with a new generation of Germans, many of the young GI's anxiously scanned the waters for any submarine looking to duplicate that feat. The lightly armored *Mauritania* was unescorted, causing it to run a zig-zag course at full speed in order to foil U-boat captains, who typically needed six or seven minutes to line up a torpedo on a moving target. Sharks ominously followed the ship, attracted by the garbage the British crew dumped overboard.

Their presence gave a chill to any man contemplating the pandemonium that would result should the ship be torpedoed or bombed.

Despite the constant feeling of dread, Norb managed to find a bit of fun. "Some kid from New York came up to me and said, 'Hey, wanna eat good?' I got a job working in the mess, had to do a little work, but we ate what the officers ate. I remember one time we were supposed to be washing dishes, and we threw 'em out of an open porthole instead. Just screwing around, you know. There was always a lot of fooling around going on, which helped relieve some of the tension and boredom we all felt."

On another occasion the men listened to a radio broadcast that had President Franklin Roosevelt assuring the country that no men under twenty-one were going overseas. This brought forth a wave of derisive cheering from the teenagers assembled aboard the *Mauritania*, including nineteen-year-old Private Schemansky. "Turn the boat around!" he shouted. "The president says we aren't supposed to be going overseas!" No luck—the transport ship continued to plow through the gray, choppy swells of the Atlantic. After nine nerve-wracking days at sea, the *Mauritania* finally docked at Liverpool. "It was dark and dreary," recalled Schemansky. "All of England was dark and dreary."

A sergeant who had been made aware that he had a state champion lifter in his midst looked over the assembled replacements for "the" weightlifter, someone surely of enormous size. "I was six feet tall and 190 pounds," said Norb. "They were looking for a big guy, maybe 250 pounds. They didn't think it was me."

Norb was assigned to Battery A of the 184th Anti-Aircraft Artillery Battalion, one of a quartet of four-gun batteries that constituted each mobile "ack-ack" unit. A headquarters battery and a medical detachment rounded out the battalion. Total strength of the 184th was about 725 officers and enlisted men under the command of Lieutenant Colonel J. S. Albergotti. Upon arrival in England they began familiarizing themselves with the newly issued .90-millimeter guns that replaced the smaller .40-millimeter weapons they had trained on back in the states. The .90-millimeter guns featured longer range, greater muzzle velocity, and a larger shell-burst area, all of which made them more effective in dealing with Germany's high-altitude bombers.

Each gun had a crew of fifteen men, of which Norb was one of two loader-gunners. Ramming a forty-pound shell into the breech at the rate of eight to ten per minute was fatiguing work, so loaders typically alternated every ten rounds, although Norb sometimes was good for up to twenty shells at a time. Some guys started calling him "Arm" Schemansky. The mobile guns were towed from place to place by heavy tractors or trucks, then positioned into firing pits made of earthworks, sandbags, concrete, or some combination thereof.

Field maneuvers, firing exercises, and the usual camp duties occupied every man's time during the miserably wet and chilly fall of 1943. Schemansky found a fellow traveler of sorts in Roman Robaszewski, a tall, slim Pole from Chicago who was the battery's first sergeant. "He liked me," said Norb. "I never did KP duty once." Instead, throughout his entire tour of duty the muscular teenager handled what other soldiers considered more onerous chores, such as helping to build roads and unloading crates of ammunition. Norb liked these activities because they helped keep the rust off his biceps.

"Arm" Schemansky already had a reputation as the battalion's strong man, thanks in part to some impromptu shock-and-awe demonstrations in the barracks.

"One time I lifted a guy who weighed 160 pounds with one hand," he recalled. "There was another guy who weighed 180 and I said, 'I can do you with two hands.'" A 230-pound corporal from Illinois named Clifton "Tiny" Voltz presented more of a challenge. But Schemansky expertly arranged Tiny's body in such a way that his weight was evenly distributed, then lifted the oversize soldier off the ground and over his head in the ultimate "military" press. Such feats of strength had Norb's pals calling him "Bronk" after Bronko Nagurski, the pile-driving fullback who was in the news at the time because of his successful comeback with the Chicago Bears. Later Norb was nicknamed "Herc," shorthand for Hercules.

One of Norb's battery mates was Frank Cwik, a slightly built Pole who came from the west side of Detroit. "I've got a picture somewhere of Norb holding a couple of those big shells," recalled Cwik, a carpenter in civilian life. "He was a good man to have around. I remember he tried to get me into lifting weights. 'They'll build you up,' he'd say. I wasn't interested. Heck, I only weighed about 135 pounds."

In March 1944, Norb and the rest of Battery A became the first American anti-aircraft battery to participate in the air defense of London. They took up position at Lippitts Hill in Essex, about ten miles northeast of England's capital city. In a bow to the fine English hospitality the Americans experienced, Norb's crew dubbed their gun "Piccadilly Lil."

By now England was fairly bursting its seams with more than a million Yanks and mountains of equipment and supplies being assembled for the inevitable invasion of Europe. D-Day finally arrived on June 6, 1944, with the first elements of the 184th going ashore at Omaha Beach eleven days later. "The beach was pretty well cleaned up by then," said Norb. "The army didn't want incoming troops and the press to see bodies."

Several anti-aircraft units dug into positions. For the next several weeks they threw up a barrage that met every attempt by German planes to bomb or recon the beachhead. Famed war correspondent Ernie Pyle spent two days and nights with one of the anti-aircraft batteries at Normandy, describing his observations in a syndicated column entitled "American Ack-Ack:"

> The Germans were as methodical in their night air attacks on our positions in Normandy as they were in everything else. We began to hear the faint, faraway drone of the first bomber around 11:30 every night. Our own planes patrolled above us until darkness. It was dusk around eleven, and we were suddenly aware that the skies which had been roaring all day with our own fighters and bombers were now strangely silent. Nothing was in the air.
>
> The ack-ack gunners, who had been loafing near their pup tents or sleeping or telling stories, now went to their guns. They brought blankets from the pup tents and piled them up against the wall of the gun pit, for the nights got very cold and the boys wrapped up during long lulls in the shooting. The gunners merely loafed in the gun pit as the dusk deepened into darkness, waiting for the first telephoned order to start shooting. They smoked a few last-minute cigarettes. Once it was dark they couldn't smoke except by draping blankets over themselves for blackout. They did smoke some that way during the night, but not much.
>
> In four or five places in the wall of the circular pit, shelves had been dug and wooden shell boxes inserted to hold reserve shells. It was just like pigeonholes in a filing cabinet. When the firing started, two ammunition carriers brought new shells from a dump a few feet away up to the rim of

the gun pit and handed them down to a carrier waiting below; he kept the pigeonholes filled. The gun was constantly turning in the pit and there was always a pigeonhole of fresh shells right behind it. The shells were as long as a man's arm and they weighed better than forty pounds. After each salvo the empty shell case kicked out onto the floor of the pit. They lay there until there was a lull in the firing, when the boys tossed them over the rim. Next morning they were gathered up and put in boxes for eventual shipment back to America, to be retooled for further use.

Each gun was connected by telephone to the battery command post in a dugout. At all times one member of each gun crew had a telephone to his ear. When a plane was picked up within range the battery commander gave a telephonic order, "Stand by!" Each gun commander shouted the order to his crew, and the boys all jumped to their positions. Everybody in the crew knew his job and did it. There was no necessity for harshness or short words on the part of the gun commander. When a plane either was shot down or went out of range, and there was nothing else in the vicinity, the command was given, "Rest!" and the crews relaxed and squatted or lay around on the floor of the pit. But they didn't leave the pit.

Sometimes the rest would be for only a few seconds. Other times it might last a couple of hours. In the long lulls the gunners wrapped up in blankets and slept on the floor of the pit—all except the man at the telephone. It was the usual German pattern to have a lull from about 2 to 4 A.M. and then get in another good batch of bombing attempts in the last hour before dawn. The nights were very short then—from 11 P.M. to 5 A.M.—for which everybody was grateful. Dawn actually started to break faintly just about 4:30, but the Germans kept roaming around the sky until real daylight came.

Our own patrol planes hit the sky at daylight and the Germans skedaddled. In the first few days, when our patrol planes had to come all the way from England, the boys told of mornings when they could see our planes approaching from one direction and the Germans heading for home at the opposite side of the sky.

As soon as it was broad daylight, the boys cranked down the barrel of their gun until it was horizontal, and then took a sight through it onto the stone turret of a nearby barn—to make sure the night's shooting hadn't moved the gun off its position. Then some of them gathered up

> the empty shells, others got wood fires started for heating breakfast, and others raised and tied the camouflage net. They were all through by seven o'clock, and half the shift crawled into their pup-tent beds while the other half went to work with oil, ramrod and waste cloth to clean up and readjust the gun.

On August 2, the 184th was moved to a position on the west side of Cherbourg with the mission of defending the vital French port. The battalion drove in trucks over ground that had cost many an infantryman his life. Villages had been reduced to rubble. Burned-out tanks and trucks smoldered. Dead, bloated cows were everywhere. But after just a couple of eventful nights, the Luftwaffe gave up on Cherbourg, turning the 184th's vigil of the skies from one of dread and anticipation to one of boredom and monotony. One month later the battalion moved on to Paris, which had just been liberated, to provide air protection there.

This was sweet duty, as enemy raids were nonexistent and passes into the French capital were soon being issued. After a few days of preparing their positions, members of the 184th could concern themselves with more serious pursuits, such as sampling Parisian hospitality and competing in an intra-battalion baseball tournament (won by Battery A).

Norb's battery was located in a large forest near Meudon. The site, formerly home to a German flak unit, contained a bombed-out barracks where Norb discovered an abandoned weight set. Battery A's commanding officer, Captain Dave Anderson, said Norb could keep the weights, assuming he was willing to lug the barbells and plates around himself. "After about two or three times, I said the hell with it," recalled Norb. Anderson undoubtedly thought the muscle-bound private was big enough without hauling a weight set all over France. Once during a German air attack, Norb had jumped over the sandbags of the gun pit, only to land directly on the captain. "He cushioned my fall," he recalled, grinning. "But I pretty much flattened him."

After a couple of months, the 184th reluctantly left Paris for Antwerp, Belgium. It was there that the battalion was introduced to a new and frightening German terror weapon, the V-1 rocket. The V came from the word *Vergeltungswaffen,* German for "weapon of reprisal." The pilotless aircraft, dubbed "buzz bombs" because of their distinctive whistling sound, had first been launched against London in the weeks following D-Day. However, starting in October 1944, the Nazis shifted their emphasis to Antwerp, hoping to destroy the Allies' key port of entry. The Allied high command scrambled to meet this new and unexpected threat.

For five months, a division-sized force of more than 22,000 American, British, and Polish troops—known collectively as Antwerp X—put up an unprecedented "wall of steel" around Antwerp, their combined 524 heavy and light guns roaring night and day. Batteries typically had only a few minutes' warning of incoming rockets.

"Shooting at buzz bombs was an assignment that required steady nerves," the 184th's anonymous chronicler (possibly its commander, Lieutenant Colonel Albergotti) wrote later in a booklet describing the battalion's overseas exploits. "As each gun fired, no one knew whether the round that was on the way would bring the bomb screaming down on top of them. It was those on duty in the gun pits, loading, firing and relaying ammunition, who realized this the most, even though the battery as a team worked to get the rounds into the air and to explode where they would do the most damage. It was a relief to all to see the buzz bomb explode in the air with a tremendous sheet of flame and cloud of smoke, followed by a mighty report. The cry of 'It's coming down!' saw many faces turned skyward watching the bomb.

"Sometimes on being hit in a vital spot, a buzz bomb would nose over and head straight down, screaming as it dove towards the ground, landing with a shattering explosion, the concussion of which smashed nearby buildings as though they were of cardboard. Sometimes with their motors off, the bombs would glide on their path until they crashed. Other times when hit, the V-1s would go into wild gyrations, turning on their backs, climbing, turning completely around or veering off to another course. When the order 'Ceasefire!' came to the gun crews no one knew what would happen to that bomb, and the sweating would begin until it crashed or went safely overhead."

Norb remembered the lethal buzz bombs as being less of a challenge than conventional aircraft. "The V-1 was easier to hit. They flew in at a constant speed—about 400 miles an hour. The radar would lock onto it and you could track it. Planes would take evasive action. You'd send a shell up to where you thought it'd be, but by then the pilot had changed altitude." He recalled the damage a buzz bomb could produce. "Each one carried a ton of explosives. When it hit, it left a hole ten feet deep and thirty feet in diameter. It could take out a couple buildings. The closest one got to us was about a hundred yards. That was plenty close."

To the world at large, the "battle of the buzz bombs" lacked the cinematic sweep and wholesale casualties of the D-Day landings. The nature of the fight meant there would be none of the territorial gains that made General George Patton's mechanized dash across France the stuff of headlines. Nonetheless, in the words of Major General William Revell-Smith of the British 21st Army Group, the defense of Antwerp was "a great victory," one as important as "any other form of major military success on the final outcome of the war." Brigadier General Clare H. Armstrong, in command of Antwerp X, was equally effusive, praising the men who had compiled "this unparalleled antiaircraft record" as "the best damn gunners in the world."

The numbers bore him out. A total of 2,183 flying bombs were destroyed by the antiaircraft units ringing Antwerp, some blown up in mid-flight and the majority clipped by gunfire and crashing in open fields short of the target. Only 211 managed to get through and land in a vital bull's eye of eight miles' circumference, the area where the most important port and warehouse facilities were located. The ports never failed to operate during the 154 days of constant bombardment, allowing millions of tons of supplies to move through without interruption. It was no stretch to say that, had Antwerp X failed, victory in Germany would have been delayed for several months and at the cost of tens of thousands of additional lives. The war could very well have stretched into 1946—and possibly beyond.

In late December 1944, the 184th was temporarily taken away from the defense of Antwerp and moved sixty-five miles to Namur, a Belgian city on the west bank of the Meuse River that was an important supply point. The epic German breakout known as the Battle of the Bulge was in full swing, and ack-ack batteries were thrown into the fight to stop the Wehrmacht. The first German planes appeared over Namur on Christmas Eve, and two nights later the 184th experienced its heaviest action of the war. Bombers came from all angles and elevations, some flying so low that the men in the gun pits swore they could feel the backwash of propellers as the Junkers roared past. By night's end the battalion claimed eight enemy planes shot down.

Confusion reigned and rumors ran rampant throughout this period. Sabotage teams were supposedly parachuting into the area. The truth was grim enough. At one point several Germans were caught crossing the Meuse in American uniforms.

"What did you do with them?" Norb asked one of the captors.

"They had the wrong uniform on," was the reply.

"You know what that meant," said Schemansky. "They took them somewhere and shot them. Spies."

Schemansky remains justifiably proud of the 184th's record. During the war the battalion was credited with destroying thirty-two enemy aircraft and more than 300 V-1 rockets from its gun pits in England and Europe. Best damn gunners, indeed. Norb estimates he alone shoved 2,000 or more shells into the breech.

However, war is never as neat and orderly as movies and official records make it out to be. In this fog of confusion, caprice, and craziness, anything could—and usually did—happen. Friendly planes sometimes strayed into the field of fire and were mistakenly shot down. Among them was a British Lancaster thought to have been knocked out of the sky by the 184th as the bomber was returning from a raid over Vohwinkel, Germany, on New Year's Day, 1945. All eight crew members, half of whom were twenty or younger, were killed when the plane crashed into the Belgian countryside. For those unfortunate British airmen, and for countless others caught up in the fury of total war, life had ended before it really had a chance to begin. In a global holocaust that claimed 50 million victims of all ages and races in every way imaginable, the sheer arbitrariness of a single death still could be confounding, as when a member of the 184th's headquarters staff survived the unit's major actions only to ingloriously drown two days after the Nazis surrendered.

By then it was May 1945, the 184th was busy disarming enemy flak batteries in occupied Germany, and the homesick Schemansky was nearly ready to swim across the Atlantic himself, back to the states and normalcy. However, it's no easier to disassemble an army of millions of men than it is to raise one, and it took until that December before he was finally able to board a Liberty ship for home. This boat was much smaller and slower than the *Mauritania* and bounced around like a cork. The constant motion caused the 200 or so returning soldiers to retch until there was nothing left in them.

Norb came back to Detroit having earned the World War II Victory, Good Conduct, and Army of Occupation medals, as well as five battle stars. Each star represented a campaign: the Central Europe, Normandy, Northern France, and Rhineland. He was also awarded the Belgian Fourragère. Many years later, when he was retired and had time to digest all that he and his unit had been through in Europe, he inquired with the Department of the Army about an additional two battle stars that surviving veterans of the 184th thought they were entitled to. The paperwork and sloppy recordkeeping were frustrating to deal with. To this day the battalion has not received official credit for its service in the Ardennes-Alsace campaign nor the air defense of England, despite obvious and overwhelming evidence that the men of the 184th were indeed there, pitching in and doing their part.

"It was a snafu," said Norb, wise to the eternal ways of the military. "Situation normal, all fouled up." It hasn't kept the slightly disgruntled veteran, sixty years removed from his wartime service, from flying the flag every day from his front porch.

Today, as members of the generation of Americans who fought World War II continue to die off at the rate of thousands each day, it's become fashionable to refer to them as "the greatest generation." The media-inspired moniker, while well-intentioned, is a conceit that former Private "Herc" Schemansky has never been able to line up fully behind. After all, previous generations were made of pretty stern stuff, too.

"I don't know how great we all were," he said. "But we won the war, so I guess you could say we were pretty good."

CHAPTER THREE

Getting Serious

If you're good at something, you should stick with it. That's what I say.

Norb Schemansky

Norb was mustered out of the army at Camp Atterbury, Indiana, a couple of weeks before Christmas, 1945. He returned to Detroit, moving back in with his sister Lillian and her husband. He had a hundred or so dollars in separation pay in his pocket and no particular plans, aside from taking his good old sweet time unwinding from more than three years serving Uncle Sam. To this end the government was happy to cooperate, making one of the features of the newly enacted G. I. Bill of Rights an unemployment provision that gave returning servicemen twenty dollars a week for an entire year. As an appreciative member of the so-called "52-20 Club," Norb bowled, shot pool, drank beer, and just generally loafed around. "I sort of drifted there for a while," he said of his first year out of uniform.

He also returned to Olympic lifting, an almost underground activity that continued to draw the disapproval of people like his dad, who saw no payoff for the amount of time and effort expended. "The old attitude back then was, 'You're wasting your time, get a job,'" Norb said. Reflective of that attitude was the fact that postwar Detroit, a city of nearly two million people, had just a couple of facilities available to dedicated weightlifters. "Guys lifted in garages and basements," recalled Norb. "It was almost like we were hiding out."

During the 1940s many of Detroit's bodybuilders ("mirror watchers" in weightlifting parlance) struck a pose at Armento's eastside gym on Woodward Avenue and Seven Mile. Lifters who were more interested in improving their strength than in sculpting the size and shape of their muscles congregated at the Yacos Gym downtown.

George Yacos, a short, stocky, and garrulous Greek, had converted a dining room inside the Taft Hotel at Woodward and Davenport, close to the campus of Wayne State University. Several championship-caliber lifters frequented the Yacos Gym, including featherweight Emerick Ishikawa, heavyweight Al Koernke, and Norb's brother, Jerome (who had won the Mr. Michigan title in 1944 before going into the service). In addition there was an interesting mix of regulars of lesser ability, such as a professional wrestler named "Crusher" Cortez; budding blue-collar poet Phil Levine; and a factory hand known only as Jack the Bulgarian. The latter character "reduced the social fabric of Detroit to colorful prejudices intricately concocted by his own odd logic, and who also advocated the daily consumption of large quantities of raw garlic to ward off a host of ills," recalled Royal Oak artist Sam Karres, who began working out at the Yacos Gym as a teenager during the war and eventually became the state middleweight champion.

Yacos' unconventional views attracted a certain bohemian element, so his gym was filled with self-styled experts on politics, labor, religion, literature, and international finance. On any given day a grunting, sweaty patron might suddenly be handed a pamphlet describing how the redistribution of the world's wealth would cure all of society's ills, or given an impromptu lecture on the solution to the eternal Arab-Israeli dispute. Yacos himself was basically a frustrated revolutionary. "I thrive on adversity," he told Norb, who began working out at the gym with his brother. "Yeah," responded the low-key lifter, "but I don't like that."

In at least one respect, Yacos was a visionary. "George was expelled from the Wayne University physical education department for advocating that all athletes exercise with weights to improve their performance," recalled Karres. "Of course, he was ahead of his time. Now nearly all sports use weights or progressive resistance in their training programs."

Yacos was a born promoter. Karres remembered one exhibition at the

Yacos Gym. "The show was terrific—everything from Olympic lifting and hand balancing to strength feats such as tearing up whole decks of cards and ripping phone books in half. The setting was friendly and intimate." Norb echoed Karres: "If the A.A.U. ran the meet, you'd hardly have anybody there. They wouldn't advertise it. If you didn't know about it, how the hell could you go to it? If Yacos promoted the meet, three or four hundred people would show up. It might be a small hall, but it looked full." Crowd size can have a positive effect on performance, he added. "Large crowds are better for lifters. It makes you feel worthy, like someone else is interested." But no matter what the size of the venue or the crowd, stressed Norb, "You still have to do it, you still have to perform."

With minimal training, Norb took first place in the heavyweight division in the Michigan A.A.U. Senior Championships, held April 28, 1946 in Detroit. It was his first competitive meet in more than three years, and he hoisted a total of 815 pounds. The following month he won the Junior Nationals in Akron, Ohio, then placed fifth at the Senior Nationals in June. Norb was a proud man, and that uncharacteristically low finish stung. He knew that if he was to become a world-class lifter he needed to get a bit more serious about his training. As he would often say in years to come, he came to meets to win, not to look good or just be competitive.

However, in the late spring of 1946 a purposeful and organized dedication to lifting was still a ways off; in fact, Norb would not compete in another major meet for almost a year. During this period the ex-soldier continued to fool around with the weights while sorting out his options, all the while continuing to collect his twenty bucks a week from Uncle Sam. "I'd try to work out two or three times a week for an hour and a half, maybe two hours," he said. "I'd spend more time on the streetcar or bus getting to and from Yacos than I did in the gym." Norb's unofficial membership in the 52-20 Club expired over the winter of 1946-47, by which time he was seriously dating a vivacious girl from the neighborhood named Bernice and casting about for meaningful fulltime employment. Soon family and factory would be taking up most of each day, leaving precious little time for what was still essentially a hobby.

Nonetheless, Norb continued to progress and to impress. Emerick Ishikawa, who worked at the downtown Statler Hotel when he wasn't training at the Yacos Gym, recalled Norb's unusally powerful grip. "Great forearm strength," said Ishikawa, who at eighty-six continues to regularly work out in his native Hawaii. "He used to do some grip feats when we went out to the bar and were messing around. He could bend a bottle cap between his two small fingers. He'd bend it right in half. No one else could do it. John Davis couldn't do it. Norb was just so naturally strong."

Although George Yacos would sometimes be referred to as Schemansky's "trainer," in reality Norb, like most weightlifters, trained himself. There was little information available, meaning lifters went through considerable trial and error regarding such basics as exercises, repetitions, sets, intensity, etc. "You basically worked out by yourself," heavyweight Al Koernke said of those days at the Yacos Gym. Koernke, today a retired barber living in Ypsilanti, Michigan, went on to offer his recollections of the up-and-coming Schemansky. "I liked Norb, he was a nice fellow. He wasn't the type of person to just walk up to someone and start offering advice, but he was available if you asked. You could tell he would go on to do great things. He was so good at the clean and jerk."

As Norb's performance at the 1947 Michigan A.A.U. Seniors indicated, he wasn't too shabby at the other Olympic lifts, either. Held in Detroit five days before his twenty-third birthday, Schemansky successfully defended his state crown by pressing 260 pounds, snatching 270, and clean and jerking 330 for an overall score of 860 pounds. He bumped his total up to 870 five weeks later at the Senior Nationals in Chicago, mostly on the strength of a 345-pound clean and jerk. After finishing fifth at the same event in 1946, this time Norb placed second to the seemingly invincible black heavyweight John Davis and won the meet's Outstanding Lifter Award. (Jerome Schemansky, who would never come close to matching his older brother's achievements in the iron game, finished a distant eighth among heavyweights with a 745 total.)

John Henry Davis, three years older than Norb, was in the midst of a remarkable winning streak. From 1938 until 1953, a span of fifteen years, Davis would remain undefeated in international competition, garnering six world championships and two Olympic gold medals during that period. He also was the perennial U.S. champion. Only the war years—during which time Davis served in the army and contracted a serious case of malaria—kept him from adding to his haul of titles and medals. "I got interested when I was 16 years old," Davis once told the *New York Times*. "During the summer of 1937

I saw a group of fellows trying to lift a cement block near a water fountain in Tompkins Park in Brooklyn. They couldn't budge it, but I was able to pick it up without trouble. There was a weightlifter watching and he asked me if I'd like to be his training partner. I tried it for a week and quit. I had become fairly good in track and gymnastics and I couldn't understand why weightlifting was so much work." A few months later, however, Davis returned to the barbells. After finishing second at the 1938 Senior Nationals, the teenager shocked the lifting world by winning the World Championships in Vienna, Austria, as a light heavyweight. "This win occurred in an era when there were no junior championships and when weightlifting was dominated by athletes in their 20s and 30s," marveled iron game historian Artie Drechsler. The 17-year-old American "had made weightlifting history by becoming the youngest athlete ever to have won a world championship. It was a distinction he was to enjoy for nearly 50 years."

Davis had his greatest success when taking the platform as a heavyweight. At the 1941 Senior Nationals, he became the first man in history to exceed 1,000 pounds in the three Olympic lifts; ten years later, he totaled a personal-best 1,063¼ pounds at the inaugural Pan-American Games. Davis, who packed anywhere from 190 to 230 pounds on his chiseled 5-foot-9 frame, was recognized as one of the greatest strength athletes in history. He could generate tremendous power in his legs, once doing a standing jump over a table 30 inches high and 28 inches wide—this while holding a 15-pound dumbbell in one hand and two 5-pound dumbbells in the other. Depending on his body weight at the time, he could crank out four or five or even six one-arm chin-ups, starting from a "dead hang" (that is, his arm straight and fully extended at the start of each pull-up). He also could pinch-lift a 75-pound barbell plate using just his thumb and two fingers. "He was a strong and pretty flexible guy," said Schemansky. "You see a 200-pound guy do a back-flip, you gotta look twice." According to Paul Anderson, the ball-shaped Georgia heavyweight who burst upon the scene in the middle 1950s, "John proved that the heavyweight was an athlete and not just a cumbersome professional strongman who moved slowly. He was a good athlete who moved fast and had strength and a good mind. He had the ability to pass mental blocks and lift weights that had never been lifted before."

Davis, who was named after the mythical strongman John Henry, is remembered as an unaffected champion who comported himself with class and dignity. His major weaknesses were opera and cigarettes. A bass-baritone whose greatest unrealized dream was to become a professional singer, Davis filled his apartment with albums of classical music and once cut a recording in Europe with middleweight Pete George. (It sold poorly.) He also smoked like a locomotive—a vice that led to the lung cancer that would eventually kill him. "You'd see him at a meet and he'd have a cigarette between his fingers, grabbing a smoke between lifts," recalled Norb.

Davis was raised by a single mother in a Brooklyn tenement and never knew his father. The high-school dropout found a surrogate father of sorts in Bob Hoffman, the colorful owner of the York Barbell Company and an attendant line of fitness publications and nutritional supplements. Hoffman moved Davis to York, Pennsylvania, where many of the country's top lifters worked and trained. He paid for Davis' schooling and promoted his career. In 1941 the color-blind Hoffman made Davis the first black to appear on the cover of a major weightlifting publication, raising the hackles of prejudiced readers. "Can you imagine my extreme repugnance and indignation when I went to purchase my favorite magazine and found J. Davis' gluteus maximus staring me in the face," complained one reader in Alabama. "I nearly went stark raving mad with insult and horror."

In 1946 Hoffman took the U. S. squad (which was comprised almost entirely of lifters on the York payroll) to Paris for the first World Championship held since the international event was suspended eight years earlier. Davis became the only champion from that last prewar meet in 1938 to repeat, while the U. S. team as a whole out-pointed all other countries, including Russia. The large and rugged Hoffman, a decorated infantry officer in the First World War, regularly employed jingoism to sell the sport (and his products) to the public. He saw his team's performance in Paris as a reaffirmation of American values in the deepening freeze of the Cold War between the Soviets and the free world. "America's victory in weightlifting more than any other thing depicts America's strength," he declared. "In France we were told by pleased French officials that the American victory was worth more to the continued cause of world peace than the display of force by a fleet of battleships, by a thousand planes or by a

Norb's mother Josephine.

Norb's father Joseph.

Norb on the day of his first communion in 1933.

Norb, at age 18, enjoying the outdoors with his brother Dennis and his two nieces.

Army Private Norbert "Hercules" Schemansky. (1943)

Norb eyes the sky for enemy planes while manning a water-cooled .50 caliber machine gun in the Meudon Forest of France in 1944.

Norb with his fellow soldiers in the gun pit in Normandy in 1944: Carl Neych, Harold Paulsen, Frank Cwik and Frank Riccio.

Norb's brothers, Ralph and Dennis, also served in the military during World War II.

Jerome Schemansky, 16 years of age, became the first Mr. Michigan. He would ultimately win a national YMCA and a North American title.

The renowned Schemansky brothers, Dennis, Ralph, Norb and Jerome strike a pose. Except for Ralph, who didn't compete, all three of the brothers would earn the title of Junior National Champion.

Bernice and Norb enjoy the summer day on the porch of their Detroit home.

Lauded by a Russian magazine as "the strongest weightlifter in the world," Norb, along with Bernice and their children Paula and Pam, prepare to leave for Sunday Easter Mass.

Larry, Pam, Paula and Laura Schemansky gather around their kitchen table in their Dearborn, Michigan home in the early 1960s. Laura blackened her nose after falling on the sidewalk.

The four Schemansky children re-create their favorite childhood photo in the same Dearborn kitchen forty years later.

Norb clowns with Bernice while his sister Esther and her son Wayne join in on the fun.

Bernice along with her mother, and her sister Winnie, enjoy a reunion with Bernice's two brothers, Ray and Chuck.

As a gifted all-around athlete, Norb could hurl a football over seventy yards and run the hundred yard dash in 10.4 seconds.

The earliest known photo of the future "Mr. Weightlifting." Norb trained at the Yacos Gym in Detroit in 1941.

Norb demonstrates his flawless lifting technique enroute to capturing 2nd place at the World Weightlifting Championships in 1947.

The Detroit born sensation, exhibiting his superbly built physique.

Norb flexes for the camera showcasing his impressively thick eighteen inch arm and solid overall body development. Many experts believe that had Norb pursued a body building career that he could have been a Mr. Universe winner.

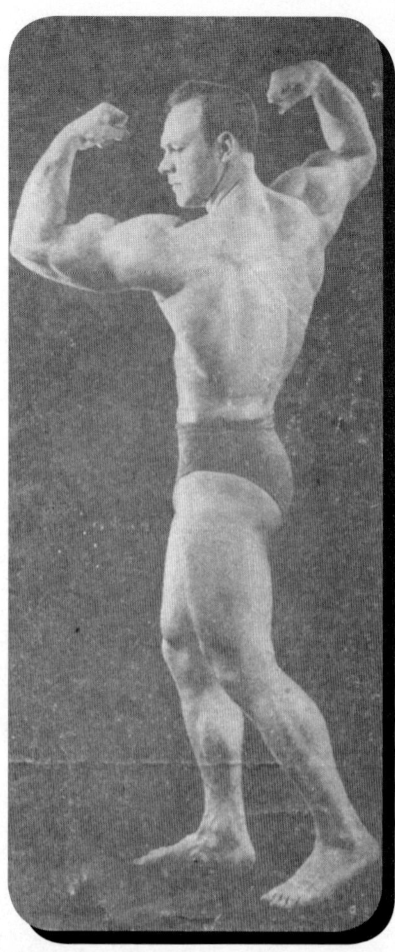

Norb reveals his championship muscles. The mild, spectacle-wearing-father recently returned home after beating the Russians again in hand-to-hand competition. Very few people in his hometown of Detroit or elsewhere in the country seemed to know that "the strongest man in the world" lived in the United States." He remained unheralded as he struggled to find a job to support Bernice and their three children.

Norb, along with 1948 Olympic weightlifting teammates Joe DiPietro, Richard Tom and Emerick Ishikawa, enjoy the camaraderie of Iran's Jaffar Salmassi in London, England.

1948 U.S. Olympic weightlifting team: (not in order) Norb, Stan Stanczyk, Johnny Terpak, Pete George, Joe Pitman, Frank Spellman, Harold Sakata, Joe DiPietro, Richard Tom, John Davis, Richard Tomita and Emerick Ishikawa.

Michigan's best weightlifters, Norb along with Stanley Stanczyk, revel in the fun times of the Olympic experience.

Norb prepares for his next record setting hoist in his first Olympic games in 1948. He earned the silver medal and impressed his contemporaries with his awesome command of the trio of difficult lifts.

Silver medalist Schemansky, along with gold medalist John Davis, and the bronze medalist Bram Charite, prepare to receive their Olympic medals in London, England.

In 1951 Norb mesmerized fans in Milan, Italy with his brilliant record-setting performance. He earned the world championship title.

“Skee” works out at the York gym in “Muscletown USA” in preparation for the impending Olympics Games in Helsinki, Finland.

Norb examines some of Bob Hoffman’s hardware in Hoffman’s mansion in York, Pennsylvania.

Arriving in Helsinki, Finland the weightlifting team, considered the greatest in U.S history, prepares to be transferred to the Olympic village. Pictured left to right: Coach Bob Hoffman, Trainer Al Roy, Pete George, John Davis, Jim Bradford, Manager Johnny Terpak, Richard Tomita, Clyde Emrich, Richard Tom, Stanley Stanczyk, Norb, and Tommy Kono.

Two of the finest weightlifters ever, Tommy Kono and Pete George both earned gold medals for the United States at the 1952 Olympic Games.

Russia's Grigori Novak congratulates the new world champion Olympic gold medalist Norbert Schemansky. Norb was greatly admired by the Russian people who revered strength above all other sports qualities. Norb's triumph was hailed as a great victory over their previously undefeated national hero.

Norb along with his beer drinking buddies and fellow weightlifters, Dave Sheppard, John Davis, Jim Bradford, Clyde Emrich, Tommy Kono, Pete George and Manager Clarence Johnson soak up the atmosphere in a German pub in the

Looking like Superman himself, Norb breaks another world record enroute to winning the Olympic gold medal and breaking the hearts of the Russian people. His triumph of the invincible Russian champion during the height of the Cold War is considered one of the greatest victories in the history of sports.

While in a stopover in Lille, France Norb used his tremendous leg and body power to lift the cumbersome 366 pound Apollon railway wheels. He cleaned it, and then jerked it three times to the amazement of all present.

After seeing Norb conquer the Apollon bar with relative ease, many spectators who witnessed the historic demonstration proclaimed it as "the greatest feat of strength ever seen." Norb's performance proved so convincing to French authorities that the Apollon bar remains retired to this day—fifty years later.

dozen divisions of soldiers. For the world knows while America has sufficient interest in developing strength and muscles to excel that they are a strong virile race."

As the country's foremost promoter of the iron game, Hoffman was able to bring the World Championships to the United States for the first time. He spared no expense, even helping to underwrite the costs of foreign lifters to the two-day event, which was held September 26-27, 1947, at Philadelphia's 15,000-seat Municipal Auditorium. Partially because the Russian and Egyptian teams decided not to participate, the venue was never more than one-third filled. But those who did show up witnessed a coming-out party of sorts for what *Iron Man* described as "America's new heavyweight sensation, Norbert Schemansky." Peary Rader, the editor of the popular fitness digest, was so impressed he led off twenty pages of coverage with a full-page studio shot of Norb posed inside the Yacos Gym.

Although John Davis outdistanced Norb, Czechoslovakia's Vaclar Becvar and Argentina's Hugo Vallarino to retain the world heavyweight crown, the "beautiful lifting of Norb Schemansky thrilled the audience due to the fine gains he has made," reported Rader. "He looks much more powerful now too. George Yacos, his trainer, was so excited he could hardly sit in his chair while Norb was lifting. Norb proved himself one of the world's strongest men and one of the most beautiful lifters. He should make a 1,000-pound total with proper training next year and should in the process make two new world records. He badly needs about 20 more pounds bodyweight. With this added bodyweight his press would go much higher. He should easily press 280 or more then.

"Norb is a family man with the obligations that go with it and can't always train as he would like. He was also suffering with a pulled muscle in his leg as was John Davis but both of them came through in great style."

In the snatch, Norb started with 264½ pounds, reported Rader, "which went easy, then a fine 275½, his former record made at the Senior Nationals. The crowd was surprised when he asked for 286½ and you should have heard the applause when he tossed this in the air for a perfect and beautiful snatch. This boy has beautiful form…he completed every lift in the meet."

Not to be outdone, Davis started with an easy 281, then snatched 308—a new world's record.

"In the clean and jerk," continued Rader, "Becvar and Vallarino both started with 314¼, then Vallarino failed twice with the 330¾ and Becvar made it but failed to make 341¾ when the weight fell on him. Schemansky was going great on the clean and jerk and started with 330¾, which went like a feather. He then made 352¾, then took the tremendous poundage of 363¾. With a tremendous pull and a great heave, he held it overhead for the count.

"The crowd was cheering so much that Davis, who had in the meantime succeeded with 352¾, decided to give them something to get excited about, so he asked for 385. I think very few there expected him to make this lift. Because of his injured leg he had been pulling the weights very high using a high split (what amazing power this man has when he wants to use it). He walked up to the weight and with very little hesitation, grasped the weight and with a wild vicious pull, brought the weight to chest with very little split. He then gave it a terrific heave to arms length overhead but the right arm bent a little, but with a battle he straightened it out again and held the lift for the clap. The crowd really went wild then. Cameramen all over the stage—officials clamoring around Davis to congratulate him and incidentally get in the pictures. I fully believe that had it been necessary, he could have cleaned 400 pounds that night and also bettered his press and snatch records."

The final tallies showed Davis had totaled 1,003¼ pounds to Norb's 909¼ "And so ended," gushed Rader, "the greatest weight lifting meet ever witnessed." Hyperbole aside, it had been a thrilling competition, one that served notice on the lifting world that a new star had arrived on the international stage—and that he was only going to get better.

As Perry Rader mentioned in his glowing coverage in *Iron Man,* Norb was now a family man. On April 28, 1947, he and Bernice Spencer were married in a small ceremony in Detroit.

Norb had first spotted Bernice inside a neighborhood drug store. The slender and sparkling green-eyed blonde working the counter at Cunningham's was of Irish, Polish and French Canadian descent and had attended Southeastern High School. "We just hit it off," said Norb. "She was nice and she was easy to talk to." In addition to Bernice's good looks, Norb was attracted to her unselfish nature, her unflagging enthusiasm, and a wide smile that never faded during their forty-nine years of marriage.

Bernice's father had died when she was young, leaving her mother to raise five children on her own. So the new Mrs. Schemansky was accustomed to doing without, an important consideration given Norb's growing preoccupation with weightlifting. "Bernice was kind of interested in the sport," said Norb. "In any event, she never told me to stop. If she had, I would have. If not for her, I wouldn't have accomplished all I did in weightlifting." Said Norb's sister, Esther: "I honestly don't think anybody else would've put up with him." (Esther held a dim view of weightlifting. Her husband Mike was a gym rat, and their son, Wayne Zoran, was a future Mr. Michigan titleholder.)

The newlywed lifter was still adjusting to married life when Paula, the first of four children born to Norb and Bernice, came along. A family meant responsibilities. Luckily for Norb, the assembly lines were humming. Years of pent-up consumer demand for automobiles (new car production had been suspended during the war) meant there was a factory job in the Motor City for anybody who wanted one. Not that Norb particularly wanted one. "Plants are oily, smelly, noisy places," said Norb, who was hired at Dodge Main. He inspected engine blocks for six or seven months before getting into an argument with a foreman and quitting. Next he hired on at Hudson Motors. "Twenty guys bumping into each other, nothing automated," is how he remembered his two-week stay on Hudson's assembly line. "One day I got hit in the head by the rack that held the car frame and I said, 'Screw this,' and quit."

Schemansky hated the mind-numbing monotony of the assembly line, but he had bills to pay and mouths to feed. He next punched the clock at the Briggs plant on Mack Avenue, where he was initially put to work inspecting windows and radio antennas. The environment was slightly more palatable at Briggs, and he would wind up working there for four years, most of that time as a stock chaser. But Norb wasn't at his new employer very long before he requested a month off. The reason? The former ack-ack gunner was going back to England. This time around, however, Norb's sights weren't trained on Nazi aircraft. They were set on an Olympic medal.

CHAPTER FOUR

Olympian

Norb had great technique. He was a super technician who made it look easy. He's the best lifter I ever saw in the whole world.

Richard Tom, 1948 U.S. Olympic Weightlifting Team

To get to London Norb first had to pass through Chicago, where he grabbed the top spot in the sectional trials, and then New York, where he was runner-up to John Davis in the final Olympic tryouts at the Riverside Plaza Auditorium. His three-lift total was up to 930, and he was jerking 352—and was confident he could do considerably more. He felt good, and his fast, fluid, clean-cut style impressed Bob Hoffman and other longtime veterans of the iron game. El Saied Nosseir, the famous Egyptian trainer and a former world heavyweight champion, would get his first look at Schemansky at the 1948 Olympics. "I wish that he were an Egyptian," said Nosseir, who had a reputation for developing stylish champions and thus knew one when he saw one.

The history of Olympic weightlifting does not, as one might suppose, stretch back to the original games in ancient Greece. Although humans have admired extraordinary strength since the first man lifted a boulder on a dare, and many nations share the legend of the boy who became a weightlifting champion by lifting his prize calf every day from the moment of the animal's birth until it was a fully grown bull, there is no record of the sport being part of any Olympiad between 776 B.C. and 394 A.D. However, when the Olympics were revived as a modern spectacle in 1896, weightlifting had developed into a popular international sport and was thus included in the inaugural program of events.

The 1896 games in Athens, Greece featured just two lifting events: the one-hand and two-hand dumbbell contests, won by an Englishman and a Dane, respectively. The sport was dropped from the 1900 Games, reinstated for the 1904 Olympics in St. Louis, Missouri (where Otto Osthoff won the first U.S. medal gold medal in the sport with a one-hand lift of 191¼ pounds), then dropped again. It wasn't until the 1920 Olympics in Antwerp, Belgium that weightlifting found a permanent place on the program. The one- and two-handed lifts were replaced by what became the three traditional Olympic lifts: the press, the snatch, and the clean and jerk. The Antwerp Games also established five weight divisions (later expanded to seven). There was no U.S. lifting team entered in the 1920 and 1924 Olympics, and the squad that participated in the 1928 Games failed to medal. Finally, in the 1932 Games in Los Angeles, featherweight Anthony Terlazzo and light-heavyweight Henry Duey won bronze medals. Terlazzo followed up with a gold in the 1936 "Nazi Olympics" in Berlin, after which war brought an end to the world's premier athletic festival for the next dozen years.

The 1940 Games were first scheduled for Tokyo, Japan and then moved to Helsinki, Finland before being canceled, while the 1944 Games were to have been held in London. Two years later, with much of Europe in shambles, Londoners agreed to host the first postwar Olympics, chiefly because nobody else really wanted to. It wasn't a universally popular decision. Some were of the opinion that the focus should be on rebuilding, not diverting funds for an athletic festival. But many others regarded renewing the Olympic games after a twelve-year hiatus as a celebration of the human spirit. According to Dominic Sutherland, who produced a documentary on the '48 Olympics, "People were really looking for something positive to celebrate against the backdrop of what was a very tough, austere time."

"Austere" was indeed the operative word of what the International Olympic Committee (IOC) officially labeled the Games of the XIV Olympiad (but which was dubbed the "Austere Olympics" and the "Spartan Games" by members of the press, the public, and the participants themselves). London was still digging itself out of the rubble caused by years of Nazi bombings and

Brits were enduring shortages of just about everything. Frugality was practiced at every level, with ration cards regulating the consumption of everything from milk to petrol. A shortage of time and construction materials meant there would be none of the building frenzy that had characterized previous Olympics. "Instead," said Sutherland, "they converted Wembley Stadium, which had been a dog-racing track up until three weeks before the Games, into the main stadium. For the Olympic swimming pool at Wembley Arena, they had to scrape the blackout paint off the glass. Herne Hill, where the cycling was held, had been a barrage-balloon site during the war. So it was really like dusting everything off to get things ready and it worked out, against the odds." In the absence of an Olympic village, athletes were housed in empty barracks, school dormitories, and private homes. British female athletes bought into the spirit of improvisation by sewing their own uniforms.

Norb admired the "Blitz spirit" that had carried the Brits through the war and now characterized their approach to the challenge of hosting the Olympics. As an amateur athlete, however, he'd already been living a life of sacrifice. In order to train and attend the final tryouts in New York, he was forced to ask his boss for several weeks off without pay, leaving Bernice—who was pregnant with their second child while also working as a secretary—to hold down the fort. (Pamela would be born the following February.) He'd had to find his own way to New York. "I went into the Paramount Hotel, broke," said Norb. "I told the desk clerk and he let me stay there." Once aboard the liner headed for England, the A.A.U. officially took over responsibility for the American athletes' welfare, passing out uniforms, patches, and so on. Norb always thought most A.A.U. executives were clueless sycophants, and his low regard for those he regarded as "deltoid warmers" was only reinforced by their suggestion that all athletes train while on the ship to England. "Weightlifting is all about balance and coordination," he said. "Now tell me, how do you lift weights with the boat rocking all the time?"

Reflecting the lingering animosity of the immediate postwar era, two of the three Axis Powers, Japan and Germany, were not invited (although the third, Italy, was). The Soviet Union and the brand new nation of Israel were not IOC members and thus not allowed to participate. Nonetheless, London attracted a record number of countries (59) and athletes (4,099) to the no-frills affair, which King George VI officially kicked off on a sun-kissed July day at jam-packed Wembley Stadium. The Olympic torch was lit, cannons boomed, and thousands of white pigeons were released. The message on the giant scoreboard read:

> The important thing in the Olympic Games is not winning but taking part. The Essential thing in Life is not conquering but fighting well.

Norb savored as much as he could of his first Olympic experience. Although he was destined to appear in three more Olympics, at the time he couldn't be sure there ever would be another opportunity like this. Snapshots of the ocean crossing and subsequent time in London show Norb and his fellow lifters cutting up, socializing with foreign athletes, and soaking in the sights like any group of tourists on extended holiday.

Coach and financial angel Bob Hoffman spent $20,000 of his own money to sponsor the team's Olympic odyssey. Norb wasn't part of the York gang that worked, lived, and trained in Pennsylvania, but there were a couple familiar faces. One was Stanley Stanczyk, who had a background similar to Norb's. The Detroit Pole had served in the army, where he earned a Purple Heart and somehow managed to drag a 330-pound weight set made of welded iron plates across the Pacific. "We ran into each other at local competitions before and after the war," recalled Norb. "He trained at the Boys' Club. He was a fast runner, a good gymnast—a pretty good all-around athlete." At the 1942 Senior Nationals, seventeen-year-old Stanczyk—competing in only his third contest—jerked more than twice his body weight to win the lightweight class, causing the press to dub him "the young Superman." The happy-go-lucky Stanczyk shattered several records as he won the national and world championships as a middleweight in 1947. That year *Your Physique* magazine published an article entitled "TERRIFIC is the Word for Stanczyk." It was tough to argue against that description, even as he moved up another class to light heavyweight for his first Olympics. By the time he retired in 1954 he had won a total of five world championships and six national titles while competing in three different weight divisions. Then, in a further display of his athletic versatility, he switched to bowling, maintaining a 190-pin average over twenty-five years. The one thing

Stanczyk didn't share with Norb was a ubiquitous nickname. Like hundreds of thousands of other Poles with an "sky" or "ski" at the end of his surname, Norb saw Schemansky corrupted to a simple "Skee." And that's what he was known as around the locker room.

The other familiar face belonged to Emerick Ishikawa, the Japanese-American featherweight from Hawaii whose ethnicity had caused him to be placed in an internment camp upon the outbreak of war. Ishikawa eventually moved to Pennsylvania to work for York and to compete, then relocated to Detroit, where he won the last of four straight national titles while training out of the Yacos Gym. (Curiously, fully one-third of the twelve-man American squad hailed from Hawaii, including Ishikawa, bantamweight Richard Tom, featherweight Richard Tomita, and light heavyweight Harold Sakata. All trained at the Nuuanu Y.M.C.A. in Honolulu.)

One of Norb's most lasting memories of Ishikawa also involves Stanczyk and a bodybuilder named Carl Magnusson. "The three of them used to do a seven or eight minute hand-balancing act around Detroit," he recalled. "They called themselves 'Rock, Stone and Boulder.' Magnusson weighed 200 pounds, so he was the guy at the bottom. They'd play at nightclubs, or any place they could to get a few dollars. Of course, they couldn't have made too much money because of the A.A.U. rules. Magnusson was Boulder because he was the biggest, but to this day I still don't know who was Rock and who was Stone."

Food was a major concern at the Games. There was some griping by the U.S. contingent, spoiled as they were by the bountiful meals—at least by London standards—they were used to enjoying at home. American athletes found Spam fritters and toad-in-the-hole (sausages baked inside a Yorkshire pudding) "laughable," said Dominic Sutherland. Everyday items like fresh eggs were a precious commodity in the dining hall. "You'd go up to the cook at breakfast and say you wanted a couple of eggs and he'd say, 'No, you get just one egg,'" recalled Norb. "I could see them being pissed off, though. They're half starving and here's some weightlifter saying, 'Gimme a steak.'" In recognition of lean times in London, many participating countries had agreed to bring supplies. Argentina had promised 100 tons of meat, Iceland was to provide frozen mutton, and Holland was on the hook for an unspecified amount of fruit and vegetables. The American contribution included 42 tons of meat, 36 tons of cheese, and 25,000 chocolate candy bars. Thousands of gallons of mineral water and 150,000 eggs also were brought in.

As the following letter from George Yacos to Norb illustrates, two of life's necessities—money and food—were never far from the mind of those competing in England.

> July 27, 1948
>
> Dear Norb,
>
> I am sending $20.00 which has been collected to date and shall try to snare more right along. Fellows are reluctant to part with money for whatever the cause.
>
> The biggest donors were Poliuto and Tony DaGutis, each shelling out $5.00 with Bidak giving $2.00.
>
> From what we read in the papers the food deal over there is stinky. It should feel fine getting back to the U.S.A. after the deprivation you experience in England. Losing weight may push Stanczyk into the middle-wgt. class. He was quoted in the News as saying he can't lift well on the food being dished out; he'll have to have good American food....
>
> Met Otto on the street car a little while ago. He says I should call Pinky and maybe there is an outside chance he might dig up a check for you in some way....
>
> Things in general are much the same as when you left. Jerome called up the other day wanting to know if I had heard anything from Eng. as well as how the final tryouts came out. I suggested he send you some dough so brace yourself in case he comes through.
>
> If you are in a position to, jot down a few items on the other lifters and things in general on lifting which you know we back here would like to hear.
>
> This is it for now so until later...So Long,
>
> Yacos

If caloric intake among individual American athletes suffered, overall U.S. performance did not. The United States won 84 total medals, nearly double the number of runner-up Sweden.

The London Olympics were the first to be televised, though the technology was still in its infancy and broadcasts were limited to the handful of sets in the British Isles. Back home, interested Americans followed events as they always had: through radio, newspapers and newsreels. Norb claimed to be neither nervous nor overly excited; instead the already worldly twenty-four-year-old directed his energy toward focusing on the details of daily preparations. "Your mind is on your training routine more than anything else," he explained. Unlike some competitors who spent several minutes psyching their self up for an upcoming lift, Norb typically began to concentrate on his pending performance only in the last few seconds before he approached the barbell. "I figured if I sat there trying to focus my mind, there was a good chance that somebody would cough or some baby would cry and all of a sudden I'd lose my concentration."

The lifting events were staged at Empress Hall, where Schemansky competed at 205 pounds. "I knew I couldn't catch Davis," he said. "I was lighter, an up-and-comer. I figured a silver medal was probably the best I could do." He was right. He pressed 270, snatched 292, and jerked 352½ to finish with 937, sixty pounds off Davis' Olympic record total. Norb also attempted a world's record on an extra attempt, barely failing with 396 in the clean and jerk.

As is always the case at the Olympics, the London Games produced its share of "feel good" tales. Among lifters, perhaps the best story involved the British lightweight James Halliday, whose experiences working the "death railway" in Siam as a Japanese prisoner during the war whittled him down to skin and bones. Halliday returned to England, where he shoveled coal all day in a power station and lifted weights in his bedroom at night. He wound up with a bronze medal for his dedication, the kind of redemptive story the world was crying out for in the immediate postwar years.

For American weightlifters, the story was the squad's near-total domination in London. Stubby-armed Joe DePietro made his first—and last—Olympic appearance a success, the 34-year-old mighty mite from New Jersey grabbing gold in the bantamweight division. The featherweight and lightweight crowns went to members of the powerful Egyptian team, but Americans were the top two finishers in each of the three heaviest classifications—middleweight, light heavyweight, and heavyweight. Stanley Stanczyk received praise for his sportsmanship, insisting that a world-record snatch judges had just passed be disqualified because his knee had touched the ground. This put American officials in the unusual position of having to file a formal protest against a member of their own team. The lift was overturned, and then Stanczyk returned a few minutes later with a second record snatch, a gold medal, and the most lopsided victory in Olympic weightlifting annals: nearly 83 pounds more than runner-up and teammate Harold Sakata.

What follows are the medal winners at the 1948 Olympics, with their three-lift totals measured in kilograms and corresponding U.S. pounds. (In international competition, lifts are always officially recorded in metric units. In converting from kilos to pounds, figures are rounded off to the quarter-pound for simplicity in comparison.)

Bantamweight		**Kgs.**	**(Lbs.)**
Gold:	Joe DePietro, United States	307.5	(678)
Silver:	Julian Creus, Great Britain	297.5	(655¾)
Bronze:	Richard Tom, United States	295	(650¼)
Featherweight		**Kgs.**	**(Lbs.)**
Gold:	Mahmoud Fayad, Egypt	332.5	(773)
Silver:	Rodney Wilkes, Trinidad	317.5	(700)
Bronze:	Jafar Salmasi, Iran	312.5	(689)
Lightweight		**Kgs.**	**(Lbs.)**
Gold:	Ibrahim Shams, Egypt	360	(793¾)
Silver:	Attia Hamouda, Egypt	360	(793¾)
Bronze:	James Halliday, Great Britain	340	(749½)
Middleweight		**Kgs.**	**(Lbs.)**
Gold:	Frank Spellman, United States	390	(859¾)
Silver:	Peter George, United States	382.5	(843¼)
Bronze:	Sung-Jip Kim, Korea	380	(837¾)
Light Heavyweight		**Kgs.**	**(Lbs.)**
Gold:	Stanley Stanczyk, United States	417.5	(920½)
Silver:	Harold Sakata, United States	380	(837¾)
Bronze:	Gosta Magnussen, Sweden	375	(826¾)
Heavyweight		**Kgs.**	**(Lbs.)**
Gold:	John Davis, United States	452.5	(997½)
Silver:	Norb Schemansky, United States	425	(937)
Bronze:	Abraham Charite, Netherlands	412.5	(909½)

Unlike today, an Olympic medal in 1948 was not a meal ticket to immediate riches. Harold Sakata was one of several team members who retired from competition soon after the London Games. As he explained at the time: "A very wise man asked me if I were happy. Sure, I said. 'And you're proud of those silver trophies?' Sure I'm proud. 'Now let's see if you can eat them,' he said." Sakata turned to professional wrestling to put food on the table, then became an actor, gaining far greater recognition and financial reward as the henchman Oddjob in the 1964 James Bond movie, *Goldfinger*, than he ever did as an Olympic medalist.

When Norb returned to his home in Detroit, there were some congratulatory shoulder slaps at the gym and some mild bragging by his brothers in local saloons, but that basically was it. As was the case with Sakata, there was no material effect on Norb's life as a result of his winning a silver medal. The Olympian and his young family were still sharing a house with his sister and brother-in-law, and Briggs Manufacturing still required Norb's presence at the plant bright and early each morning.

"I came home," he recalled with a shrug, "and put the medal in a drawer."

In the wake of the Olympics, family responsibilities kept Norb close to home except for thrice-weekly training sessions at the gym and an occasional road trip to compete in a major meet. In the spring of 1949 he traveled to Cleveland for the Senior Nationals. There, with John Davis absent, he won the first of his nine national titles despite having to lift with a badly sprained right hand and wrist. The following year he took first at the inaugural Y.M.C.A. Championships in Baltimore (he would repeat the next two years), placed second to Davis at the Nationals in Philadelphia, then won his second straight North American Championship in Montreal with a tournament-record 380 clean and jerk. He was edging towards the 1,000-pound mark, typically finishing in the range of 940 to 960 total pounds.

In 1950 Norb moved his young family out of his sister's house and into a lower flat at 3373 Charlevoix. The rent was reasonably cheap—thirty dollars a month—and the house was directly across the street from the Franklin Wright Settlement, a respected nonprofit neighborhood center that offered day care for the Schemanskys' two little girls when Norb and Bernice worked. He'd also shifted his training from the Yacos Gym to a more convenient location, the Northeastern Y.M.C.A. on Harper at Cadillac. There he worked out with his brother Jerome and a couple of firefighters who were also well-known bodybuilders, Don Van Fleteren and Vic Seipke.

Typically, Norb's heaviest training night was Monday. His routine included three or four presses at 240 pounds to start, increasing in 15- to 20-pound increments to his limit. He did the same with the snatch. For his cleans, he would begin with 325 pounds and then jump up to 370 or 380. If he was successful at cleaning that amount, he'd jerk the weight two or three times. On average training nights, he worked in sets of three while pressing and snatching amounts not too close to his limit, saving his energy to "push" a little on the clean and jerk. "The jerk always came natural to me, so I didn't practice it that much," he recalled. "About two or three times a month I'd practice jerks with weights up to my top clean." Norb could continental and jerk 430 pounds. (The "continental" was a variant of the clean, allowing the lifter to pull the barbell up to his belt, where it could rest before being moved up the torso until the barbell was in position to be jerked overhead. This two-step pull to the shoulders was a slow and clumsy movement and usually only done in training or exhibitions.) Although Norb was primarily a three-lift specialist, he could dead-lift 600 pounds and squat almost 500.

During this period Skee attracted the notice of Clarence Johnson, a lifting enthusiast who ran an accounting business on Woodward Avenue in Highland Park. In the 1920s Johnson became active on the board of the Northeastern "Y" and was elected the A.A.U.'s local representative, often serving as a referee at meets. "I couldn't afford the monthly dues, so he started letting me in for free," recalled Norb. "He was a good schmoozer, a social climber. He'd pick up tabs for local lifters, play golf with guys from the Internal Revenue Service." Johnson often would prevail upon Norb to give an exhibition before a church group or at a local school. Although their friendship would later sour, in these early years both men enjoyed a mutually beneficial relationship.

In 1951 the International Weightlifting Federation created a new classification, the middle-heavyweight division for lifters up to 198¼ pounds (90 kilograms). The overdue change allowed Norb to compete in the new bracket or as a heavyweight, depending on the circumstances, though training down to contest weight as a mid-heavy would soon become problematic. For the first couple years, however, it proved to be his most effective weight. He left the heavyweight division to John Davis (who lifted a world-record 1,062 pounds at the '51 Pan American Games in Buenos Aires, Argentina) and Jim Bradford. Slimming down to 196 pounds, Skee took that year's Nationals at Los Angeles in grand style, setting new world marks in the fledgling class in the snatch (295 pounds) and the clean and jerk (370¾). Some of those in attendance at the June meet clutched copies of the prior month's issue of *Strength & Health,* which featured Norb on its cover for the first time.

That fall, Norb accompanied the U.S. team to Milan, Italy for the World Championships. The three-day competition began October 26 at the Milan Ice and Sports Palace. Norb was still burned up about being passed over for the previous year's tournament in Paris, when Davis, Stan Stanczyk and Pete George had led the American team to an upset win over the favored Egyptian squad and the Russians. Norb felt sure he could have beaten Davis as a heavyweight, but Bob Hoffman wasn't convinced. He was spending in the neighborhood of $15,000 to bring the American entourage overseas, and once again his money spoke loudest.

The Russians, evidently stung by their third-place team finish the year before, sat this one out, though their imminent arrival was rumored for days. Skee had some fun with it, at one point sidling up to a teammate as somebody pounded on a door during a training session and whispering, "Don't look around for a second—the Russians have arrived." The lifter turned around anyway, just in time to see two elderly spectators, one leaning on a crutch, the other sporting a white beard, shuffle into the room.

Hoffman had his own opinion about why the Russians opted not to compete. "They've heard about Schemansky," he said, "and they don't want their great hero, Grigori Novak, beaten by him. It would be a terrible thing for the Russians if their invincible champion was beaten by an American."

Norb's powers of concentration impressed observers like Charles Coster, who was on hand to report for *Muscle Power* magazine. He saw Norb fail in his first attempt at a 280-pound snatch. He described what happened next.

"Before taking the same poundage once again," wrote Coster, "he spent the time almost completely enveloped in a huge blanket while he concentrated upon the task before him. When he was ready, the blanket was thrown off, those long powerful legs propelled him forward…and he ripped the bar aloft to score a perfect lift. This was followed three minutes later by another magnificent success with 292 lbs. The same evening he recorded three successful clean & jerks with 352-363-374 lbs.—the last poundage being a new world record.

"Not content with this, he asked for 385 lbs. for an extra attempt outside the championships. His first try with this weight was a failure to 'clean' by a narrow margin…so once more the blanket was brought out, and once more he spent a few minutes of precious meditation and mental concentration. This time he made a magnificent success, and he received a standing ovation from an appreciative audience."

Skee totaled 942¼ pounds to become the first middle-heavyweight champion of the world. He, John Davis, and all other winners were presented with their prizes during a banquet held in the Giardino d'Inverno (Winter Garden) of the Odeon. "Pete George had a beautiful silver cup as the outstanding lifter," observed Oscar State in a wrap-up for *The Weightlifter & Bodybuilder,* "but Schemansky was the most envied, because he received a first-class miniature camera."

Norb continued to lift like a man possessed. In a local meet in December 1951, he competed as a 207-pound heavyweight and scored a 280 + 310 + 390 = 980, his best total yet. On an extra attempt he made what was thought to be a 405-pound clean and jerk. When the barbell was weighed, however, the scales showed it was only 400½. That wasn't quite enough to break John Davis's record of 402, but it was just enough to establish Norb as the lightest man ever to clean and jerk 400 pounds.

Skee won a third straight national Y.M.C.A. championship as a heavyweight in April 1952, then began the process of getting in middle-heavyweight trim for the upcoming Senior Nationals and Olympic trials, to be held in June in New York. Once again he needed about six or seven weeks off from work.

This time, however, his request for an unpaid leave of absence was met with hostility from his boss.

"Tell him he can have all the time off he wants," was some bigwig's response. "He's fired!"

Norb went upstairs, exchanged a few harsh words, then left Briggs Manufacturing for good. Whether he was fired or quit didn't really matter. He was more concerned about winning the Nationals and grabbing gold in Helsinki, Finland.

Revisiting the Yacos Gym

by Phil Levine

Working-class poet Phil Levine was easily the most literary lifter at the Yacos Gym in postwar Detroit. Levine, who left Detroit to pursue an academic career, would go on to receive the National Book Award and the Pulitzer Prize. He currently teaches at New York University.

My twin brother Eddie and I joined the Yacos Gym in 1946 while attending Wayne University. Eddie had seen a show that George Yacos put on at the Jewish Community Center on Woodward near Northern High School. The stars of that show were two bodybuilders, Bill Hooper and Bill Ghesquire, and the great Hawaiian lifter, Emerick Ishikawa, all of whom worked out at Yacos Gym. Eddie marveled at the perfection of Hooper's physique and assured me we would do well to look that good. We were eighteen years old, students of course, but also in hot (if often useless) pursuit of female company and still young enough to put some dwindling faith in the precepts of Charles Atlas.

The Yacos Gym was located in what had been the ground-floor dining area of the Taft Hotel on Davenport near Woodward. This was not prime real estate, but it was a short walk from Wayne and by no means forbidding. On our first visit to the gym George Yacos greeted us at the desk, which sat near the entrance, and explained the charges –it cost something like $10 a month—as well as the benefits. For 25 cents a visit you got a towel and the use of the shower, you could come as often as you wanted, and the gym stayed open until 9 p.m.

Where the walls were not plastered with mirrors they were covered with photographs of weightlifters and bodybuilders of the past and present, from Eugen Sandow to Tony Sansome to John Grimek. There was nothing that in the least resembled those weight machines that crowd today's gyms and so-called health clubs, for this was basic stuff. The only machines were the human bodies, and there were plenty of those, all male. Before we escaped into the locker room to dress for our initial workouts George gave us his lecture on the only political course that made sense to him; alas, he was a devotee of Technocracy, Inc., and believed the reins of society should be handed over to the technocrats, the trained engineers and scientists responsible for the miracles of modern life—the light bulb, the telephone, the radio, the automobile, the airplane, the atom bomb, the death camps. (Those last two are my inclusions.) Was George a fascist? I think not; I think he was a good-hearted working-class guy who'd read a few books and fallen for some zany notions. He was clearly a racist, but displayed no animosity toward Asians and Jews. He was a typical Detroiter of that era.

I settled on a Monday-Wednesday-Friday workout schedule, for the most part during the afternoons, and it was during a workout within that first month that I discovered two of the strongest men I'd ever seen: Al Koernke and the still unknown Norbert Schemansky.

They could not have looked less alike. A big man, large chested, with an imposing presence, Koernke had almost black hair and spoke with a deep and penetrating voice. Before I learned his name I took Schemansky to be Nordic with his fine light brown hair, light eyes, and a voice that, though breathy, was surprisingly gentle. With his dark-framed glasses he had the look of a college professor and a body out of classical sculpture. He was by far the more powerful looking of the two with enormous sculpted thighs, great broad shoulders, and an almost flat chest. He moved with great precision and care. Poised over an Olympic barbell, arms relaxed, he seemed to go into what I can only describe as a trance for close to a minute before he plunged to initiate the lift. The weights he handled with such ease—practice snatches with over 200 pounds, clean and jerks with almost 300—were to me astonishing. The two were in training for a national competition, both were heavyweights (technically, though neither weighed over 200 pounds), and were two of the finest lifters in the country. Often Norbert's younger brother Jerome would show up at the gym. Although taller than Norbert—he was over six feet and probably weighed about 210—he lacked Norbert's athleticism and determination. In character he was nothing like his brother. Unlike Norb, he swaggered about the gym with great joy in his strength and ferocity.

Later I saw Norbert compete in the U.S. Nationals, held in Detroit. All the heavyweights lifted against John Davis—then regarded as the strongest man in the world—who outweighed Norbert by probably 20 pounds. I doubt Norbert was even 200 then. It was clear that Davis had greater brute strength and pressed substantially more, but Norbert was the better athlete. His technique with the split snatch has never been excelled, and his quickness was awesome. I can no longer recall where Norb and Koernke finished in the competition which Davis won easily. Two years later they would compete in the 1948 Olympics and Davis would take the gold medal, Norbert the silver.

It was not long after Norbert's return from London and those Olympics that I saw him one afternoon in Yacos sitting in a very untypical and seemingly morose mood. I asked him what was wrong. A man of few but always friendly words, he asked me how I would like to be the second strongest man in the world. I howled with laughter, and answered that I'd love it since presently there were a couple hundred million men who were probably stronger. Norbert laughed too, for he immediately recognized the question was ridiculous when addressed to a 160-pound college student of middling strength.

At that time the Hoffman publication, *Strength & Health,* often featured a column by a salesman who traveled with his "trusty 75s," a large fellow who claimed he worked out every day with these monster dumbbells. I've long ago forgotten the fellow's name, but I clearly recall his appearance one afternoon at Yacos. In sweatpants and tee-shirt he did indeed present a large but not impressive figure. I watched him demonstrating to George Yacos his curls with the 75s; his form was awful, requiring a great deal of body swings—which even we beginners regarded as cheating. When he went to one-arm overhead presses his body leaned so far to the side he was only lifting the weight a foot or so.

Watching from the wooden lifting platform, Norbert—whose lifting form was as close to perfect as anyone could get— saw all he could take. In his quiet voice he told the fellow you could not build strength by cheating. He then took both dumbbells and curled them while holding his body perfectly upright and without pausing went to alternating overhead presses with no sideways leaning. What startled me the most was the fact I'd never seen Norbert do either of these exercises, which were usually performed by bodybuilders. The whole gym enjoyed seeing the *Strength & Health* blow-hard taken down a peg.

One day the light-heavyweight lifter and bodybuilder Leo Maryck brought a column of machined steel into the gym and asked if anyone could lift it merely by gripping it at the top, which was about five inches in diameter. Everyone tried—Leo included—and because it was so smooth and slippery it was simply too much to get a decent purchase on. I don't know what it weighed—at a height of 18 inches it was formidable. I will never forget Norbert's effort. He entered the gym at the point of maximum drama—this part may be enhanced by the distance of almost sixty years—fully clothed in his familiar checked wool jacket. George Yacos called him over to give it a try. He studied it for a full minute, chalked his hand as the rest of us had done to no effect, gripped it with his right hand, squatted down, and in one burst of power not only lifted it off the floor but flipped it in mid-air and stood upright with the steel column balanced on the palm of his hand. The whole gym gave him an extended burst of applause.

The last time I saw Norbert lift was in a two-man competition some months before he won his gold at Helsinki. I was working days and came into the gym about 6 p.m. to see Norbert going head to head with the Olympic light-heavyweight champion Stanley Stanczyk. At the time there was no more than a ten-pound difference in bodyweight. Stanczyk—a great lifter in his own right –had enormous brute strength, and that evening he out-pressed Norbert as both handled over 275 pounds. After the snatch they were even, and Norbert with his perfect split-legged technique won with a clean and jerk of 375 pounds. Stanczyk was a very handsome man. Like Norbert, had he turned to bodybuilding he could easily have been a champion. It was a display of competition, sportsmanship, athleticism, and strength never to be forgotten. My brother Eddie, then a fine-art student at Wayne, likened it to something out of the epic encounters of mythology, and it remains for me frozen in the dramatic light that dreams give, something like a painting by Caravaggio, a moment both in and out of time: competition in its purest form.

I can recall with what glee I read the Detroit papers and discovered Norbert had won a much-deserved gold medal at the 1952 Olympics. By now I was out of college and working fulltime at some industrial job and whatever time I could find to myself I spent on my life's true work, poetry. I'd drop into the gym only occasionally. I don't recall when I finally stopped going to Yacos. It was probably in 1954 when I went off to study poetry at the University of Iowa. A measure of how much I missed the place and the people I knew there is the fact that it's still there in my dreams. At least once every few years in my sleep I'm vividly there at the long dismantled Taft Hotel huffing and puffing along with the greats: Emerick Ishikawa, Stanczyk, Al Koernke, Sam Karres the painter and lifter, Leo Maryck, Jerome, the bodybuilders Bill Hooper and Pete Jacobs, and that great athlete and gentleman who put the place on the map of weightlifting, Norbert Schemansky.

CHAPTER FIVE

Good As Gold

I am told that Norbert is a married man with a family.... He has to earn a living like the rest of us, and it is a great tribute to his character and will-power that he has persevered and triumphed with his training despite the setbacks and discouragements which are the common lot of the worker in his daily battle for life in this cock-eyed old World.

Charles Coster, Muscle Power (November 1952)

The 1952 Olympics represented a nice change of pace for Norb, who had successfully defended his middle-heavyweight title at the Senior Nationals before heading off for Finland. For the first time in his life he was making an ocean crossing in an airplane instead of a boat. He tried out the camera he had won in Milan during the long flight, though what he mostly captured were photographs of the wings. "Tommy Kono was the real photographer in the bunch," he admitted. "He was always taking pictures and movies."

The team that flew to Helsinki in July 1952 was worth preserving on film. It was the greatest collection of lifters ever to represent the United States in the Olympics, as well as one of the strongest squads ever assembled anywhere in the history of international weightlifting. Among the bicep-bulging passengers were Norb, John Davis, Stanley Stanczyk, Tommy Kono, Pete George and Jim Bradford, each of whom would make the return flight to America with either a gold or silver Olympic medal tucked securely into their baggage.

Skee would come to enjoy the company of Bradford, a quiet, friendly

African-American from Washington, D.C., who "liked to drink beer with me." The broad-shouldered, 285-pound Bradford—one of the most powerful pressers in iron game history—had exhibited great sportsmanship in Milan. He withdrew from the heavyweight competition at the very end to prevent Davis, who was competing with a badly hurt leg, from risking further injury. The gesture cost Bradford the world title and kept alive Davis's unbeaten streak in international competition. "Aw, shucks," he said at the time. "I'm young yet. I'll get my chance again in a couple years." Although Bradford would remain a force on the heavyweight scene for another decade, many experts believed he could have done more. "Jim never got out of it what he should have," said Norb. "He wasn't as serious about his training as others were."

In a figurative sense, Kono had already traveled a long way before boarding the plane for Finland. As a sickly Japanese-American youngster forced to spend the war in a relocation camp near Tule Lake, California, he had been inspired by the lifting feats of fellow intern Emerick Ishikawa to improve his body. Kono would one day be recognized along with Schemansky as the icons of U.S. lifting in the '50s and '60s. For now the modest and likable twenty-two-year-old, on leave from the military, was being asked to win gold in the lightweight bracket. He wouldn't disappoint, and neither would Pete George, who competed as a middleweight. The former "wonder boy of weightlifting"—still a schoolboy in Akron, Ohio when he won his first national title in 1946—also would capture gold.

Helsinki, which had been awarded the 1940 Games only to then lose them because of the war, had waited twelve long and difficult years for a second chance to host the world's finest amateur athletes. Finland was a country of barely four million people still burdened by rationing and war reparations, but energetic and resourceful organizers managed to put together a smoothly run Olympics. A new airport and quay were built, elaborate flower beds were planted, and the country's first traffic lights were installed. One of the big improvements the Finns touted over the 1948 London Games was the construction of an Olympic village. "Yeah, those were some apartments," Norb quipped. "Seven big guys in one room."

The Olympics officially opened on July 19, 1952, as nearly 5,000 athletes from 69 countries marched in pouring rain into the 70,000-seat Olympic

Stadium. The parade of nations included participants from Japan and Germany, who were welcomed back after being excluded from the '48 Games.

Russian athletes competed in the Olympics for the first time in forty years, since the country's last pre-Communist appearance in 1912. Displaying the mix of paranoia and secrecy that had come to characterize the Cold War, the Soviet Union originally announced it would house its athletes in Leningrad and fly them in daily for events. The Reds soon settled on building their own Olympic village in Otaniemi, near the Soviet naval base at Porkkala. Athletes from other Communist nations also stayed there.

A symbol of the deepening U.S.-Soviet rivalry was a large scoreboard Russians erected at the Otaniemi complex that prominently displayed the countries' respective medal counts. Thanks to their domination of the wrestling and gymnastics events, the Soviets surged into the lead in the first couple weeks of competition. Propagandists from Eastern Bloc countries used the favorable results to help tout the superiority of communism over capitalism. Officials of Western nations naturally fretted. Caught in the middle were the athletes. "There were many more pressures on American athletes because of the Russians," Bob Mathias, who in Helsinki became the first person to win a second consecutive decathlon, later said. "They were in a sense the real enemy. You just loved to beat 'em. You just had to beat 'em...."

The weightlifting competition was held in Messuhalli Arena. Norb had tremendous respect for the Russians, who were chaperoned everywhere to discourage fraternization with Western athletes. To this day he maintains the most impressive feat of strength he ever witnessed was during a rare open training session when Grigori Novak cleaned 281½ pounds and pressed it. "I mean back when a press was a press," Norb said. "Then just for the hell of it he lowered the weight down behind his neck and pressed it three times."

Clyde Emrich, a member of the U.S. squad, was there watching that day with Norb. "It was a terrific lift," he recalled. "I think when Novak did that he was trying to send a message to Norb. Norb was impressed, but in his typical way he didn't show it or let the Russians know it. He told me he would get Novak on the other two lifts—the snatch and the clean and jerk—and he did."

Novak, the man Norb had to beat to win gold, was one of Russia's most venerated sports heroes. He had yet to be defeated in international competition, though this distinction has to be qualified with the reminder that the war had caused all but two of the world championships between 1939 and 1945 to be canceled, as well as two Olympics. And, of course, the Soviets had sat out the first postwar Olympics and several other international meets. This meant there were limited opportunities for anyone to defeat Novak. (The same qualifier applied to John Davis, whose equally remarkable unbeaten streak included several major tournaments lost to war, injury, financial difficulties or some other reason.) Nonetheless, when Novak did compete, he won, often convincingly.

Six years earlier, in 1946 at Paris, he had pressed 309 pounds at the World Championships en route to winning the light-heavyweight title. As wards of the government, favored athletes like Novak enjoyed numerous perks while pursuing their fulltime livelihood in the gym. The going rate for a championship or a new record reportedly was 25,000 rubles, about $500 in American dollars. Soviet lifters quickly got wise, choosing to set individual records incrementally, collecting a new bonus each time, instead of lifting all that they were capable of at one time. "It is this professionalism, as we would term it in this country, which makes it increasingly difficult to outperform the Soviet athletes," complained Bob Hoffman. "The Russian lifters travel around in a group month after month and year after year. In Paris in 1946 there were at least 20 lifters who came with the Russian party of 38." By comparison Hoffman could afford to bring only six American lifters, all of whom had just a few days together to train, while he himself served as the squad's coach, trainer, manager, and delegate to the international convention held in conjunction with the tournament.

Norb was the underdog in his head-to-head match with Novak. "Most people in Europe didn't think I could beat him," he reflected many years later. "Few men today could beat him at strict pressing." Handicapping Norb's chances was the painful muscle pull he suffered in his right thigh during training. He did it while attempting to jerk a barbell loaded with 341 pounds. A worried trainer told the press, "We hope to get him back in shape for the contests but cannot make any predictions." Those who expected Norb to be apprehensive didn't know their man. He made his own prediction. "I'll send him to the salt mines," he reportedly said.

The lifting events began at 9 o'clock in the morning of Sunday, July 27 and continued into the wee hours of the following day. Novak was expected to press 319, but the best the world's record-holder in the slow lift could do was 308. Norb got up 281, which gave the Russian a 27-pound cushion heading into the quick lifts. Novak started with 275 in the snatch, but it wasn't until his third try that he was able to make it. Meanwhile, Norb went on to snatch 308½, wiping out Novak's advantage and setting a middle-heavyweight record in the process. In the clean and jerk, Novak lifted 319, but Norb created a stir in the hall by jerking 391¼, a record for the mid-heavy class. Skee, who weighed in at 196 pounds in his socks and trunks, thus became the heaviest man to clean and jerk double his body weight. He wasn't through, however. He called for 402 pounds on his third attempt, but couldn't quite pull off the lift.

By the end of the competition Norb had lifted a total of 981 pounds, shattering his own world's record by forty pounds and easily capturing the gold medal. Novak, the silver medalist, finished far behind with a three-lift total of 904. "Norb was the sensation of the meet," declared Hoffman, extending his own records in the snatch, jerk, and total and "showing such strength, super speed and lifting skill" while doing so.

The final weightlifting results from the 1952 Summer Games revealed the Americans and Soviets between them had seized two-thirds of the medals, including all of the golds and all but two of the silvers. In the unofficial team totals (which could be scored in any number of ways, depending on which country was trying to claim supremacy), Norb's gold medal gave the American lifters a narrow victory over the Soviets. Schemansky "broke the Russians' hearts," claimed Dietrich Wortmann, chairman of the American weightlifting committee and incoming president of the International Weightlifting Federation. "Novak is a legend in the Soviet Union....He's such a big man he eats with Stalin. But our champion, Norbert Schemansky, spotted the Russian a big edge in the press and then won with a world record lift...and it hurt." The Russians, who appreciated brute strength over all other qualities, were impressed enough by what they considered the biggest upset of the entire Games to invite the Detroiter and his teammates to their embassy for an official reception. Tellingly, no such offer was extended by the U.S. embassy.

Bantamweight		**Kgs.**	**(Lbs.)**
Gold:	Ivan Udodov, U.S.S.R.	315	(694½)
Silver:	Mahmoud Namjou, Iran	307.5	(678)
Bronze:	Ali Mirzaii, Iran	300	(661½)

Featherweight		**Kgs.**	**(Lbs.)**
Gold:	Rafael Chimishkyan, U.S.S.R.	337.5	(744)
Silver:	Nikolay Saksonov, U.S.S.R.	332.5	(733)
Bronze:	Rodney Wilkes, Trinidad	322.5	(711)

Lightweight		**Kgs.**	**(Lbs.)**
Gold:	Tommy Kono, United States	362.5	(799¼)
Silver:	Yevgeny Lopatin, U.S.S.R.	350	(771½)
Bronze:	Verdi Barberis, Austria	350	(771½)

Middleweight		**Kgs.**	**(Lbs.)**
Gold:	Pete George, United States	400	(881¾)
Silver:	Gerard Gratton, Canada	390	(859¾)
Bronze:	Sung-Jip Kim, Korea	382.5	(843¼)

Light Heavyweight		**Kgs.**	**(Lbs.)**
Gold:	Trofim Lomakin, U.S.S.R.	417.5	(920½)
Silver:	Stanley Stanczyk, United States	415	(915)
Bronze:	Arkady Yorobyev, U.S.S.R.	407.5	(898½)

Middle Heavyweight		**Kgs.**	**(Lbs.)**
Gold:	Norb Schemansky, United States	445	(981)
Silver:	Grigory Novak, U.S.S.R.	410	(904)
Bronze:	Lennox Kilgour, Trinidad	402.5	(887¼)

Heavyweight		**Kgs.**	**(Lbs.)**
Gold:	John Davis, United States	460	(1,014)
Silver:	James Bradford, United States	437.5	(964½)
Bronze:	Humberto Selvetti, Argentina	432.5	(953½)

The strong showing by Americans in lifting, as well as in other events like boxing and basketball, helped to narrow the gap in the overall medal standings in the final days. By the time of the closing ceremonies one week later the United States had out-medaled their super-power rivals, 76-71, including a 40-

22 edge in gold medals. Russian officials quickly and quietly dismantled their scoreboard.

The Russians' performance raised suspicions. Wortmann told the press of a secret weapon—a vial filled with a mysterious substance that the Soviets sniffed between lifts.

"I don't know what it was," he said. "It was a drug, or a stimulant, or something. Anyhow, before each lift a bottle of the stuff would be put under the competitor's nose and he'd take a deep whiff. Then his eyes would become glassy and he'd start lifting like a maniac. I don't think it gave them any strength but it probably relaxed them and made them not afraid of the bars. It made them seem unconscious of anything else about them. They looked dazed. But after a while the effects would wear off and the fellows would get back to normal. Then they'd take another whiff."

Norb was on a natural high. After years of being viewed as John Davis's understudy, winning the gold medal was immensely satisfying. "When you start training, that's what you think about from the very beginning. You want to be the best. So when you're up there, and you know you are the best, it's a pretty nice feeling."

The view from Olympus, however, was again a bit of a letdown. Norb wasn't quite sure what an Olympic gold medalist was supposed to receive in terms of acclaim or material reward, but he wasn't prepared for the decidedly underwhelming reaction he experienced in his own hometown.

"I got off the plane from Helsinki and took a bus downtown," he recalled. "Then I got on another bus and went home. Nobody knew who the hell I was except this porter at the bus terminal. He said, 'Nice going, Schemansky.' He even mispronounced my name. And that was it."

Norb had never finished his secondary schooling. But on August 27, 1952, not long after his return from Finland, he easily passed the Detroit Public Schools' General Educational Development (GED) test to earn his equivalency diploma from Northeastern High School. Perhaps not too surprisingly, the deadpanned Schemansky's lowest score was in the category of "Correctness and effectiveness of expression." However, he scored in the 90th percentile in "General mathematical ability." This meant his score was higher than, or as high as, 90 percent of others who had taken the test. He scored a similarly impressive 86th percentile in the category of "Interpretation of literary materials." In the army Schemansky had taken a battery of tests that revealed an I.Q. of 132. These results dispelled any notion that the Olympic champion weightlifter was just some monosyllabic bohunk whose only options in life involved either carnival work or pulling out tree stumps on a dare.

Interestingly, Briggs Manufacturing offered Norb a job when he came back from the Olympics. Proud and stubborn, he turned the company down. Instead he went to work for Clarence Johnson.

The position didn't amount to much. He did odd jobs, ran errands, and supervised a bunch of high school kids at the local hall when one of the unions Johnson did work for held an election. For this Johnson paid Norb a few dollars each week. He even bought the family their first television set, which throughout the decade let Pamela and Paula eat lunch with Soupy Sales and mom and dad catch the latest episode of *Dragnet* and *I Love Lucy*. The best part of working for Johnson was the freedom it allowed Norb to train.

At this point in the narrative it's tempting to simply stop and ponder where Norb was headed at this moment in his life. Why continue to expend so much time and effort throwing around cold iron plates when new opportunities were there for the asking? Millions of discharged servicemen were taking advantage of education benefits under the G.I. Bill to get a college degree or attend a trade school. Other veterans were making use of low-interest government loans to start businesses. In retrospect, Schemansky might have been wise to retire from competition right then and there. He was at the top of his game, and ultimately—even if it took another fifteen or twenty years—there would be nowhere to go but down. He was only twenty-eight years old and had already been crowned a national, world and Olympic champion. Other lifters with lesser credentials had given up the iron game. "There was no money in lifting in those days," said Al Koernke, who finished second in the Senior Nationals in 1949, got married the following year, and soon left the sport to concentrate on a new livelihood as a barber. It was the only way he could see to raise three kids. "You just had to have a great passion for lifting to continue," Koernke said.

Asked about such things today, Schemansky gave it a few seconds' thought, then twirled a finger around his temple: *Crazy.* Lifting had become an opiate.

"Once you're hooked on it," he said simply, "you're hooked on it."

Hooked as he was, Norb put on nearly twenty pounds within three months of returning from the Olympics in order to compete as a heavyweight at the North American Championships in Montreal. There he established Canadian Open records in the snatch (295 pounds) and total (965). A couple of weeks later he was at a Mr. World contest in Philadelphia, fully intending to break John Davis's clean and jerk record. Skee called for—and successfully raised—405 pounds, but when weighed it was found to actually be 408, a new world's record in the heavyweight class.

Then, on January 17, 1953, at an A.A.U. Open in York, Pennsylvania, he handed Davis his first loss in fifteen years of big-time competition. Davis pressed 310 and snatched 290, but he missed jerking 380. Meanwhile, Norb pressed and snatched 310 each and jerked his 380 for an even 1,000 pounds. On a fourth try, Norb jerked 412½ in his characteristically smooth style. "He was famous for his speed and technique in the split style, being as fast and agile as the best lifters in the lighter weight classes," recalled one admirer. "He could get lower under a weight, particularly in the jerk, than anyone if he had to and still get up with it. This required incredible speed, leg strength, balance and control." The 412½ broke his own three-month-old record.

By June Norb had trained back down to 198 pounds bodyweight, enabling him to win the Senior Nationals in Indianapolis and the World Championships in Stockholm, Sweden, as a middle-heavyweight.

The 1953 World Championships in Stockholm represented a changing of the guard. The cry in the past had been, "The Russians are coming." Now the Russians were here—to stay. Their nationalized sports program, which made permanent "students" and "army officers" out of their most promising athletes, put the under-funded, disorganized American amateur system to shame. Just a few months earlier, Tug Wilson, president of the U.S. Olympic Committee, had addressed the national meeting of the A.A.U. Athletes were "drifting away from amateurism," he warned the delegates. "Certainly we have gone far from the days when a boy would walk five miles for a chance to run in a race." Wilson, who'd been a member of the U.S. squad at the 1912 Olympics, urged the A.A.U. to expand its activities, especially youth developmental programs. But American weightlifting was doomed by numbers even then, said Norb. As the '50s wore on, standouts like Davis and Stanczyk were past their prime and there wasn't a deep roster of talented young lifters to replenish the ranks. Even when the U.S. was doing well in international competition, it had only a fraction of the number of registered lifters that Russia had.

Per their style, the Russians trained in seclusion. The Soviets "do nothing but lift," Bob Hoffman moaned later. "At Stockholm they were fresh from three months of special training at an athletic camp where they trained fourteen times a week, twice each day." When the Russians finally let the Americans in to observe a training session, it quickly became apparent the tight-lipped Reds were simply going through the motions. A couple of the lifters started a game of ping-pong. "They're just playing around," said Clarence Johnson, who'd accompanied the team as a manager. "Now that they let us stay to watch them they won't show off what they really can do."

As a team, the Soviets beat the Americans for the first time, thanks to a Canadian. Doug Hepburn, a brooding colossus with a club foot, whipped John Davis and Jim Bradford to capture the heavyweight title and deprive the U.S. of the points it needed to edge out a win. Norb did what he could do, compiling a 975¼ score while successfully defending his mid-heavy crown. He jerked 396¾ and officials awarded him an additional two pounds after weighing the barbell. The 398¾ was just Skee's latest world's record.

Not long afterwards, Norb sustained a minor injury that prevented him from competing in the state meet in Detroit. Almost on a whim, he decided to enter the Mr. Michigan contest that was always part of the proceedings. He was never comfortable parked before a mirror, so he got someone to take several snapshots of him in various poses and he studied those. "I was in good shape," he later explained. "Didn't know anything about posing—some spend hours in front of a mirror practicing. Gave them a back pose or two and a couple of arm shots and that was it." Norb was voted Mr. Michigan 1953 and the photographer won a blue ribbon. It wasn't much, but then again Norb was used to nothing.

On the last day of 1953, the A.A.U. announced the recipient of that year's James B. Sullivan Memorial Trophy: Major Sammy Lee, a 33-year-old Californian who had won the platform diving events at the 1948 and 1952 Olympics. At the time of the announcement, the diminutive Korean-American was serving in the army medical corps in his ancestral land. A total of 631 ballots were cast by sportswriters and officials. Five points were awarded for a first-place vote, three points for second, and one point for third. The results (including the total number of first-place votes in parentheses) were as follows:

Athlete	Sport	Points
1. Sammy Lee	Diving	1,676 (247)
2. Patricia Keller McCormick	Diving	1,045 (94)
3. Charley Capozzoli	Track	990 (123)
4. Jimmy McLane	Swimming	734 (82)
5. Norb Schemansky	Weightlifting	345 (33)
6. Gail Peters	Swimming	307 (24)
7. J. Lewis (Poppa) Hall	High jump	303 (20)
8. Nancy Cowperthwaite Phillips	Track	206 (8)

The Sullivan Award was first presented by the A.A.U. in 1930. By definition it goes annually to "the amateur athlete who, by performance, example and good influence, did most to advance the course of good sportsmanship during the year." Candidates are nominated by the regional A.A.U. district associations and affiliated organizations, with a committee then paring candidates to a list of finalists. Norb was a finalist in 1953 and again in 1954. He didn't fare very well in the balloting either time, finishing fifth one year and sixth the next, though it's worth noting that even making it onto the short list has always been an achievement in itself for lifters. Only one other weightlifter besides Norb has ever been a finalist in successive years: Tommy Kono, who was runner-up four times in a five-year span (1959 through 1963).

Most striking is that in the long history of the Sullivan Award, no lifter has been selected the country's top amateur athlete—in Norb's opinion, just one more indication of the sport's lack of stature and exposure in the United States. Even scullers and wrestlers have won the award three times apiece.

"It's more of a popularity contest than anything," he said. "I never even knew I was a candidate until practically the last minute. Typical A.A.U. stuff." The late notice was designed in part to prevent electioneering by finalists, but exposure obviously is key. "You figure swimmers and sprinters get the most publicity, so they're better known to the voters." In fact, half of all Sullivan Award winners have been track and field stars, including Mal Whitfield. In 1954 the two-time Olympic 800-meter champion became the first African-American to be presented the silver trophy:

Athlete	**Sport**	**Points**
1. Mal Whitfield	Track	1,689 (252)
2. Patricia Keller McCormick	Diving	1,328 (149)
3. Tom Gola	Basketball	682 (82)
4. Bud Held	Javelin	600 (47)
5. Bob Backus	Discus	472 (41)
6. Norb Schemansky	Weightlifting	390 (39)
7. Shelly Mann	Swimming	316 (22)
8. Art Bragg	Track	269 (18)
9. Don Schlundt	Basketball	111 (7)

As always, Norb got more respect from international judges. In 1954 he was the top U.S. finisher (and sixth overall) in a poll conducted by a respected German news agency that asked sports authorities in 24 nations to select the best sportsmen around the globe. By then, however, Schemansky's name carried a more marketable cachet: "The Strongest Man in the World."

East vs. West

by Frank Spellman

Frank Spellman, a 30-year-old middleweight from Pennsylvania, was competing in his second Olympics in Helsinki. Today, the 84-year-old fitness enthusiast still works out three times a week at the gym.

When you looked at Norb you saw power, absolute power. I always thought Steve Stanko, the great heavyweight of the '40s who was also the first Mr. Universe, was the most athletic weightlifter I had ever seen, but then Norb came along. He was in a class all by himself when it came to having speed, coordination, and explosive power. He had everything it took to be a champion. After a while the Russians started getting deeper into lifting and Norb started looking small compared to them. He was competing against guys almost a hundred pounds heavier than he was.

I remember at York we had a solid barbell. It had these balls on the ends and an extremely thick handle. In fact, I could barely get my hands around it. There was a trick to cleaning it. The first time I pulled up the weight it knocked me right down on my back. Later I found out you pull it and catch it and then you'll be okay. Don't you know Skee snatched it!

Norb and I were at the London and Helsinki Olympics together and more than a few other meets over the years. He basically trained in Detroit, while I was part of the York Barbell Club and stayed in Pennsylvania. I worked at York, the barbell factory, for eight years.

I started competing in 1941 and, outside of some time in the Army Air Corps during the war, kept competing for 30 years. I still work out. Bob Hoffman was like a father to me. A lot of guys came to York—young lifters, muscleheads who wanted to meet the champions. Bob would put these guys up, feed them, and when they got ready to leave he would give them a book—Bob wrote a bunch of books on fitness—and tucked inside of it was some money. That was the kind of guy he was.

It was like the United Nations at York. Hoffman didn't care who you were; we were all Americans on the lifting platform. I was Jewish, Jim Bradford and John Davis were black. Skee, of course, had Polish blood, and so did Stanley Stanzcyk, who could speak the language. Tommy Kono and Emerick Ishikawa were Japanese-American. Johnny Terpak was Ukrainian and he spoke a little Russian. Stanko's parents came over from Hungary. We had several lifters from Hawaii, and so on. We all lifted because we loved it. We would've done it for nothing. As a matter of fact, we did do it for nothing.

I remember the '48 Olympics. Hoffman came up to me when I was getting ready to go up to the platform to do my last lift, a record clean and jerk. He said, "Frank, if you make this you will be Olympic champion for life." I did make it and won the gold medal. I got so excited I didn't watch the rest of the competition. After the Olympics Bob sent the team to Paris, where we got wild and woolly.

The Russian system obviously was different. After the World Championships in Paris in 1946, the American and Russian teams went to the Louvre, the famous art museum. Grigori Novak and I sat together. He was really and truly a nice guy. He was Jewish, so he said a few words I understood and we used a lot of hand signals. He said by winning the championship he was paid off. He took out a roll of bills that must have been five inches in diameter.

CHAPTER SIX

World's Strongest Man

The big champ waited for the Apollon bell. "Skee" eyed it confidently and then took his normal knuckles front cleaning grip with no preliminaries. He pulled that great awkward and twisted weight, that unliftable barbell, to his shoulders as easily as most of us would clean 100 pounds.

Bob Hoffman, Strength & Health (February 1955)

The new year of 1954 saw Norb Schemansky once again gracing the front of *Strength & Health*, a harbinger of great things to come for the twenty-nine-year-old cover boy. He would be at the peak of his ability that year, though away from the lifting platform he remained all too often a famous unknown.

In April, Norb won yet another Y.M.C.A. championship, this time in Providence, Rhode Island. By now he had made the decision to compete exclusively as a heavyweight. Judging by results, it was a wise and logical move. His body was filling out as he matured, and there was now a better understanding about the relationship between size and power. The extra body weight barely affected his speed and precision; as a technician he was still a marvel to watch. Weighing in at 220 pounds, Skee raised a personal-best 1,035 pounds at Providence, including a 400-pound clean and jerk. Several weeks later, at an exhibition in Arizona, he cleaned that amount and jerked it twice, as if it were a signal to the lifting world that more remarkable feats were down the road.

They literally were. He traveled from Tucson to Los Angeles for the Senior Nationals. There he broke his own clean and jerk record with a 416½-pound effort on an extra try. He raised his total to 1,050 while winning the event and was named Outstanding Lifter.

What accounted for Norb's continued progress as he passed his thirtieth birthday? There were several factors, but in one of its early issues a brand new magazine called *Sports Illustrated* explored an essential but frequently overlooked aspect of the iron game—powerful thought, the kind of intense concentration that sports psychologists would come to term "positive visualization."

"The only way to raise a 400-pound barbell over your head is to think it up there," Ezra Bowen wrote in 1954. "It helps to have several cubic feet of muscle packed around the shoulders and loins, but the muscle becomes superfluous if the thought is missing.

"This, at least, is the conclusion of Norbert Schemansky, who can lift more pounds of barbell overhead than anybody else on earth. Not long ago, he gave a rather awesome demonstration of the power of thought at a YMCA in his native Detroit. After tossing around some trifling 200—250-pound weights in a conventional warmup—'to draw the blood'—Schemansky attacked a 400-pounder. He walked slowly up to the bar, like a massive mahout approaching a truculent bull elephant. Placing his shins next to the bar, he squatted, wrapped his hands around the bar, and then stared pensively ahead in what appeared to be a two-second prayer for success."

"Suddenly he had the bar off the floor, then at waist level, then overhead; and just as suddenly, back on the floor—set down as gently as if he were shooing a kitten.

"Later, he explained his moment of prayer. 'If you go up there and you're not thinking, the thing'll seem pretty heavy. You just can't get coordinated. Before you start, you got to try to get all your thoughts into seeing how much drive you can put into the lift, so you have a pretty good idea you can do it. Then, in those last couple of seconds, your mind's almost a blank, just thinking about getting that thing up there. If you make it right, you don't even feel the weight. Just use your legs to come erect and there you are.'"

It wasn't that simple, of course, though Norb often made it look so. This was particularly true that fall as he took Europe by storm, wrecking the record book as he went along.

The 1954 World Championships were scheduled for Vienna, Austria. Instead of working out in York before heading overseas, as was the Americans' habit, the U.S. squad gathered in Copenhagen, Denmark, to train in privacy. On October 4, just before leaving for Vienna, Bob Hoffman's men put on an exhibition at the request of Danish sports officials. That day Norb attacked the bar, pressing and snatching 325 pounds each, then jerking the unprecedented figure of 418¾ pounds. His unofficial three-lift total was 1,068¾ pounds. This shattered the 1,037 pounds Doug Hepburn had recently lifted at the Commonwealth Games in Vancouver, British Columbia. Six days later in Austria Norb upped his performance, this time officially setting a new standard.

Hepburn, the defending world's heavyweight champion, had concentrated on winning the Commonwealth Games in his hometown and did not make it to the World Championships. Hepburn or not, the crowd in Vienna naturally rooted for a local favorite, Karl Holbl. But Norb out-pressed the Austrian and five other heavyweights with 330½ pounds. He moved on to the snatch, where he progressed from 308½ to 325 on his first two attempts. On the third he called for a couple of small discs weighing a half-kilo to be added to the bar—at 330½ pounds it was just enough to break John Davis's world record by a pound. After Jim Bradford and Holbl had finished the clean and jerk, Norb took his turn, asking for 396¼ on his first try. "This looked absurdly easy and brought laughter from the crowd," George Kirkley reported in the London-based digest, *The Bodybuilder*. "On to 413¼, which he dealt with just as comfortably, and bringing his total up to the new record figure of 1,074¼." It would have been even higher, but after cleaning 424¼ on his third attempt, Norb barely missed the jerk. Nonetheless, at 224 pounds body weight, Schemansky was the lightest world champion heavyweight ever.

The competition may have been over, but Norb was just warming up. "Put 200 kilos on the bar, and I'll continental and jerk it," he said. Then Norb left observers slack-jawed by ramming 440¼ pounds overhead. "A pull to the belt, a little dip, and then to the shoulders and the weight was jerked solidly to locked arms," was how Kirkley described it. His adrenalin racing, Norb then asked for an additional five kilos, making the weight a stupendous 451½ pounds. Spectators chanted, "Can't beat 440...can't beat 440." This time the bar was a little off balance and it crashed to the floor. After five straight attempts Norb had been stretched to the limit of his capabilities. He was drained but carried a wide smile throughout all the congratulatory backslaps and handshakes that followed. His successful 440¼-pound effort had wiped out the seemingly untouchable mark of Austria's Karl Swoboda, who had jerked 429 pounds with the continental method forty-two years earlier. The spectacle of Norb's amazing lift was preserved on newsreels, which wound up being shown in theaters around the globe. Norb Schemansky was undisputably "the world's strongest man," as the Russian picture magazine *Ogonyek* and many other publications proclaimed. His performance took some of the sting out of the Russians out-pointing the Americans for the second straight year at the World Championships.

Tommy Kono enjoyed a remarkable barnstorming tour across Europe himself, becoming the first lifter to win three straight world titles in three different classifications, setting several records, and for good measure winning the Mr. World crown at Roubaix, France. He and Clyde Emrich acted as spotters for Norb's post-contest continental and jerks at Vienna—dangerous duty considering the stupendous weights involved, recalled Kono. But Norb was a performer, he noted. "Whether it was in a contest or an exhibition, Norb went beyond the call of what he was supposed to do. Taking a fourth attempt outside of the contest or after the meet is over—he didn't have to do it but he did it. He could've hurt himself. He was always giving of himself to the public. Nowadays you'll see some lifters, if they've already won their class, not even take a third attempt. They've already won, so they quit. They're not pushing themselves. They're getting paid, so their attitude is completely different."

Norb wasn't through. On Thursday, October 14, the Americans made their way to Lille, France, where some world record attempts were scheduled for that Sunday. Hoffman decided to have the gang drop in at Robert Cayeaux's

Paris gym for a workout. While making arrangements to use the gym with his old friend, Hoffman inquired about the famous Apollon barbell.

The Apollon bell was a ponderous 366-pound weight made of two giant boxcar wheels with a thick bar thrust through them. The improvised barbell had originally belonged to a 6-foot-6, 300-pound French giant named Apollon, who had actually never lifted it overhead but had instead used it in various stunts. While a generation of strongmen had deadlifted the weight, only two men had ever been able to lift the train wheels overhead. The first was the French professional strongman Charles Rigoulot, who did it in 1930—but only after practicing for weeks beforehand. In 1950 John Davis gave it a go, and his small hands and the chunky circumference of the bar caused him much grief on his hold. After several failed attempts, Davis finally cleaned the bar by flipping it up to his shoulders, and then reversing his grip in mid-air in order catch the bar at his shoulders. After this he was able to jerk the train wheels overhead. During one of Davis's unsuccessful tries the weights had crashed heavily to the ground, badly bending one end of the bar and making it that much harder to grasp for anyone who might want to replicate the feat in the future.

It turned out the Apollon bell was no longer at Cayeaux's gym, but was being stored in the basement of another local gym. When Hoffman suggested the sensation of the recent World Championships might be interested in attempting to lift the "unliftable" Apollon bell, volunteers were quickly mustered to move it via truck to its former home. "It was a very impromptu arrangement," Norb recalled. "I had no idea I would be asked to try it. But what the heck, I was game."

Word spread rapidly. By the time the Americans arrived at Cayeaux's gym, a large crowd had gathered, including a number of reporters and photographers. "It is too bad that what followed could not have taken place in a big hall and been witnessed by thousands of people," Hoffman later wrote, "for we were to see the greatest display of strength which ever has taken place in the world; a feat of strength which is unsurpassed and which gives Norbert Schemansky just claim to the mythical title, 'World's Strongest Man.'"

The American lifters warmed up with snatches, presses, and jerks with a standard plate-loading Olympic bar before taking turns attacking a 358-pound weight with a thick non-revolving handle. As was the case with the Apollon wheels, only Rigoulot and Davis had ever succeeded in jerking this particular barbell overhead. On this day, however, Dave Sheppard, Clyde Emrich and Tommy Kono all joined the exclusive fraternity, though the latter needed assistance in cleaning. Pete George also gave it his best shot, continentalling it to his chest but missing the jerk. Davis, who been through all this four years earlier, just watched.

At this point the Apollon wheels were rolled out. Could Norb possibly clean and jerk this misshapen 366-pound weight? Like the 358-pound barbell his companions had just finished with, the Apollon bell's handle did not revolve, making the lift that much more difficult to pull off.

Photographers readied their large box cameras. For Norb it was a relatively simple lift, devoid of the drama that had accompanied the triumphs of his predecessors. Unlike Rigoulot and Davis, who had succeeded only after several failed tries, Norb took the Apollon wheels and lifted them on his first attempt, jerking the weight overhead—not once, not twice, but three times—before setting the bar back down. He had "literally handled the famous weight like a toy," said one observer. It was over so quickly—wham, bam, thank you Stan—that a moment of stunned silence filled Cayeaux's gym. "My God," said Hoffman, "that was terrific." Recalled Clyde Emrich: "Norb just stood over it, did a slow dive, whipped it to his shoulders, jerked it three times, and set it down. I said, 'Jeez....' It was tremendously impressive." A half-century later, Pete George had basically the same memory of the event: "Norb just walked up to it and whipped it up like nothing. He really awed everyone in the gym." The spectators, Hoffman later wrote, "were overwhelmed. The French all seemed to shout at once, 'He is greater than Rigoulot.' That, I would say, is the height of praise from a Frenchman, for Rigoulot is a national hero."

Norb felt like he could have done six or seven reps with the Apollon bell. The most difficult part was the bend in the bar. "The bend made it hard to hold because it slips in your hands and the weight turns and shifts around," he explained.

Asked countless times over the years how he did it, Norb's answer has always been the same: "I squeezed like hell and pulled." The wheels were rolled back into storage and have not been used since. "The Frenchmen decided I did it too easily and put the Apollon bar away for good," he joked.

Having conquered the Apollon wheels, Norb pulled off another sensational lift at a follow-up exhibition in Lille on October 17. Officials from the International Weightlifting Federation were on hand. This time Norb clean and jerked 424¼ pounds, making the record lift he had narrowly missed at Vienna and causing the crowd of 4,000 to go wild. Bob Hoffman had to rescue Norb from the mob of autograph seekers that pressed him into a corner. "I still remember the referee," Clarence Johnson said many years later. "The guy cried. It was so emotional."

It was an amazing thirteen-day trip, one that made Norb Schemansky a familiar name in several countries. The one lift Skee remains proudest of after all these years is the 440-pound continental and jerk in Vienna. "I just missed 451, and that was at a bodyweight of 220 pounds and with no special training. When Paul Anderson did 450 the following year, he weighed well over 300 pounds and was called 'a wonder of nature.'"

A *Detroit News* reporter looked up the Schemansky family not long after Norb's return from Europe. What Pete Waldmeir discovered was the husky hero and his wife sharing a crowded flat with three children and an overflowing china cabinet serving as a trophy case. "Mrs. Bernice Schemansky enjoys her role as wife of 'the world's strongest man,' even if she has to live on a slim budget and spend many lonely weeks while he's off on missions of goodwill for the United States," he wrote.

"Norb enjoys the competition and I'm just as happy," Bernice told Waldmeir. "I guess he'd be out bowling or doing something else."

Bernice came across as almost unbelievably understanding and supportive, even when her peripatetic husband was a couple of thousand miles away when their third child was born.

"I once resented his long trips," she said, "but I've grown accustomed to them now. I missed Norb when our son, Lawrence, was born six weeks ago. He was in Vienna, but it couldn't be helped." As for past suggestions that Bernice accompany Norb on one of his trips abroad, she said she'd rather stay home with five-year-old Pamela and seven-year-old Paula. "Frankly, I'm glad it never materialized," she confessed. "I'd just as soon spend a vacation at Traverse City."

Even in a major sports town like Detroit—justifiably referred to as "the city of champions"—weightlifters were given comparatively little coverage. Whether this was fair or not, the slight was to be expected. After all, there was so much going on and only so much space to devote to the many individual stars and great teams of the period. The Detroit Red Wings, boasting superstars like Gordie Howe, Ted Lindsay and Terry Sawchuk, alone won seven straight National Hockey League titles and captured four Stanley Cups in the 1950s. At the same time the Lions, featuring the likes of Bobby Layne, Doak Walker and Joe Schmidt, were a perennial powerhouse that played in four NFL championship games during the decade. The middle-of-the-pack Tigers fielded such fan favorites as Al Kaline and Harvey Kuenn; enthusiasm for the game on all levels reflected the fact that baseball was still by far the favorite pastime. In addition, Detroit was the acknowledged bowling capital of the world, a rabid fight town that had given the world Joe Louis and Sugar Ray Robinson, and was a hotbed for high school and college sports. Even someone with Norb's massive deltoids could expect a hard time muscling his way onto the sports pages back then. As it was, he appeared periodically on local radio-TV sports shows and was invited to the big annual All-Sports luncheon at the downtown Statler Hotel. Norb certainly was considered a champion on the local sports scene during the Eisenhower decade. It's just that in a city that had given the world so many great athletes and produced so many championships, he wasn't *the* champion.

Perusing the three Detroit dailies of the period—the *News*, the *Free Press*, and the *Times*—reveals sporadic coverage, but also a true civic pride in Schmensky's achievements in whatever was written. There were columns, human interest features, and news items describing his performance at major competitions. Headlines emphasized his title as "the world's strongest man" and he was invariably photographed flexing in his street clothes or "stripped for action" in a gym pose. Often Bernice or an available beauty queen or actress was pictured *oooh*-ing as she felt Norb's bicep. Chevrolet's ad agency employed Norb to introduce a new sports car called the Corvette in an advertisement that had him lifting its fiberglass underbody over his head. Much of the mainstream media exposure appeared after the newly acclaimed "conqueror of the Russians" returned from Vienna.

Because Norb's vanquishing of the Soviets came at a time when the U.S. was involved in a stalemate with Communist forces on the Korean peninsula (Jim Bradford was just one of many athletes to serve there during the war), the media relished playing up the cold-war angle. "Detroiter Breaks Heart of Russia" was a typical headline. One unidentified clipping from the period that Norb's niece, Mary Beth Fox, has held onto all these years carries the headline, "It Takes a Detroiter To Beat Those Russians." There was the obligatory Herculean pose of her Uncle Norb, his massive arms flexed as if ready to deliver a couple body blows to Joseph Stalin, along with text bemoaning the victorious American's anonymity:

> It was a small story on the second page of the Sports section. The head said "Schemansky Outlifts Reds in World Meet." Then it went on to say that Norb Schemansky, a Detroiter, had beaten the Russians again in hand-to-hand competition. In the process he had set another world record in world weight-lifting championships. He met the Russians in Vienna over the weekend. He set a world record of 330 pounds in the press and 412.5 [sic] pounds in the lift. Not a Russian came close to Detroit's Norb. Not many people in Detroit know that the strongest man in the world lives here. Not many seem to care. Because Schemansky will come back to town, unheralded as usual, to go about the business of finding a job to support his wife and two children. A lot of people will have forgotten the story which said, "Schemansky Outlifts Reds in World Meet."

Being prohibited from capitalizing financially on one's hard-won athletic skills was frustrating. Amateurs were not allowed to accept money or any gifts (except those of a token value) for performances or endorsements; to do so risked being declared a professional and therefore forfeiting the right to participate in A.A.U.-sanctioned meets. As the national governing body for most amateur sports in the country, the A.A.U. arbitrated any disputes involving alleged violations, and their recommendations regarding issues of eligibility were readily accepted by the national and international Olympic committees. Everybody was aware of the sad example of Jim Thorpe, who was stripped of his medals from the 1912 Summer Olympics after the A.A.U. discovered he had once played professional minor league baseball for a few dollars a game under an assumed name. More recently, Olympic track star Mal Whitfield had been investigated by the A.A.U. for a European trip he made in the summer of 1953, a probe that resulted in his name being removed from that year's list of Sullivan Award finalists. (The investigation turned up no wrongdoing and Whitfield went on to win the Sullivan in 1954.) In early 1955, after competing in (and winning) just two international tournaments, Doug Hepburn gave up his amateur status in Canada to pursue a career as a professional wrestler, an occupation he hated but which earned him $15,000 his first year in the ring. Hepburn's decision removed one of Schemansky's key rivals from the heavyweight ranks, but it also deprived the lifting world the opportunity to see the two champions go *mano a mano* on the world stage.

With few exceptions, even professional athletes had relatively modest incomes in the 1950s. Johnny Podres made $7,500 in 1955, when he was named *Sports Illustrated* Sportsman of the Year for pitching the Brooklyn Dodgers past the New York Yankees in the World Series. That same year Lions running back Doak Walker led the NFL in scoring and was named All-Pro for the fifth time in his six seasons, then quit at the pinnacle of his career. The laurels and championship rings were nice, but he could make a better living for his family outside of football. Many members of the Lions and Red Wings earned just a few thousand dollars a year while helping their teams win titles during the decade; to make ends meet, most pros sold cars or worked other jobs in the off-season. The mind-bending salaries, multi-million-dollar endorsements, and overall sense of entitlement that even "amateur" athletes enjoy today in every sport simply did not exist back when Norb was in his prime.

Norb regularly blasted the A.A.U., his criticism growing more strident with age. In *Tales of Gold*, an excellent oral history of the Olympic Games published in 1987, the now-retired lifter offered his unvarnished views of the organization to interviewers Lewis H. Carlson and John J. Fogarty. "The only thing anyone was doing for me in those years was, when I got on a plane to go to a big meet, they'd give me an A.A.U. emblem and tell me to put it where it belonged—over my heart. I'd tell them that I'd put it where it belonged—in my back pocket."

"Bob Hoffman...used to pick up the tab for the trips, but you would get to go only if you at least had a chance to get one of the top three places. Sometimes they wouldn't even pay unless you were going to be a winner. When I won the World Championship in Vienna in 1954, I came across the border, and they wanted to know how much money I had. I told them, 'Nothing.' They pulled me aside. They thought I was joking. I told them, 'I don't have any money. I'm broke.' They couldn't believe that I could be a world champion and not have any money. I had traveled all the way to Europe with empty pockets."

Beer on the House

by Jim Bradford

Jim Bradford, who began lifting in 1944, won several national titles and a pair of Olympic silver medals during an age filled with storied heavyweights—one of whom was his beer-drinking companion, Norb Schemansky.

For years it was kind of the accepted thing that Norb and I would be in a contest somewhere. I always thought that if you could have combined the two of us you would have had one terrific lifter. He had the flexibility, the agility, and I had the old-fashioned brute force. I know they used to say about me, "If Jim can clean it, he can press it."

The catalyst between the two of us was Johnny Terpak, who won a bunch of championships while working for Bob Hoffman at York. I lifted for the York Barbell Club. I think he got a kick out of pitting the two of us—me and Norb—against each other whenever they'd get everybody together for training before a big meet. Terpak knew I was a good presser but he knew Schemansky was a great snatcher and good at the clean and jerk. So he was always kind of pitting me against Norb. He would drive Norb to do more in the quick lifts. He'd say, "Well, you know Jim is going to do maybe 350 in the snatch." I couldn't do 350; the highest I ever snatched was 330 or something. But he'd say, "Jim is going to do so-and-so," and so Schemansky would get out there and try some phenomenal weight and half the time he got it. Schemansky thrived on challenges. You just never knew what he'd do. You'd be watching him in a contest and you'd say, "He just might get it."

It really didn't matter to me. I lifted for the fun of it. I used to look at the other guys and they would be training like mad, especially Schemansky. I could never understand that. I just came to a contest and said, "Hey, Terpak, what do you want me to lift?"

Maybe that's why I wasn't too good in what they call the quick lifts—the two-handed snatch and the clean and jerk. Skee was really the master there. I used to marvel at his ability to split. That was the style in those days; we didn't do the squat style. Boy, that guy could get so low I thought his fruit salad would scratch the floor.

It's a shame we couldn't adjust to the squat style. I used to tell Tommy Kono and Ike Berger that they were cheating because all they did was a high dead lift and they would just sneak up under the weight. But, of course, that was the squat style. I don't know how much I could've done or Norb could've done if we could've adjusted to the squat style. On the clean you had to pull the barbell much higher in the split style than in the squat—probably at least a foot higher.

Norb and I used to hang out together. We had fun. We'd drink a little beer together. Of course we didn't have much money so we had to improvise. I can't remember what city this was...maybe somewhere in Germany. Anyway, we'd go around the city and go into these bars. Norb would walk in and say to everybody, "This is John Davis." You know, this is John Davis so give the guy a free beer. And of course people didn't know for sure, but I was this big black American weightlifter and there sure weren't that many of us in Europe.

Once in a while somebody might say, "I thought John Davis was a little...."

"No, no, this is John Davis," Norb would insist, and they would roll out the free beer. And then I would say, "Give my friend here a free beer," and Norb would get to drink on the house, too. People would keep feeding us beer and we'd tell a lot of stories and after we got all filled up, we would go. But we used to do that all the time.

I never used steroids or that kind of stuff. As far as I know, the other guys on the team weren't, either. That's one of the reasons I don't have as great an admiration for the Russian team as some seem to have. I would see the Russians giving their lifters needles and taking pills and stuff. I couldn't understand what was going on until later. I thought maybe the guy had some sort of ailment or something. Meanwhile the guys on the American team figured you were heavy into drugs if you took No-Doze! No-Doze was nothing but a bunch of caffeine.

Norb really loved weightlifting. He wasn't too particular about what effect it might be having on him. His main concern was to get that weight up and succeed. In fact, I wish I'd had his innate drive for success because I was more laid back. How I did in a meet didn't really matter all that much to me, but it sure mattered to Schemansky. He definitely wanted to be the best that he could be. Kind of like that army commercial: "Be all that you can be."

We weren't making any money then. We were true amateurs. By the 1960 Olympics in Rome it was costing me two to three thousand dollars a year to compete. I had a family and after awhile I said, "This doesn't make any sense." In 1961 I was invited to Russia to compete,

In 1954 Norb was universally hailed as "the world's strongest man" and "the Heavyweight Champion of the World." With great power and speed, Norb snared the world championship title in Vienna, Austria. Here he holds a sculptured bust he was awarded in recognition of his world record lifting. Bob Hoffman and Clarence Johnson enjoy the adulation Norb receives from the European audience.

At a body weight of 225 pounds, "Skee" hurls 440 pounds skyward. His record setting hoist is considered one of the greatest feats of strength ever. Norb was mobbed afterwards by the thrilled European audience members.

With the help of teammates Clyde Emrich and Pete George, Norb attempts to continental and jerk a world record 450 pounds! In 1954, Norb was possibly the world's most publicized athlete except in his native country of the United States.

Many experts in international weightlifting believe that Norb may be the all time greatest master of the split snatch. Lifting incredible poundage, he was famous for diving very low to the ground and then exploding upward, defying gravity, and hurling the weight nearly seven feet in the air.

Weightlifting legends Dave Sheppard, Tommy Kono, Pete George, John Davis, Clarence Johnson and Jim Bradford enjoy the European scenery with a couple of fans in the early 1950s.

Detroit's YMCA standouts Glenn Breuhan,Vic Seipke, Norbert Schemansky and Don Van Fleteren pose with their trophies.

York Barbell legends: Norb Schemansky and Steve Stanko.

Norb continues to reach the victor's podium after winning the gold medal at the Pan American Games in Mexico (1955). It was the extension of his victory streak which included world titles in Italy, Sweden, and Austria.

1960 U.S. Olympic weightlifting team: Back row, left to right, Coach Bob Hoffman, John Pulskamp, Jim Bradford, Norb, Richard Zirk, and Manager Johnny Terpak; front row, Chuck Vinci, Ike Berger, Tony Garcy, Tommy Kono, and Jim George.

After overcoming two serious back injuries and resisting his doctor's advice, Norb's performance at the 1960 Olympic Games in Rome was called by the Russian team "the greatest comeback in sports history." Norb, the "miracle man," earned the bronze medal. He competed at a much lower body weight than the other medalists and was pound for pound the strongest man in the entire competition.

Olympic teammates Joe Puleo and Norb check out the landmarks in Budapest, Hungary with the Russian champ Leonid Zhabotinsky.

Continuing to prove the skeptics wrong, Norb pushed harder and harder challenging world record benchmarks. Lifting at a bodyweight considerably less than Paul Anderson, he hoists overhead more than 400 pounds in his latest world record performance!

The "Old Master" performs a brilliant split snatch while establishing another one of his 26 world records—eclipsing the famous Russian champion Yuri Vlasov's best. Bob Hoffman proclaimed the exceptional feat "the greatest lift of all time."

Norb became America's first weightlifter to ever total 1,200 pounds in the three Olympic lifts.

A legend in his time and for all time, no other strength athlete in organized world competition ever dominated his sport for so long, and as well, as the incomparable champion Norbert Schemansky.

Norb Schemansky's triumphs over adversity and serious injuries became an inspiration for many people.

Bob Hoffman, Johnny Terpak, Norb, Bill March, Gary Gubner, Tony Garcy, Ike Berger, Gary Cleveland, Louis Riecke, and Norb visit the United States space facility.

Two weightlifting immortals: Norbert Schemansky and Yuri Vlasov meet together in Tokyo, Japan. Although Norb was outweighed considerably in his career by Vlasov and other storied heavyweights, Vlasov in an interview once stated: “Norbert Schemansky is the greatest and strongest athlete I have ever seen.”

Norb mounts the podium while receiving his silver medal at the World Championships in Budapest, Hungary. In the highly controversial “Match of the Century” between American Norb Schemansky, age 38, and the Russian Vlasov, age 26, many witnesses believe Norb was robbed of the gold medal by the judges. Also pictured is American Gary Gubner.

In 1964 Norb astonishes the weightlifting experts by winning a bronze medal at the Olympic Games in Tokyo, Japan. He was the oldest athlete to win a medal at the games. Once again, he competes against Russian Olympic medal winners Zhabotinski and Vlasov who both weighed considerably more than him.

Norb and Ike Berger check out a Los Angeles club's weightlifting equipment during a goodwill tour.

In 1965, at age 41, Norb continued to astonish those who thought he would retire. Amazingly, he continued to improve each year in his three lift totals.

Karo Whitfield Presents

STRENGTH AND HEALTH SHOW

GRADY HIGH SCHOOL GYM

ATLANTA, GA.

SAT. MAR. 23

7:30 P. M.

WEIGHT LIFTING BY WORLD'S CHAMPIONS

PAUL ANDERSON

HARRY JOHNSON

—o—

"MR. ADONIS"
PHYSIQUE
CONTEST

—o—

"MISS VENUS"
BEAUTY
CONTEST

—o—

WEIGHT LIFTING
IN 148 POUND
CLASS BY
SOUTH'S BEST

—o—

GYMNASTIC
EXHIBITION
BY
SOUTHERN
CHAMPIONS

—o—

Norbert Schemansky

JOE ABBENDA

Exhibition Weight Lifting By Paul Anderson & Norbert Schemansky
"World's Strongest Men"

Joe Abbenda "Mr. America" & "Mr. Universe" 1962
Doing His Title Winning Poses

Harry Johnson "Mr. America" 1959
Doing His Fabulous Muscle Control Act

ADVANCE TICKETS ON SALE AT 106½ FORSYTH ST., N. W.

General Admission: $2.00 - Reserved Seats $2.50

Two weightlifting icons meet face-to-face for the first time. In 1963 Norb appeared with Paul Anderson, a professional, in a venue in Atlanta, Georgia.

Norb is likely the most massively muscular heavyweight of all time. After one of the hundreds of free exhibitions he gave during his career, he poses here with Michigan State University's Biggie Munn after his weightlifting demonstration.

"Mr.Weightlifting" sets another world record while becoming the first man in history to pass the 350-pound mark in the snatch.

Photo by Joe Puleo

Astro Gym's Jack Katchmar and the legendary Bob Bednarski visit Dr Russell Wright's clinic in 1969.

Jack Katchmar provided the above photo showcasing the unbelievable exploits of one of history's all-time greatest and least known athletes.

Norb's training philosophy was simple: train hard, and don't worry about any kind of special diet. Norb's workout favorites: beer, pizza and hamburgers.

Swimmer and Olympic gold medalist Clark Scholes of Michigan and Norb recall their Helsinki experience.

In 1980 Norb coached this team in Mexico City. Winners included Steve Mansour and Dr. Bob Suchyta.

Norb retired at age 72 after working for the city of Dearborn for nearly a decade. Only later in life did he catch any type of break when it came to gainful employment.

so I went over there and I won it. After that I figured, "Let's just come home and pay my bills and not worry about this lifting anymore." That's when I retired.

Guys like Norb and me did what we did for the love of it. We sure weren't doing it for the money. You can say what you want, but we loved the idea of lifting for the United States of America. That was more important to us than anything else—doing the best for our country.

CHAPTER SEVEN

Setback

Personally, when I think of the world's leading strength athlete, I think of Schemansky, the man who can clean and jerk the most, not the man who has the highest total or the best press, snatch, bench press or squat.

Peary Rader, Iron Man Lifting News (December 1956)

In the fall of 1954, with no real job prospects on the horizon, Norb went back to working odd jobs for Clarence Johnson. Meanwhile he applied to the Detroit Police Department.

Norb had always had a mild interest in police work. One of his cousins was a bodyguard for Detroit's depression-era mayor, Frank Murphy. And like many kids back in the days when patrolmen actually walked a beat, he had grown up admiring the neighborhood cop. "He was a big guy named Roger," he said. "I guess his uniform and all that made an impression on me." Norb took the written and physical tests, passing both with flying colors, and it was soon announced that he would enter the academy for eight weeks of training beginning February 28, 1955. Photographs of the bare-chested candidate being weighed and trying on a patrolman's hat appeared in the local papers. "When He Pounds a Beat," declared one bemused headline writer at the *Detroit News*, "It'll Stay Pounded."

Having the world's strongest man and the conqueror of the Russians wearing a badge was considered quite a coup for the department. "One cop said, 'We're not going to waste him on the streets,'" recalled Norb. "The plan was to use me in some kind of public relations." The square-jawed sports figure seemed to have the makings of an ideal role model. The police commissioner reported receiving a letter from a youngster who wrote, "If the police force is good enough for the world's strongest man, it's good enough for me."

Unfortunately for all involved, Officer Schemansky was out of a job before he ever had one—again because of his preoccupation with lifting. He put his entrance into the police academy on hold in order to compete at the Pan-American Games in Mexico City. There he posted a first-place total of 1,041¼ pounds, including a record 333 on the snatch. He was successful with 336 on a fourth attempt, but the lift was never officially credited by the International Weightlifting Federation. Norb also came close to completing a continental and jerk of 452 pounds, but lost it by being off balance.

Given his own predicament, Norb could commiserate with Humberto Salvetti, the disappointed runner-up. "I heard that the Argentina government was going to give him a house if he won the gold," he said. "I couldn't believe it. If that was true I should've let the guy win. All I got out of it was the gold medal and a world record in the snatch that they never bothered to submit. It wasn't until three or four years later than somebody finally topped it."

His ballyhooed plans for joining the police force died on the vine. At a luncheon where Clarence Johnson and Norb presented a set of barbells to the Highland Park Boys Club, Johnson told reporters the lifter needed to concentrate on defending his crown at the upcoming Senior Nationals in Cleveland and the World Championships in Munich, Germany. Following that was a goodwill tour of Russia and the Middle East that was being organized by the U.S. State Department. "If Schemansky goes," said Johnson, "he probably won't be able to enter the academy at all."

"I kept putting it off, putting it off," recalled Norb. "And then I hurt my back…."

Norb had started experiencing problems with his lower back shortly after returning from the Pan-American Games in March. He suffered from numbness in his legs and back spasms that kept him awake at night. Two years earlier, a spell of similar symptoms had occurred while he was preparing for the '53 Senior Nationals. The pain had caused him to miss five crucial weeks of training, but the Thursday before the meet the sciatica left as abruptly and mysteriously as it had appeared and he was able to still take first place in Indianapolis.

This time around, however, the pain would not go away. He tried to remain optimistic, describing the problem as a "kink in the hip" to Charlie Ward of the *Detroit Times*, who was profiling local athletes for the following summer's Olympic games in Melbourne, Australia. "I had one of these things before and it disappeared practically overnight," Norb told Ward, hopefully. "This one has proved more stubborn but I think it will disappear just as the other one did."

Not only did the pain not go away, it got worse. Neither Norb nor Bernice had health insurance. There was no money to spare on a doctor, and Norb was unaware that he was entitled to free medical care at the local Veterans Administration hospital, so he resigned himself to somehow *willing* his way through the spasms and sciatica. "I was in misery all the time," he recalled. "I was doing some exercises, trying to work it out. I was trying a little bit of everything." On really bad days the pain had him doubled over and scuttling about like Quasimodo. The so-called kink had reduced his lifting ability by about a hundred pounds. Soon he was forced to quit training all together. The national and world championships went on without him, as would the Russian tour and the Olympics. He also had to kiss the police academy good-bye. "I missed a lot," he said, his voice tinged with regret a half-century later.

By the fall of 1955 Skee had lost twenty pounds—and nearly his mind. Then came a chance meeting with Dr. Russell Wright, a pioneer in sports medicine who was able to get the hunchback of Charlevoix Street the career-saving help he needed.

"I was on Woodward Avenue, just leaving Clarence Johnson's office, when I ran into Dr. Wright," Norb said. "Turned out he had an office just a half-mile down Woodward. He was the doctor for some of the local pro teams, and he could tell right away by the way I was all hunched over what was wrong with me. This was on a Thursday. Two days later, that Saturday, I was being evaluated at Detroit Osteopathic Hospital."

Dr. Wright's diagnosis was a severely herniated lumbar disc. He explained to Norb that the gel-like discs in the spinal column act as a form of shock absorber between the vertebrae. When a disc "leaks" or "bulges" it can rub against the nerves in the spine, causing loss of sensation and muscle control in the legs as well as sharp shooting pains that radiate down the back and the buttocks. It would be a simple matter to say that years of lifting heavy iron plates had thrown Norb's back out of whack, but the root cause of back trouble is not always as obvious as it might seem. There actually are dozens of possible causes, including a genetic predisposition to the condition or a muscle imbalance that produces uneven wear and tear on the body. In Dr. Wright's opinion, weightlifting in and of itself had not caused Norb's back problem. The condition can be found in people in all walks of life, whether they are active or sedentary.

Today's method of treating a bulging disc—minimally invasive endoscopic surgery, in which the surgeon's tools are inserted directly to the problem area through tiny incisions—was unknown in 1955. Norb's condition required major open surgery, followed by substantial bed rest to give his body a chance to recover from the trauma. Dr. Wright's colleague, Dr. Paul Leonard, performed the operation just five days after Norb's fortuitous encounter on Woodward. Dr. Leonard made a six-inch incision in the patient's back, cut through the underlying muscle and ligaments, and carefully pulled aside the nerves in order to gain access to the damaged disc. Then he meticulously trimmed the part of the disc that had moved into the nerve canal and was causing the impingement. Finally, he sewed up the incision. Thanks to pain-killing drugs Schemansky was feeling practically giddy when he woke up in his hospital bed. But when the moment arrived for him to leave nine days later, he got a sobering introduction to the long road to recovery that lay ahead.

"Here I am, the big strong guy, right? When I got of bed that first time, I took one step and almost collapsed. Two attendants had to grab me." A look at the bill for the operation and the hospital stay might have produced a similar reaction, except that for once Norb's fame paid off in something more tangible than a trophy or medal. "The doctors and the hospital knew I didn't have any insurance," he said, "so they picked up the tab. You know what the whole thing cost? Three hundred bucks. It's a lot of money when you don't have it."

Norb returned to the flat on Charlevoix a semi-invalid. It took considerable therapy before he was able to resume simple everyday activities, and months before he was able to start a graduated program of rehabilitation in the gym. Meanwhile, the lifting world moved on without him. There was a new name on everybody's lips: Paul Anderson, a kindly, affable and deeply religious country boy who had the brutish, primitive strength of a mastodon.

Norb recalled first hearing of Paul Anderson in 1953, a couple of years before his name became a household word through newsreel, newspaper and magazine features and appearances on *The Ed Sullivan Show* and Steve Allen's *Tonight* program. Anderson was born in 1932 in Toccoa, Georgia. His father, a construction engineer who worked on hydroelectric dam projects, moved the family frequently. Anderson had Bright's disease as a youngster and was afflicted with kidney ailments his entire life. He was powerfully built but not particularly athletic, attending Furman University in South Carolina on a football scholarship but soon dropping out.

It was at Furman that Anderson first raised eyebrows, almost nonchalantly doing several deep knee bends with 400 pounds one day in the corner of the gym. Upon returning to his parents' home in east Tennessee, Anderson hooked up with storied strongman Bob Peoples, who became his promoter. Peoples' specialty was the dead-lift, but he soon had his protégé working on overhead movements. At the 1952 state meet, Anderson broke tournament records in all three Olympic lifts, then added a 660-pound squat—eighty-five pounds more than the unofficial world's record—as an exclamation point to an already spectacular performance. By early 1953, *Strength & Health* was reporting on this "new strength phenomenon" and "natural powerhouse" who packed about 360 pounds on his 5-foot-9 frame and trained with concrete-filled floor safes. In 1954 Anderson won the Junior National heavyweight title with a 1,030 total.

A series of injuries kept Anderson from competing in any major meets until 1955, by which time Norb was sidelined by his own physical woes. At the Senior Nationals that year, Anderson supplanted the absent Schemansky as heavyweight champ with a 436-pound clean and jerk that broke Skee's world record. A couple of weeks later Anderson and the rest of the American team were in Moscow to kick off the government's goodwill tour of Russia and the Middle East. Fifteen thousand people waited in a cold rain for the chance to watch the Americans and Russians go barbell-to-barbell at the open-air Zelyony Theater. Those who couldn't get a ticket stayed home to watch the encounter on television. Middle-heavyweight Arkady Vorobyov, a three-time Olympic medalist and five-time world champion between 1952 and 1960, was as astonished as anyone by Anderson and later recorded his impressions of the genial goliath and the excitement he generated.

"To be honest," Vorobyov wrote, "if the match itself had not taken place and only one man had remained on the platform, thousands of spectators would have still stayed in their seats, if that man had been Paul Anderson. When he stepped out of the airplane and onto the gangway an enthusiastic 'exclamation' was heard from our side. The 'Dixie Derrick,' as Anderson was nicknamed, really staggered the imagination. Powerful arms, somewhat reminiscent of a bull's leg in shape, bulged beneath the short sleeves of his shirt….He had a rolling gait that reminded one of a pair of compasses: one leg stood firm while the other drew an arc and bore it forward. This gait underlined even more his bulk and power. Immediately, when he set foot on Moscow soil, Anderson became extremely popular. Scientists and pensioners, schoolchildren and housewives followed the news of this miracle man with great interest….

"With his unusual strength and size, Anderson became a living legend to be touched and pinched. He once joked to a journalist that several cows grazed on his front lawn so that he could drink three gallons of fresh milk each morning. The journalist duly reported this to his readers in complete seriousness. If Anderson had said that each morning he ate a whole roast lamb for breakfast, no one would have dared doubt him. We went to the joint training session with the Americans as to a revelation, once again because of Anderson. The question everyone wanted to solve was: what was this — a miracle or a triumph of methodology?"

Workouts preceded the U.S.-Soviet exhibition. Without even bothering to warm up, Anderson started off by pressing 325 pounds above his head six times. He asked for more plates to be added. To everybody's amazement, he pressed 380 to break Canadian strongman Doug Hepburn's world record—pressing it not once, but three times. Moving over to a bench, he pressed 451 pounds three times. To top off this incredible exhibition, the barefooted Anderson hoisted 600 pounds and change off of a rack and onto his shoulders. "The bar bent with the weight," reported Vorobyov.. "He did five knee-bends without difficulty, and it was quite obvious that this was not his limit. There was a ripple of applause in the hall which was crowded with people, as the training session had turned into a performance. The good-natured, curly-headed lad toyed with them like he would with a dumbbell.... Anderson returned to America leaving behind the belief that it would take a superman to compete against another superman." Astonished Russians called Anderson *chudo prirody*, "a wonder of nature."

U.S. embassies wired home reports of the unprecedented excitement Anderson was generating as the American lifters continued their triumphant tour through the Middle East, where they put on a private demonstration for the Shah of Iran, a weightlifting buff. When the squad returned to the states, Vice President Richard Nixon welcomed them to the White House and the governor of Georgia announced that, henceforth, July 5 would be known as Paul Anderson Day.

That fall, at the World Championships in Munich, Germany, Anderson totaled 1,130 pounds to eclipse the world's record Norb had set a year earlier in Vienna. He also became the first man ever to elevate more than 400 pounds in the military press. "The thrill of the evening was furnished by the heavyweights," reported the *New York Times*. "Whenever Anderson went on the platform to make a lifting attempt, the 4,000 fans went wild." Members of the international lifting community were ambivalent about Anderson's effect on the sport. On one hand, his popularity was raising the iron game's profile with the general public. On the other hand, many potential converts were put off by the idea that lifting weights might cause one to grow to Anderson's monstrous proportions, such as his 36-inch thighs and 42-inch waist. "But whatever your views are," decided *Health & Strength*'s George Kirkley in his review of the weightlifting world in 1955, "it must be admitted that Paul is something in the way of being a freak. No normal 23-year-old, even with intensive bulk or bodybuilding training, weighs that much or has such measurements." Personally, added Kirkley, he preferred his heavyweights to be built along the more defined lines of John Davis and Norb Schemansky.

Short on technique and relying almost entirely on his bull-like strength, Anderson extended his own record total to 1,175 pounds at the 1956 National Championships before heading to Melbourne for the Summer

Games. Disappointment and drama attended his much anticipated Olympic performance. Anderson was vulnerable to minor sicknesses, and some malady affected him in Australia. Instead of making a run at the magical 1,200-pound mark, he implausibly failed to complete six of his nine attempts and could only compile 1,102 pounds, a mark matched by Argentina's Humberto Salvetti. However, Anderson—who competed at a "mere" 308 pounds—won on the basis of lower body weight. It came down to his very last lift, with Anderson power jerking 413¼ pounds after twice failing at that weight. Anderson's narrow and impossibly dramatic victory gave the U.S. team four gold medals to the Russians' three and earned American weightlifting bragging rights for the last time during the Cold War era.

In his brief spell of major amateur competition, Paul Anderson had claimed three national titles, a world's championship, and what would turn out to be the last Olympic gold medal ever won by a U.S. heavyweight. Along the way he had set several world records and profoundly changed the sport. According to historian John D. Fair, "Anderson's size and strength represented a new standard, almost a quantum leap, in lifting. Henceforth most heavyweight champions would follow the Anderson model of bulk training and become super heavyweights, virtual giants of sport."

With nothing more to prove, and anxious to use his fame for a greater purpose, Anderson became a professional strongman in 1957. He put his superhuman strength on display for a price, staging exhibitions around the country. He would use his fist to hammer nails through thick boards or employ his broad back and sequoia-like legs to lift thousands of pounds of human cargo off the floor. The *Guinness Book of World Records* credited him with a 1,200-pound squat and a 6,270-pound back lift—the most weight ever hoisted by a human. He also had brief flings at professional wrestling and boxing. Anderson, a devout Christian, had long entertained the dream of starting a foundation for homeless boys. To that end he used his earnings from hundreds of exhibitions a year around the country to bankroll what became the Paul Anderson Youth Home. He and his wife, Glenda, opened it in Vidalia, Georgia in 1961. Anderson died of kidney illness in 1994, having spent the last several years of his life in a wheelchair, but the home continues the good work he and his wife started. At last count more than 2,000 troubled young men had passed through its doors.

U.S. weightlifting, already beginning a slow slide into mediocrity, keenly felt Anderson's loss after he left the amateur ranks. "Once he retired," observed Arkady Vorobyov, "America could find no successor to the great man, and for a time the records of 'wee Paul' stood like a rock....In time, of course, many great lifters...exceeded Anderson's lifting, but the legendary lifter left quite a 'legacy' for the strong men who followed in his footsteps."

It's one of the quirks of iron game history that the time Norb lost to injury between 1955 and 1957 roughly paralleled the period Anderson spent in major amateur competition before turning pro, meaning these two storied heavyweights never got a chance to go head-to-head when it counted. There had been an earlier missed opportunity at the 1954 Senior Nationals, when the anticipated "heavyweight contest of the century" failed to materialize after neither Anderson, John Davis nor Doug Hepburn could make it to Los Angeles. And Anderson also did not attend the Pan-American Games a few months later, Skee's last competition before his back blew out.

Throughout his long career, Norb shared a venue with Anderson only once. Karo Whitfield held a strength and health show inside a high school gym in Atlanta in March 1963, and the "World's Strongest Men" were invited to put on an exhibition. Aware of A.A.U. regulations, the promoter made sure the amateur and professional participants were separated by a curtain and a one-hour intermission. As a professional, said Skee, Anderson's lifts didn't have to be officially verified, so it was hard to know exactly what to believe when word of his latest amazing achievement passed through the gym. "It seemed that every time Vlasov or somebody set a world's record, Anderson's publicity handlers would announce, 'Paul did that two weeks ago.'" When Norb became the first American amateur to total 1,200 pounds in 1964, it was pointed out that three months earlier Anderson had lifted 1,205 pounds as a professional at an exhibition in Coral Gables, Florida.

When asked about his missing the Melbourne Olympics, Norb always maintained he lost out on a second gold medal. In his estimation he would have pressed and snatched between 341 and 352 each, while jerking somewhere in the range of 430 to 441. This would have given him a total of anywhere from 1,113 to 1,146 pounds—less than Anderson's record 1,175 at the '56 Senior Nationals, but more than the 1,102 Anderson put together on an "off" day in Australia. "I think I could've beaten him if I'd stayed healthy," said Skee. "Anderson was outstanding in the press, but he was not as good in the quick lifts. My lifts were more balanced. And I always liked the challenge of people saying I couldn't beat some guy. For me, that was extra motivation."

Of course, nobody can say for certain who would have prevailed in a *High Noon*-style shootout between Norb and Anderson, though those who lifted alongside both legends would never lay odds against Schemansky. "The greatest quality Norb had was that he was a great fighter," said Tommy Kono. "He was the greatest competitor you could find. He wouldn't shy away from anybody. He could be the underdog and he wouldn't care. His attitude was: 'Let's show the people, let's make this guy work for his trophy.' A great weightlifter is a performer. He goes out and does things because he *has* to do well." Jim Bradford also spoke to Norb's determination. "I said it so many times: You could never count Norb out. You never knew what he might end up doing in a contest. He was never afraid to try, and when he tried you never knew but he just might succeed. I would imagine that a lot of times Norb surprised himself with what he was capable of. And that's what it takes to win."

While Anderson mania continued throughout 1956, Norb quietly concentrated on getting well. He returned to the gym and discovered to his satisfaction that lifting weights did not harm his back. That spring Reg Park, the English bodybuilder who would go on to star as Hercules in a series of Italian sword-and-sandal movies, dropped in on Norb during a tour of the states. Park had endured back problems of his own, so he suggested the name of his physiotherapist back in Leeds. Meanwhile, Park reported in a journal of his travels, "Norbert contented himself with bench presses around 300 pounds and presses with approximately 200 pounds from squat stands. His bodyweight was down to 200 pounds. In view of the fact that he had won world titles, and had snatched and clean and jerked almost as much as Anderson whilst weighing 140 pounds less, it amazes me that the A.A.U. weightlifting authorities have not had him to America's leading spine specialists." Norb, who knew the A.A.U. far better than Park, was anything but amazed.

Although Norb didn't give it any thought, it was his name—not Paul Anderson's—that remained the popular synonym for strength around his hometown and which still carried the biggest wallop with some impressionable kids in need of a role model. One was a beanpole of a youth named Don Howard, who was growing up on the west side of Detroit.

"During those years 'Schemansky' was a household word," recalled Howard, today a retired purchasing agent for General Motors. "His name was as big as Willie Mays or Sugar Ray Robinson. It was common vernacular to refer to some show-off flexing his muscles in the school locker room as a 'Schemansky.' We'd yell, 'Hey, Schemansky! Sit down!' Or when someone lifted something very heavy—like the day four of us kids jokingly tried to lift a Volkswagen—we were called 'little Schemanskys' by our peers."

Howard admits he was a gawky, uncoordinated kid who failed miserably at every sport he tried. He finally opted for the music program, a popular refuge for non-athletic types, and did well in the marching and concert bands. "But I always wished I was bigger and stronger, like Norb Schemansky, the world's greatest weightlifter. He was my secret hero."

At the very time Norb was recovering from his back injury, Howard was in intermediate school, where the skinny twelve-year-old made friends with "some really big guys" who protected him from the bullies who had picked on him for years. "They were the Schemanskys of my life," said Howard. "They were my pseudo heroes, the Norb Schemansky I could never become."

Fifty Years Too Soon

by Pete George

Dr. Pete George, a three-time Olympic medalist turned dentist, had a front-row seat for many of Norb Schemansky's historic lifts during America's golden age of weightlifting.

I admired Norb greatly. We were contemporaries, teammates on several world championship teams. We started about the same time but he just went on and on. He was a few years older than me, but he had an endurance that just wouldn't quit. We thought he was all washed up after 1955. I admit that I sort of gave up on him; I thought he was finished. He'd won the heavyweight championship and then Paul Anderson came along, so I thought Anderson would completely replace him and Norb would slip out of the picture. Instead it was the other way around—Norb came back stronger than ever from his back operation.

There is no question in my mind that he was the greatest unsung hero in Olympic history. There is no one who has accomplished what he has and yet been so unknown, even in his own hometown. Norb's biggest problem was he was born fifty years too soon. If we were doing now what we were doing then, we would be national heroes. But at that time there was no television coverage. Sportswriters knew very little about weightlifting. Today, thanks to people like Arnold Schwarzenegger and others, the sport's on everybody's mind. We just came along too soon.

I was there when Norb lifted the Apollon railroad wheels in 1954. I'd been there five years earlier when John Davis had lifted them, too. Norb did it much easier. He just whipped it right up there and jerked it three times. There was a great big *"aaahhhh"* when he whipped it up. He really awed everyone there with it. He had a workman's attitude about lifting. He wasn't the most dramatic lifter. He just more or less went about his business, went at it in a workmanlike way, and accomplished all his lifts. He was a natural. He was not one to push himself into the limelight. We were good friends. I enjoyed his friendship and admired him. He was very witty. Sometimes his wit was sarcastic, but I always enjoyed it.

Norb and I both won gold at the '52 Olympics. His battle with Grigori Novak was hailed as the battle of the century as Novak was at that time considered the world's greatest weightlifter. When Norb defeated him it really crushed the Russians. As you know, Norb had to train on his own. Every time he took a trip to compete he had to worry if he had a job waiting for him when he got home. By comparison, when the Russian lifters returned home they got all sorts of prizes—apartments and cars and so forth—and were hailed as heroes, whereas our guys were unknown.

For me, weightlifting was a different life back then. I had school and a career to worry about. But for Norb, weightlifting *was* his life. It was everything to him.

CHAPTER EIGHT

A Roaring Return

We classify Schemansky as one of the greatest weightlifters of our time. Not only because he makes world records and amazingly heavy lifts but because he does this at an age when most men are thinking of the rocking chair, and because he does this great lifting in spite of two serious back operations.

Peary Rader, Iron Man (August 1962)

On March 30, 1957, Norb took first place at the state Y.M.C.A. championships in Detroit. It was his first competition in two years, and he managed to ring up a 285 + 280 + 350 = 915 effort. Later that year, on June 23, the thirty-three year-old brewery worker arrived in Daytona Beach for the Senior Nationals. Twenty-five hundred fans were astounded when "the miracle man from Detroit" won the gold medal with his 990 total. A number of awestruck enthusiasts proclaimed Schemansky's triumph: "The greatest comeback in sports history." The bespectacled "man of steel" continued to astonish the weightlifting world when he reached the top in Montreal at the North American Championships. Hoisting an even 1,000 pounds, he won the event for the third time.

Things were definitely looking up in 1957. That year Bernice gave birth to their fourth (and last) child, Laura, and Norb followed up on a tip from one of his mother-in-law's friends and got hired at Stroh's brewery on Detroit's near east side. During his four years there his duties included custodial and maintenance work, everything from cleaning out tank filters with long-handled brushes to stacking large aluminum barrels of Detroit's famous fire-brewed beer.

For all the sweat involved, working in Stroh's basement was still considered a plum job. It was a union position that paid more than $100 a week, not counting overtime, with benefits that included free beer throughout the day for all employees. "There were a couple of barrels on every other floor," said Norb. "When I got hired they gave me overalls, boots, and a glass." Norb chose not to drink on the job, but thirstier types would arrive at work an hour early to take full advantage of the tap room. "Then I'd have to work all day with these guys," said Norb, wincing at the memory. With Bernice continuing to work as a secretary, the family income had doubled. There was now enough money, if not always time, for Norb to travel to distant meets. He and Bernice also were able to sock something away for the house they hoped to someday buy.

Then, one November day in 1957, Norb was running up the brewery stairs when he felt a sharp, familiar pain in his back. "I said to myself, 'Uh-oh, what's that?' So it was back to Dr. Wright again."

An examination revealed scar tissue had formed around his damaged disc and was pressing on the spinal nerves. Once again Dr. Leonard performed the surgery, cutting through Norb's muscular back and reopening the original six-inch incision to get in and clean up the problem area. This time the brewery workers' union covered the costs, including a weekly disability payment while Norb recuperated.

The common wisdom in weightlifting circles was that a lifter, even one with Norb's demonstrated grit, would be forced to toss in the towel after a second major back operation. Among doctors there was some doubt that the patient could even resume a completely normal lifestyle, much less return to the grueling demands of Olympic lifting. Norb, always happy to prove the "experts" in any field wrong, had other thoughts.

Instead of simply laying immobile in his hospital bed for several days, as he did after his first operation, he began doing simple exercises to keep his muscles from freezing up. He did them in secret, away from the disapproving eyes of the medical staff, concentrating on keeping his back stiff while gingerly working his legs. "I'd push my legs against the foot of the bed, keeping them limber," he said. When it came time to leave Detroit Osteopathic Hospital, Norb surprised everybody by practically walking out on his own. In less than two months he was back at the Northeastern gym, planning his second comeback.

Mike Kuhne, who worked out at the Northeastern "Y" during the 1950s, remembered the prevailing sentiment in the local gyms about Schemansky's second comeback. "We knew he never actually gave up, but the likelihood of his appearing once again on the world stage seemed remote, given his condition and the facts. All of his world records had been broken since he last competed, and the latest crop of world championship competitors were younger, bigger, and on steroids. Jim Bradford had come back from the army bigger and stronger than ever, and he did not have the back problem. No one took the old champion very seriously. It just seemed impossible."

During his rehabilitation Norb consulted with Bob Hoffman, asking for a frank appraisal of his chances to once again be a force on the international stage. The dean of U.S. weightlifting didn't want to dampen Norb's enthusiasm, so he just laid out the facts. For starters, there was his age. Schemansky was now thirty-three, older than most other lifters in his class. There also were the intertwining issues of his relatively light bodyweight and ordinary pressing ability. In 1954, when Norb won his last world title, he weighed in the range of 219 to 227 pounds and his best competitive press was 330 pounds. Just three years later, those numbers seemed almost quaint. Jumbo heavyweights were pressing 60 and 70 pounds more than Norb's best efforts. Catching up seemed an insurmountable task for a modest-sized heavyweight like Skee. The overriding concern throughout was his damaged back. How would it react after two surgeries, especially as Norb piled on the poundage? Some alarmists feared the strain on his lower spine could actually cripple him.

Norb rehabilitated in his usual methodical fashion. As he explained in a letter to *Strength & Health*'s Bob Haase: "After my second back operation in November 1957, I started training in January 1958 for a second comeback. I did mostly bench pressing, press off rack, rowing motion, and curls. Using light weights such as 250 pounds for 10 sets of 3 reps in the bench press, 175 for 10 sets of 3 regular presses taking the weight off the rack, rowing motions with 70 to 100 pounds, 5 reps and 10 sets, and a few curls were enough to get me back on the right path. During these first few months of training I made sure I did everything with a very straight back."

"He began with exercises such as the bench press, press from the rack, rowing and curls," observed historian Artie Drechsler. "Over time, he began to 'pull' or deadlift by starting at the top and taking the bar from a rack, then lowering the bar to perform a partial deadlift or pull. As his training continued, he progressively lowered the bar closer and closer to the platform, until he was able to lift it from the floor. Norb also worked his press and his squat harder than ever before. This great emphasis on assistance exercises eventually led to a substantial gain in bodyweight."

In early March 1958, less than four months removed from his second operation, Norb started training in earnest for the upcoming state championships. He was anxious to see what his body was capable of in an environment that didn't figure to be as competitive as the national meets. He did light cleans of up to 250 pounds, working them into his routine of presses, curls, and rowing exercises. At the tournament three weeks later he compiled a 300 + 260 + 320 = 880. Nothing spectacular, until one considers how far Norb had bounced back in a short time. The total was good enough for him to regain Michigan's heavyweight title.

Norb's recovery continued, cautiously and incrementally. He perfected his version of the new "layback" style of press, which involved more body movement than the strict presses of the past. In order to build up strength in his slow lifts, he incorporated more squats, standing presses and bench presses into his routine. Within a few weeks he was able to bench press 440 pounds and had worked his standing press up to 345 pounds, his best ever. A new device called the power rack had gained popularity. The four-pillared cage-like apparatus allowed a lifter to safely perform partial movements with heavier weights than would have been possible if executing the full movement. Norb used it extensively with good results.

In the spring of 1959 he embarked on a robust victory streak that, to the astonishment of doctors and many of his contemporaries in the lifting community, put him on the road for a return trip to the Olympics. On April 18 at the Great Lakes Weightlifting Tournament in Erie, Pennsylvania, he pressed 330, snatched 275, and jerked 370 for a winning total of 975 pounds.

Eight days later, he scored 340 + 300 + 380 = 1,020 at the Mid-States A.A.U. Championships in Whiting, Indiana. All were tournament records and Norb was chosen the Outstanding Lifter. Then in May he grabbed another first at the Ohio Valley Open in Louisville, Kentucky. Once again he was named the Outstanding Lifter. He could place only third at the Senior Nationals in York in July, but he rebounded to close out the year with first-place finishes at the A.M.A. Open in Pittsburgh and the North American Tournament in Quebec. Both times he received kudos as the meet's best lifter. In addition, his 310 pounds in the snatch set a new Canadian Open standard. The countless arm curls, bench presses, standing presses and partial deadlifts had paid dividends. The extra pounds came in the form of muscle, a solid base that produced a substantial increase in strength and a chiseled physique that was an aberration in the emerging era of super-sized heavyweights. To Norb's relief, the pain that had been predicted for his back failed to materialize.

Factoring into Norb's comeback was an elevated mood, the result of a major shift of scenery. In early 1959, he, Bernice and the four children happily moved into a small house in the west end of Dearborn. Norb and a friend had been driving around the leafy Detroit suburb one day when he sighted the little bungalow on New York Street. There was a municipal pool on the corner, and a hockey rink and woods nearby—all in all, a more inviting and tranquil setting than the east side of Detroit. The three-bedroom house featured only 900 square feet of living space, but after spending a dozen years in cramped flats the humble-sized new home seemed as big as a castle. "It was like moving to a whole other world," is how the oldest daughter, Pamela, described their domestic upgrade. At long last, the Schemanskys had a place to truly call their own. Although at times it would be a struggle paying off the $10,000 mortgage, on balance it felt good to be a homeowner.

They soon welcomed the first family pet, a black and tan German Shepherd named Venus. "We got her from a neighbor," said Norb. "Bernice wanted her, so she became part of the family." The dog hung around throughout the 1960s. The younger kids in the neighborhood certainly knew a local celebrity lived inside the bungalow, Norb remembered with a chuckle. "I'd hear them walking past on the sidewalk. 'That's Venus's house,' they'd say."

♦ ♦ ♦

In June 1960, Norb finished second by ten pounds to Jim Bradford at the Senior Nationals and Olympic Tryouts in Cleveland. The already heated competition for an Olympic berth turned raucous after A.A.U. national chairman Clarence Johnson, responding to protestations from several people at the scorekeeper's table, overruled the judges and declared one of Skee's snatches "not good" because of a knee touch. "There was a good deal of commotion among lifters, judges and audience from here on out," observed one correspondent, "with Schemansky's anger carrying him to lifts he hadn't made in years." By now Norb had 240 pounds of solid muscle packed onto his frame. The extra heft, coupled with his wounded-bear indignation, allowed him to set new personal highs in the press and three-lift total, with 355 and 1,075 pounds, respectively. It earned him a spot on the Olympic squad for the Summer Games in Rome.

More than two years into his comeback, Norb still had people doubting him. In York, where Bob Hoffman assembled the U.S. team for several days of concentrated workouts before heading to Italy, one lifter confided in Bradford that he thought Schemansky was just about through. After all, Norb was now thirty-six years old with a history of serious back problems. "Skee isn't in the mothballs yet," Bradford responded.

Along with more than 5,300 other athletes from 83 nations, Norb, Bradford, Tommy Kono, and the rest of the American weightlifting squad marched into the sun-baked oval of the Stadio Olimpico for the gala opening ceremonies on August 25. The following days provided some memorable moments for the international television audience, including polio survivor Wilma Rudolph capturing three gold medals in track and a brash young boxer named Cassius Clay winning light-heavyweight laurels. On a more ominous note, Danish cyclist Knut Jensen, his system filled with amphetamines and nicotinyl tartrate, collapsed and later died in a hospital—only the second death ever in Olympic competition, and an early, tragic indicator of the drug use that was creeping into sports.

Norb prefers more light-minded memories of the 1960 Summer Games. "The Italian government gave everybody in the country two weeks off to watch the Olympics and instead it was so hot they went to the beach," he recalled with a laugh. On one occasion, the Americans saw a couple of trucks loaded with "good looking broads. We were thinking, 'What gives?' Turned out they were shipping all the prostitutes out of Rome. They still managed to straggle back in."

Asked if accommodations had improved since his last trip to the Olympics eight years earlier, Norb quipped, "Yeah, instead of six or seven big guys squeezed into an apartment, now it was three guys." Even a goodwill gesture by Norb's employer had comic overtones. The Stroh brewery shipped three cases of beer to Rome, two of which were pirated by Italian and Olympic officials. Norb wasn't able to employ his "church key" on an unopened bottle until he had shelled out $17 duty on the third, remaining case. "So much for the 'free' beer," he said.

The war of the weights played out inside the 5,000-seat Palazzetto dello Sport. There were so many nations competing, the contests often lasted from afternoon through the wee hours of the following morning. As was usually the case at the Olympics, the most anticipated battle involved the heavyweights. Eighteen men competed in the class, the largest contingent of heavies yet in a major international competition, but once again it boiled down to a duel between the U.S. and the U.S.S.R.

The Russian grizzly was Yuri Vlasov, a 25-year-old *girevik* ("kettleball man") who had become acquainted with the famous handled cannonballs as a teenager in military school. He moved on to the Zhukovsky Air-Force Academy, where he studied engineering and mastered "the jolly game of taming iron." At the 1959 World Championships in Warsaw, Poland, the cerebral strongman tamed 1,101¾ pounds of iron to wrest the crown from fellow countryman and two-time champion Alexei Medvedev. He also snatched a world record 337¼ pounds. Vlasov's success—he would not lose a single competition between 1959 and 1963—made him the idol of millions, including an Austrian teenager named Arnold Schwarzenegger.

Although technically rivals, Vlasov and Schemansky were much alike. In fact, their physical resemblance was so strong people in Rome often mistook one lifter for the other. They were relatively small heavyweights of exceptional strength and ideal proportions who put a premium on mental toughness (though the Russian would gradually increase his body mass to more than 300 pounds before retiring in 1967). Vlasov maintained that judging a man's strength by his size was like judging a book by its thickness. It was not beef, but "mind muscle," that determined victory. "At the peak of tremendous and victorious effort," he wrote, "while the blood is pounding in your head, all suddenly becomes quiet within you. Everything seems clearer and whiter than ever before, as if great spotlights had been turned on. At that moment you have the conviction that you can contain all the power in the world, that you are capable of everything, that you have wings. There is no more precious moment in life than this, the white moment, and you will work very hard for years to come to taste it again."

Like his American counterpart, Vlasov wore horn-rimmed eyeglasses even when lifting, giving him a slightly nerdy look. The bookish image wasn't wholly misplaced as Vlasov would go on to a second career as an author and political dissident. His most famous moment would come in 1989, when he criticized the KGB during hearings inside the Kremlin. Tens of millions of his countrymen watched on live television as Vlasov accused the infamous state-within-a-state of blocking the rising tide of reform in Russia and of sowing "grief, cries, torture on its native land." The critic's status as a national hero was probably the only thing that kept him from disappearing.

Although nobody at the Rome Olympics was aware of it, Vlasov was already a conflicted man. Seven years earlier his father, a career Communist diplomat, was summoned by the secret police. He was never seen again. As the Soviet Union hailed Yuri Vlasov as "the strongest man on the planet," the bones of his father lay buried somewhere in a Moscow forest.

Vlasov put all of that out of his head to concentrate on experiencing the "white moment" in Rome. On September 10, the day before the closing ceremonies, United Press International sent this report over the wires:

> Russia's fantastic heavyweight, Yuri Vlasov, broke the world's weight-lifting record three times in three hoists tonight to win the Olympic gold medal.
>
> With a calm confidence that was almost frightening, the red-clad Russian stepped briskly to the bar, grasped it and raised it above his head in three

> final jerks for a total of 1,182½ pounds, fifty-five pounds above the five-year-old world record set by an American lifter, Paul Anderson.
>
> James Bradford of Washington equaled the 1955 world's record of 1,127½ pounds with his press, snatch and jerk total, but it was only good for second place in the heavyweight class. Norbert Schemansky of Dearborn, Mich., hoisted a total of 1,100, equaling the existing Olympic record, for third place.
>
> In the snatch, Vlasov lifted 341 pounds to 330 pounds by Bradford and Schemansky.
>
> The Russian waited until after Bradford had finished his lift, equaling the world's record, before he began his last campaign—the jerk.
>
> The first time on the platform the giant Russian lifted 407 pounds and broke the world's record. He came back again with the same deadly calm and hoisted the weights for 429 pounds breaking the record again.
>
> In the final lift, Vlasov lifted 445½ pounds.
>
> The little sports palace where the weight lifting ended at 3 o'clock in the morning exploded into wild applause for the Russian.
>
> Schemansky also attempted to equal the previous world record on his last jerk but failed.

Norb, who competed at a body weight of 247½ pounds, jerked 396 ¾ on his first attempt. Had he made 424¼ in either of his two failed tries, he would have tied Bradford's three-lift total but won the silver on the basis of lower body weight. "I made that lift a few years earlier," said Norb, "but with my back I didn't have the technique."

The Red juggernaut continued. All told, the Russian contingent took five out of a possible seven gold medals in weightlifting at Rome:

Bantamweight		**Kgs.**	**(Lbs.)**
Gold:	Chuck Vinci, United States	345	(760½)
Silver:	Yoshinobu Miyake, Japan	337.5	(744)
Bronze:	Esmaiil Elmkhah, Iran	330	(727½)

Featherweight		**Kgs.**	**(Lbs.)**
Gold:	Yevgeny Minayev, U.S.S.R.	372.5	(821¼)
Silver:	Isaac Berger, United States	362.5	(799¼)
Bronze:	Sebastiano Mannironi, Italy	352.5	(777¼)

Lightweight		**Kgs.**	**(Lbs.)**
Gold:	Viktor Bushuyev, U.S.S.R.	397.5	(876¼)
Silver:	Howe-Liang Tan, Singapore	380	(837¾)
Bronze:	Abdul Wahid Aziz, Iraq	380	(837¾)

Middleweight		**Kgs.**	**(Lbs.)**
Gold:	Aleksandr Kurynov, U.S.S.R.	437.5	(953½)
Silver:	Tommy Kono, United States	427.5	(942½)
Bronze:	Gyozo Veres, Hungary	405	(892¾)

Light Heavyweight		**Kgs.**	**(Lbs.)**
Gold:	Ireneusz Palinski, Poland	442.5	(975½)
Silver:	James George, United States	430	(948)
Bronze:	Jan Bochenek, Poland	420	(926)

Middle Heavyweight		**Kgs.**	**(Lbs.)**
Gold:	Arkady Yorobyev, U.S.S.R.	472.5	(1,041¾)
Silver:	Trofim Lomakin, U.S.S.R.	457.5	(1,008½)
Bronze:	Louis Martin, Great Britain	445	(981)

Heavyweight		**Kgs.**	**(Lbs.)**
Gold:	Yuri Vlasov, U.S.S.R.	537.5	(1,185)
Silver:	Jim Bradford, United States	512.5	(1,130)
Bronze:	Norb Schemansky, United States	500	(1,102¼)

Vlasov was named the outstanding sportsman of the Summer Games. As they had in 1956, Soviet athletes outdistanced the Americans in the overall medal count; they also grabbed the most gold medals. U.S. domination of the heavyweight ranks was ending and the overall quality of the program was in the midst of a steep, almost unimaginable decline. Proof of the latter was in bantamweight Chuck Vinci's gold medal; nearly a half-century later, it remains the last an American weightlifter has won at the Olympics.

Lauded by the Russian athletes as "the wonder of the games", Norb had to be satisfied with getting a bronze to complete his "hat trick" of three medals in three Olympic outings. He now had one of each color. "Norb's bronze medal is almost as good as a gold one because of the training he had to do after his two operations," Bernice told reporters after her husband returned home from his seven-week absence.

Like Bernice, Norb recognized that vindication was nearly as sweet as a higher podium finish. Far from being through, he had set a personal best for the three-lift total, and he had done it on the world's largest stage.

Skee was back. The mothballs would have to wait.

CHAPTER NINE

Battling the Russians

Vlasov has the Order of Lenin. I go around unrecognized.

Norb Schemansky, 1962

While Yuri Vlasov returned from the Rome Olympics to a hero's welcome in Russia, Norb came back to Michigan uncelebrated but rejuvenated. At the state tournament in January 1961, he set new records for the event with a 380-pound press and a 320-pound snatch. Feeling good that day, he snatched 343½ on an extra attempt for a new world's record, but failed at 348½ when his knee swiped the floor. Six weeks later at the Baltimore Open, he became the first man in history to pass the 350-pound mark in the snatch when he ripped up 351—this despite a bad shoulder that prevented him from pressing or jerking.

Norb always maintained that setting a world's record gave him the most satisfaction. "That means you're the best of all-time, you've done something no other man has ever done before. It's better than winning the Olympics. I always figured the Olympic champion is probably the best guy on that particular day. Who knows, somebody else who was better might have had an off day during the tryouts and not made the team."

On April 28, 1962, Norb executed what some veteran observers present called the greatest lift ever made—a 362-pound snatch at the state championships in Detroit. As with all of Norb's lifts, it was a thing of beauty, performance art that even spectators with little knowledge of the sport could appreciate. Per his style, he kept a wide handgrip on the bar, which cost him some leverage but also reduced the distance the weight had to be hoisted over his head. Using his powerful back and shoulder muscles, he flipped the 362-pound weight off the floor and in one swift unbroken movement carried it all the way up, doing a lightning split to get under it before straightening out his oak-like legs to reach a standing finish. There he stood, as implacable and imposing as the Colossus of Rhodes astride the harbor mouth, until the judges signaled a legal lift. "Everybody went crazy," recalled one observer. "It was a perfect lift. His knee was probably only an inch from the floor."

Norb's extraordinary effort obliterated the best Vlasov could do at the time and would turn out to be the only world's record set by an American that year. Bob Hoffman was so impressed he immortalized the historic moment on the cover of that September's *Strength & Health.* Norb's training regimen and increased bodyweight—he had bulked up to nearly 260 pounds while adding tremendous power in his legs and hips—also paid off in his slow lifts. At the same meet he pressed 390, then just missed 410. His 1,160 total was his best yet, and despite his age (he would turn thirty-eight in a month), he just seemed to keep getting better and better.

But all was not well. Following his record-setting snatch, Norb unburdened his thoughts on a writer for the Associated Press. He had been in a funk for some time. Three weeks earlier, leg cramps had caused him to withdraw midway through a meet in Brooklyn, New York. It was doubly frustrating because a shoulder injury had plagued him throughout 1961, forcing him to miss almost a year of competition. There also was his continuing feud with the A.A.U., which seemed to have cost him a recent trip to the Soviet Union for the annual Prize of Moscow tournament. For some inexplicable reason he had been passed over in favor of York heavyweight Dick Zirk when the U.S. squad was selected—this despite the fact that Norb had won the qualifying event in Wilmington, Delaware. He kept his mouth shut until he learned Zirk had finished a dismal fifth in Moscow, an offensive showing that pricked Norb's national pride. When he tried to get an answer from the A.A.U. and York Barbell, all he could learn was that Zirk was chosen because he had a visa, suggesting Skee might have had a problem in getting one. This was news to Norb, who had competed all over the world for years without once encountering any difficulty with visas or passports.

Norb also was out of work again, having left the brewery when the company refused the ailing worker's request to be transferred to a less physically demanding sales job. "They said they didn't hire athletes as salesmen," Norb said. "A few weeks after I left, they hired a football player."

With all this gnawing at him, Norb cut loose. The New York bureau of the Russian news agency, Tass, picked up the wire service report detailing Schemansky's chronic unhappiness and gleefully gave it a socialist spin for Moscow's *Sovietski Sport.*

"This American is 38 years old," the story began. "He has four children. He has been looking for a job for a long time.

"This is a common story for this country where over four million cannot find work to feed themselves and their families.

"This is the condition of the famous American weightlifter of world renown. Just recently he established a new world record in the snatch with 362 pounds, a full kilogram over the record of the Soviet 'bogatyr' Yuri Vlasov.

"The athlete, who captured a bronze medal in the Rome Olympics, told a correspondent of the *New York Times:* 'I have been busy looking for a job, but finding one is becoming harder. Besides that, employers are afraid that I must take off too much time for weightlifting.'

"These are the bitter thoughts that are burdening this manly person and great athlete. In the same interview, Schemansky complained that at the same time his colleague in weightlifting, Yuri Vlasov, receives widespread respect and was awarded the Order of Lenin, he, in the USA, does not attract the slightest attention—even when he was seriously ailing.

"Two countries—two fates. The story of Schemansky reflects the attitude toward man in a capitalistic society."

In what had become almost a stock headline for stories involving Skee, the Russians labeled the propaganda piece "The Bitter Thoughts of Norbert Schemansky."

Left out of the Tass report was Norb's determination to beat the Russians in the upcoming World Championships in Hungary, where he was looking forward to a rematch with the seemingly invincible Vlasov. The Soviet hero was in the process of gaining additional bulk, to the point that he could correctly be described as "the Russian behemoth" in newspaper accounts. En route to Budapest, Norb won the Senior Nationals in June, totaling 1,140 pounds inside a high school auditorium in the Detroit suburb of Highland Park. His total slipped ten pounds at the team tryouts, held in York in September, but it was still good enough for Bob Hoffman, coaching the U.S. squad, to hand Norb a plane ticket to Budapest for his first crack at the world's title since the glory days of 1954.

"We thought he was through as a lifter," Hoffman would remark of Norb's performance in Budapest, "but this indomitable man trained on with a will. Who could expect that this injured, battered old champion, who participated in his first World Championships in 1947, would be in the 1962 championships and outpress 'the world's strongest man,' Vlasov, the man who had erased the record Paul Anderson had held for years?" Unfortunately for Norb, he lost the championship in what Hoffman termed "the great heavyweight robbery."

Fourteen lifters representing a dozen countries competed in the premier event, the heavyweight contest. For a long while it seemed that Norb would pull off an upset of the man, eleven years his junior, who had not lost in over three years. He began by out-pressing Vlasov, 402½ to 391¼. This shocked many, as Vlasov was the current record holder and Norb hadn't been known as a particularly strong presser until the last two or three years. Moving on to the snatch, Norb and Vlasov both started with 330½, then moved successfully on to 341½. With 352½ on the bar, Norb again made the lift while Vlasov failed—another eleven-pound gain to give Schemansky a comfortable margin with the decisive final event, the clean and jerk, still to come.

"I had him by twenty-two pounds going into the last lift," Norb recalled a few years later. "He was draggin' his ass all night. When he came out for his last attempt, he had a patch on his leg and popped the lift up like nothing. Without some 'outside' help, he was a beaten man." Hoffman saw the same transformation. "Vlasov had been going along at about half steam," he wrote, "but he came out to the platform now like a demon. I don't know what they gave him to charge him up, but he was like a raging maniac, and he cleaned and jerked 440¾ like it did not weigh anything. All we could do was watch, for our men were through."

Vlasov also received unexpected help from the weather and the judges. On this final night of the championship, promoters decided to move the battle of iron-game giants from an indoor hall to an open-air arena to accommodate the large crowd of 9,000 people. The wet September chill affected Norb, the oldest lifter, more than anyone. His right leg cramped during his first attempt at 418¾ in the clean and jerk, causing his knee to hit the platform and the lift to be disqualified. He went inside to the dressing room, where the team doctor, Dr. Russell Wright, feverishly massaged his leg. Norb hobbled out and was forced to power clean a second attempt at 418¾, then returned inside for more massaging. Then it was back to the stage, where he again had to power clean the weight so his leg wouldn't bend and cramp. Norb successfully managed 429¾, giving him a new American record total of 1,184¾ pounds that eclipsed Paul Anderson's best officially sanctioned effort by nearly ten pounds. But it could have been more, had a healthy Norb been able to jerk 440¾ on his third attempt, as originally planned. This would have forced Vlasov to make a world-record lift to win, something he didn't seem capable of at this tournament.

Instead the suddenly re-energized Vlasov jerked 440¾ on his first try, cutting Norb's advantage in half, then asked for 457¼. "A success with it would mean victory," Hoffman reported in *Strength & Health*. "He cleaned the weight easily, got set for the jerk, made a false attempt, settled himself again, and then jerked the weight." Such a double dip was in clear violation of the rules. But two of the three judges signaled the lift was good, sealing the Russian's win by the slimmest of margins—a quarter pound. According to Hoffman, one judge "later said that he thought Vlasov was merely adjusting the bar, but the facts are that Vlasov was in position, then bent his legs, straightened up, and finally jerked the weight, and this lift was definitely not correctly performed." George Kirkley, another weightlifting authority in attendance, recalled: "Many people around me…were complaining about Vlasov being allowed the lift, but there was nothing that could be done about it. The American camp could not appeal to the jury as at that time no appeal could be made by another country against a lift that was passed by the referees."

Norb had to settle for silver while a teammate exactly half his age—

nineteen-year-old Gary Gubner, the world indoor shot-put champion—took bronze. "And so it ended," Hoffman continued, "with Vlasov at the top on the victory stand with our lifters second and third. The championships were over, and we listened to the Soviet national anthem instead of 'The Star Spangled Banner.' It is a tragedy that Schemansky, this determined man, had to lose by the barest margin."

Norb felt as if his pocket had been picked. Never mind that at this stage of his life Skee's pockets were nearly always empty; this time something of value had been stolen from him. "The A.A.U. claimed they would dispute the double jerk, but they never did that I know of. I should've been world champ then at thirty-eight." It was no consolation that the Middle Atlantic A.A.U. Weightlifting Association nominated Norb for that year's Sullivan Award, and no surprise—at least to Schemansky—that this time around he didn't even make the list of finalists.

While the lifting world slowly changed around him, Norb's stubbornness and outspokenness remained intact. Strength training was becoming more sophisticated as the 1960s wore on, with such trendy techniques as "periodisation" and "plyometrics" finding an audience. A couple of musclemen, Bill March and Lou Riecke, attributed their well-publicized strength gains to "isometric-contraction" workouts—that is, employing maximum force against a fixed object—with Riecke performing the full lifts only on weekends. Sales of isometric power racks soared in the early '60s.

Schemansky kept to his old routine, with slight variations. "It was working for me, so why change it?" he asked rhetorically. Even at his age he was America's top international lifter and setting world records. And Norb got considerable satisfaction from beating the young pups. "I remember the Russians used to point at me and say, 'Everybody hits their peak at twenty-seven—except him.'"

During the 1960s Norb's typical weekly training routine began with a Monday session of pulls from the rack. He would perform three repetitions each of low and high snatch pulls (at 315, 365, and 400 pounds), low clean pulls

(375, 450, and 525), and high clean pulls (400, 475, 550). He would conclude with a dozen standing presses, doing three reps each in 25-pound increments (250, 275, 300, and 325). On Tuesday he started where he had finished, doing three presses each at 250, 275, and 300 pounds, before moving on to the squats (three reps at 315, 405, 455, and 505 pounds). Finally it was on to the power rack, where he'd do one quarter-squat at up to 800 pounds and also some presses. Thursday was reserved for power snatches (two reps at 205, 225, 245, and 265), power cleans (two reps at 300, 320, 340, and 360), and presses (five reps at 205, 225, 250, and 275). On Saturday, Norb would end the week by concentrating on the Olympic lifts up to 90 percent of his maximum, sometimes throwing in some squats or deadlifts.

About three weeks before a meet, Norb began eliminating power exercises in favor of Olympic lifts. He also cut his schedule back to three workouts a week: Monday, Wednesday, and Saturday. In the final few days he focused on form, style, and speed, not poundage. For lack of a better term, Skee exhibited "smart power." He didn't attempt maximums in the gym. Instead, he concentrated on doubles, which saved energy and helped him hone his technique.

"Some guys couldn't believe how much more I could do in competition, which is when it counts," he said. "I remember Bob Hoffman once said, 'In training Norb looks like he's dying, but in a contest he's a dynamo!' That's because I never burned myself out, never left my best lifts in the gym. I figured I could always lift 10 percent more in competition."

Norb's home away from home during this period was the Astro Gym, which one of his friends, Jack Katchmar, opened in the basement of Detroit's Normandy Hotel in 1959. Katchmar, who had been seriously wounded as an infantryman in Europe, used some of his disability checks to get the private gym up and running, then depended on the kindness of strangers, minimal monthly dues from members, and the drawing power of Norb's name to keep the threadbare operation afloat.

The gym was a converted kitchen, which accounted for its narrow rectangular dimensions. "It was about 600 square feet," Norb remembered. "A couple lifting platforms, a couple squat racks. It had to be for Olympic lifting only—there was no room for anything else." The Astro Gym was an undeniably masculine enclave that was a notch or two above a deer camp. Some battered lockers and an old sofa were jammed into the makeshift dressing room, while *Playboy* pin-ups adorned the peeling walls of the main room. Drunks stumbling along Woodward Avenue occasionally beat on the locked door. The Astro was just a mile down Woodward from Clarence Johnson's office, though neither Johnson nor any other A.A.U. official ever saw fit to drop in. However, *Detroit News* columnist Doc Greene paid a visit and declared it the poor man's version of the tony downtown Detroit Athletic Club. The Astro, Greene decreed, was the city's other D.A.C.—the "Derelicts Athletic Club." While admitting the seven-story Detroit Athletic Club obviously had superior facilities, Greene pointed to the fetching centerfolds and said, "You have better wallpaper."

Some promising youngsters frequented the Astro, including lightweight Zuhair "Steve" Mansour, whom Norb had met in Rome. "I was very impressed with his style and power and made a point to introduce myself," recalled Mansour, who emigrated to Detroit after the 1960 Olympics and is today a successful businessman in the area. "I was competing for Iraq at the time, knowing I would be moving to Detroit. Norb said, 'Look me up when you get here.' I did, and Norb offered me to come work out with him. It was a great opportunity as well as a good learning experience. He took weightlifting to the next level. He was a no-nonsense guy. He lived and breathed everything weightlifting. That's what made him a champion." Under Norb's guidance, Mansour was able to achieve some of his best performances, winning two national championships and competing in two more Olympics.

Joe Puleo, a local middleweight whose father installed the showers at the club, was another notable Astro lifter. "Norb came to all of the local meets in Detroit and that's where we got to know each other," said Puleo. "Eventually, he invited me to work out with him. We trained together, off and on, for the next eight years." Puleo became a six-time national champion and a member of the 1968 and 1980 U.S. Olympic teams. He also earned a law degree and opened a practice in Florida, where he is now retired.

"Being around Schemansky was quite a learning experience for a young weightlifter," he said. "Watching a great Olympic and world champion going through his training routine provided me with an in-depth education about real weightlifting. His training methods were not theoretical or subject to question.

They were solid and successful. His training methods made him stronger and led him to win world championships.

"Norb's greatest asset was his superior mental approach to the sport. He had an amazing ability to focus on winning and being the best. You could see it in his training and in his preparation for competition. When you watched him in competition, you knew that something great was going to happen. He was going to win or break records, or both. There would be no 'psyching him out' or distracting him. He was there to win. Much is made of mental attitude and sports psychology today. There are a lot of experts out there. Books have been written about the subject. However, it's doubtful that any of the experts will ever understand the depth of Schemansky's mental strength."

Whatever the caliber of the individual Astro lifter, Norb grunted and pulled right alongside them at training sessions and at tournaments. Memories are fuzzy and records are incomplete, but everybody seems to agree that Astro's contingent absolutely dominated the state championships during the dozen or so years the gym operated. The story is that the Astro Gym became so crowded with trophies, the Michigan A.A.U. quit handing them out. Norb himself remained untouchable, winning the last several of his seventeen state crowns during this period.

Charles Fraser was a Michigan State University student who would go on to organize the Olympic lifting program at the school, as well as translate Yuri Vlasov's book, *The Justice of Strength.* Fraser recalled the awe in which Schemansky's protégés at the Astro Gym held him.

"We Olympic lifters who trained with him back in the '50s and '60s were so dominated by his greatness that we elevated him to the status of a semi-god of mythic proportions," said Fraser, who as a boy had been inspired by Schemansky's performance in the 1952 Olympics. "We wanted to be like him, even though we knew we could not. He was more than a great weightlifter. He was a great athlete. He was masculine, the prototypical strong, silent hero. He demonstrated his greatness by action, not words.

"We watched his every move when he came into a gym or a room. Even if we pretended not to notice, we were more fully aware of him than what we were doing ourselves. He was the best self-coached athlete I have ever known in a lifetime of athletics. And being true to himself, a man of few words, he did not like to coach others, at least verbally. He coached by example. When we asked him for training advice, he would give a brief, terse answer, alarmingly simple and often blunt, as if to say, 'It's obvious. You should have figured it out for yourself.' Although a man of few words, when he spoke, everyone listened."

Fraser commented on Norb's remarkable physique, as well as his "charisma"—a word not often used in connection with Schemansky. "He was the best-built heavyweight ever to hoist a barbell on the world stage. He had the proportions of a world-class bodybuilder. Many observers claimed that he would have been the dominant physique champion of his era, had he chosen to pursue it.

"In addition to his marvelous physical presence there was his exquisite personal comportment on the lifting platform. He wasted no time with dramatic 'psyching up' or other platform histrionics before attempting a lift. When he missed a lift, which was rare, there was no cursing or temper tantrums or self abuse. If one of his lifts was turned down by the judges, another rarity, Norb never complained. He would just stare for a moment at the head judge, then walk off the platform."

In 1963, Norb twice walked off the platform the runner-up to Soviet rivals. In March, at the Prize of Moscow Tournament, he admittedly was "in pretty bad shape" but still managed some decent lifts while compiling a 1,102¼ total, trailing behind Leonid Zhabotinsky. This was Norb's first trip to the Soviet Union, and the Russian people impressed him with their passion and knowledge of the sport. "The turnout was something, not like here in the states. I remember when the Russians came to Detroit [for an exhibition in May 1958], they couldn't believe how small the crowds were. The papers said 2,000 people were there, but there might've been 400, no more than that." In September at the World Championships in Sweden, Norb upped his total to 1,184¾, but Yuri Vlasov had improved to 1,228½ to win handily.

Afterwards, Norb and Vlasov and several others shared a few beers inside a Stockholm hotel room. According to Lou Riecke, Vlasov had a personal trainer in tow. "He was a little bitty guy," said Riecke. "Vlasov would point to his shoulder and the guy would rub it, he'd point to his leg and the guy would rub it. Whatever Vlasov wanted, this guy took care of it."

The upcoming Olympics were to be held in Tokyo, Japan, which gave Norb an idea. Through Jack Lipsky, the American squad's Russian-speaking trainer, Norb playfully issued a challenge to his nemesis. Recalled Riecke: "Schemansky told Lipsky, 'You tell Vlasov that he beat me tonight, but I challenge him next year in Tokyo. We are going to go to the geisha house and he'—Norb points at Vlasov's little trainer—'he can keep score.' Vlasov throws up his arms, starts waving them back and forth as if to say, 'No, no.' Norb, of course, wasn't serious. It was typical Norb—very deadpan but funny."

By now Schemansky was using the squat style in his cleans, an attempt to avoid the cramps he often experienced in his back leg when splitting with heavy weights. Despite the aches and pains and pulls and strains that were becoming more frequent with age, he kept rolling right along. Between July of 1963 and the following June he won several tournaments. He was named the best lifter at meets in Chicago, Dallas, and Canada, as well as at the '64 Senior Nationals, where he avenged a five-pound loss to Sid Henry in the previous year's championship. At the Michigan Teenage State Championships at the Northeastern "Y" on February 2, 1964, Norb became the first American amateur to reach the magical 1,200-pound mark. His 445-pound clean and jerk also toppled the existing U.S. mark. However, because he was an extra lifter (meaning he was not on the official list of entries for the event), neither record was recognized by the A.A.U. When weightlifting's version of Ol' Man River rolled into New York for the Olympic Trials in August 1964, the *Times* was intrigued enough to lead off its coverage with him. "The 40-year-old Schemansky was the oldest man in any of the seven classes during the two-day competition," reported Frank Litsky. "He lifted like a youngster as he pressed 396¾ pounds, snatched 330½ and clean and jerked 418¾. His total was 1,146 pounds." Sixteen years after being selected for his first Olympics, Norb was headed for his unprecedented fourth.

First he assembled with other American lifters in York. Norb's stopover in "Muscletown, U.S.A." had been a regular feature of his itinerary for major meets since he began representing the barbell company in 1960. Unlike many members of the team who lived and trained in York, Norb flew in a week or so before a big national or international championship. While in Pennsylvania, his and other out-of-state lifters' hotel and meal expenses were paid for by Hoffman. That was perfectly fine with the A.A.U. board of directors. But Hoffman also regularly slipped a few dollars to his lifters to help out at home or as an incentive at a critical stage of a meet. "There's a little extra in it for you if you make this one," he was known to say before a lifter approached the barbell. Strictly speaking, such handouts violated amateur rules, Norb admitted. "But Hoffman and all the other amateur officials were on the same boards, and he was paying the way for everybody in those days, so they had to play ball with him. Hell, without Hoffman there was no U.S. weightlifting."

By now Hoffman was making as much money selling his line of health products as he was weight equipment. Hoffman, possibly a medicine show pitchman in a previous life, wasn't above attributing a portion of Norb's success to his alleged use of such concoctions as Hoffman's Super Hi-Proteen, Hoffman's Energol Germ Oil Concentrate, and Hoffman's Rub. While Norb was undecided about the value of supplements—he could take them or leave them and in any case he thought they tasted terrible—he had always scoffed at the idea of a special diet for lifters. A good deal of his caloric intake revolved around hamburgers, pizza, Polish sausage and beer, and it became a standard line of his that "If someone needs a special diet to compete, then I've got him beat already." He did make good use of all those free cases of Hi-Proteen tablets Hoffman regularly shipped to the Astro Gym. "I'd sell them to members of the Wayne State track team," Norb said. "Hey, it kept me in gas money during the '60s."

The Games of the XVIII Olympiad, held October 10-24, 1964 in Tokyo, represented the first time a country in the Far East had hosted the Olympics. The Japanese pulled out all of the stops to impress on the rest of the world how far it had come since the war. Memories were stirred when nineteen-year-old Yoshinori Sakai, who was born in Hiroshima on the day that city was obliterated by an atomic bomb, lit the Olympic Flame. Norb wasn't overly impressed by the American squad's accommodations in the Olympic village, which was a redeveloped barracks that formerly housed U.S. occupation troops. "It was still three big guys squeezed into a room," he said.

It could have been worse. He could have been sharing a sofa and a kitchenette with the two Russian super-heavyweights, Yuri Vlasov and Leonid Zhabotinsky. Norb, who was competing at 265 pounds, described Vlasov's appearance at the Games. "I'll never forget him in Tokyo, at a bodyweight of roughly 310 pounds. It was hard to believe he weighed that much." Zhabotinsky, a former tractor factory worker who swore by his wife's Ukrainian *borshch*, was even bigger at 341 pounds.

Norb felt he was lifting better than ever, and in training sessions in Tokyo he measured himself against Vlasov. The Soviets trained in the morning, before the Americans, so Skee knew going into each day's workout what he needed to keep pace. Informed that Vlasov had pressed 352½ pounds five times, for example, Norb did the same. This went on until the Russian coaches started to feel their man was no longer a lock for the gold medal.

Then came the big day. Norb, with a history of saving his best lifts for competition, wanted to start with 407¾ pounds on the press, figuring he could work his way up to as much as 424¼. However, the American coaches—who had not attended his training sessions, and didn't know what he could do—wanted him to start much lower, at 391, figuring that 402 would be his best. After debating the issue back and forth, everybody finally compromised on a starting weight of 396¾—which wound up being all that Norb was able to press, and that after two failed tries. Norb seethed. The arguing had destroyed his concentration and timing, as well as any real hope of winning gold. Nonetheless, he went on to snatch an American record and personal-best 363¾, then requested a fourth attempt at a world's record 380¼. To Norb's dismay there was a long delay before he could make the attempt, stalling his momentum, and after a half-hour wait his cold muscles couldn't pull it off. In the final event he clean and jerked 424¼, then asked for 451¾, which would have been a U.S. record. Twice he cleaned the bar with ease, but missed the jerk. His three-lift total went into the books at 1,185 pounds—an impressive figure, but still more then seventy pounds behind the two much heavier Russians.

Meanwhile, a subplot involving the Soviet heavies played out. With the gold medal resting on the outcome of the clean and jerk, Zhabotinsky failed on his second attempt. The tubby and expressive twenty-six-year-old was obviously discouraged. He went over to Vlasov (some accounts had him hobbling, as if he had injured himself) and told him he was a beaten man. Vlasov, in the lead and assuming his countryman had reached his limit, played it safe on his third and last attempt—only to then watch as the suddenly rejuvenated Zhabotinsky produced a world's record jerk on his final attempt to edge him for the gold. Vlasov was so furious over being dethroned by what he considered an unsportsmanlike trick, he later threw his silver medal out a window. "The Great Zhabo" would go on to set nearly a score of world records over the next several years and capture gold in the '68 Olympics with a score identical to one he rang up in Tokyo.

Norb never thought Zhabotinsky played possum in order to set up Vlasov. "He didn't miss it on purpose," he said of Zhabo's failed second attempt. "He was off-balance. And the guy still had to make that final lift to win."

Norb finished third to win the bronze. However, in terms of amount lifted in relation to bodyweight, Skee was again pound-for-pound the best of the heavyweight bunch, just as he had been four years earlier in Rome.

The final results at the Tokyo Olympics showed how far U.S. lifting had fallen. Other than Norb, only featherweight Ike Berger brought home a medal. Dominance in the sport continued to belong to Russia, as the Soviets' medal bonanza included four golds and three silvers.

Bantamweight		**Kgs.**	**(Lbs.)**
Gold:	Aleksey Vakhonin, U.S.S.R	357.5	(788¼)
Silver:	Imre Foldi, Hungary	355	(782¾)
Bronze:	Shiro Ichinoseki, Japan	347.5	(766)

Featherweight		**Kgs.**	**(Lbs.)**
Gold:	Yoshinobu Miyake, Japan	397.5	(876¼)
Silver:	Isaac Berger, United States	382.5	(843¼)
Bronze:	Mieczyslaw Nowak, Poland	377.5	(832¼)

Lightweight		**Kgs.**	**(Lbs.)**
Gold:	Waldemar Baszanowski, Poland	432.5	(953½)
Silver:	Vladimir Kaplunov, U.S.S.R.	432.5	(953½)
Bronze:	Marian Zieliwski, Poland	420	(926)

Middleweight		**Kgs.**	**(Lbs.)**
Gold:	Hans Zdrazila, Czechoslovakia	445	(981)
Silver:	Viktor Kurentsov, U.S.S.R.	440	(970)
Bronze:	Masashi Ohuchi, Japan	437.5	(964½)

Light Heavyweight		**Kgs.**	**(Lbs.)**
Gold:	Rudolf Plyukfelder, U.S.S.R.	475	(1,047¼)
Silver:	Geza Toth, Hungary	467.5	(1,030¾)
Bronze:	Gyozo Veres, Hungary	467.5	(1,030¾)

Middle Heavyweight		**Kgs.**	**(Lbs.)**
Gold:	Vladimir Golovanov, U.S.S.R.	487.5	(1,074¾)
Silver:	Louis Martin, Great Britain	475	(1,047¼)
Bronze:	Ireneusz Palinski, Poland	467.5	(1,030¾)

Heavyweight		**Kgs.**	**(Lbs.)**
Gold:	Leonid Zhabotinsky, U.S.S.R.	572.5	(1,262)
Silver:	Yuri Vlasov, U.S.S.R.	570	(1,256½)
Bronze:	Norb Schemansky, United States	537.5	(1,185)

Norb's feat of winning an individual medal in four Olympics was, at the time, unprecedented. Since then the four-timer club for lifters has grown to include Germany's Ronny Weller, Greece's Pyrros Dimas and Croatia's Nikolay Peshalov. Today, after more than sixty years, Schemansky's name is still in the *Guinness Book of World Records* as the oldest weightlifter ever to win an Olympic medal. There was a disappointing footnote to what turned out to be

Norb's last Olympic appearance, though. Nobody in his family was ever able to travel to any of the Games to watch him compete. The closest somebody in the Schemansky clan got to the action, he said, was the living room TV.

From Russia, with Love

by Ike Berger

Isaac "Ike" Berger emigrated from Israel to New York in 1949, when he was twelve. Berger, widely considered the greatest featherweight lifter in history, won eight U.S. titles and competed in three Olympics, medaling in each.

Norb and I were on the U.S. squad for the Rome and Tokyo Olympics. I think he was one of the greatest lifters ever. He was fantastic. In Rome there were so many lifters, you could be lifting at 3 a.m., but I still made it a point to stick around to watch Norb lift. You always wanted to watch him every time he stepped on that platform. The way he looked—his massive arms—he was just so impressive. You always wondered how he could do it, lifting such tremendous poundage with that split style of his. You really have to be strong to lift the weights he did.

Norb was an easygoing guy. He doesn't like any waves. A very down-to-earth guy. I always liked watching him, even in training. His way was completely different than others, but his way worked for him. He used to do a lot of repetitions with heavy weights. Instead of lifting it completely, he would do it half-way, half-way, then he would finish it: *One-two, boom-boom-boom*, then finish it. Then he'd do *one-two, boom-boom-boom-boom,* finish it, and so on. It was like explosive repetitions. We never did that. He was a heavyweight and he wanted to get used to the heavy poundage.

He was very popular with lifters all over the world. They all knew him and respected him. Even the Russians. I was there once when Yuri Vlasov said through an interpreter, "I followed your career. I have tremendous respect for you." Of course, Norb liked the thought of Yuri saying that. Yuri was so much younger. Heck, Norb was almost twice the age of some of the guys he was lifting against.

We were treated very well in the Communist countries. You could pick out any person on the street and they would know who you were. In Europe weightlifting was huge. Whenever we competed in Russia the place was packed. I mean, not an open seat anywhere. They loved the sport. So many weightlifting enthusiasts. Not only did they love the sport but they knew everybody's name. They followed all the guys' careers, knew the history.

I remember one time the Russian coach came up to Norb and said through an interpreter, "Tell him, 'I love you, Mr. Schemansky.'" In Russia they don't say "I admire you," they say "I love you." So the coach kept telling Norb, "I love you," and Norb would say, "Okay, okay." "But I love you," and the Russian coach gave Norb his watch. Norb was embarrassed by it. But it was understandable. Remember, Norb was well known in Russia because he had defeated Novak in the '52 Olympics and he had battled Vlasov and lifted all these tremendous weights. The Russian people knew all about him. So the Russian coach gave him the watch out of respect. He was just trying his best to show how much respect and admiration he and the rest of the country had for him.

CHAPTER TEN

Last Lifts

I now wonder why the hell I did it, training for all those Olympics and losing all those jobs and money. I was just hooked on lifting, and I did like to win. I always liked the challenge of somebody telling me I couldn't beat some guy or other.

Norb Schemansky

Bruce Randall's feature in the December 1964 issue of *Iron Man*, headlined "Norbert Schemansky—A Marvelous Physical Speciman," came out just a few weeks after Norb returned to the states from the Tokyo Olympics. It was typical of the adulatory coverage lifting magazines gave the sport's elder statesman, even while the mainstream press continued to all but ignore him. "Anyone who has had the opportunity to witness the lifting of Norbert Schemansky can well consider himself a very privileged person," Randall wrote, "for here is not simply another man lifting another weight…he is a masterpiece of human mechanism in motion.

"By what yardstick do we measure a champion? By the rule of winning? Then Schemansky is most certainly a great champion for he is a man who has won world titles and broken world records in his chosen sport. Do we measure a champion by his triumph over formidable adversity? Here's a man who has won fight after fight and battle after battle against the odds of injury and disappointment. Several years ago, everyone assumed that his best lifting days were well behind him. Schemansky was told by medical doctors that because of a severe back injury he would never lift again, yet here he is, in the year of 1964, the United States Heavyweight Weightlifting Champion."

Randall, a former Marine who had won the Mr. Universe title in 1959, was downright rhapsodic in his head-to-toe description of Norb's physique. "Have you ever seen Schemansky's back?" he gushed. "It is truly a sight to behold!"

> Supporting this back is a pair of legs which are, by any standards, simply incredible. I honestly wish that mine were only half as great. To look at him is to see the best built heavyweight of this or any other century. His body is like that of the Faranese Hercules come to life, only much improved! Without a single doubt, his legs are the greatest pair, from a combined standpoint of both strength and development, that any man has ever possessed. The shape is simply super classical. Certainly, size by itself is impressive but here are legs in a combination of size and shape to a degree heretofore deemed impossible. The wonderful sweep of the quadriceps, the fullness above the knee, the terrific line and shape of the leg bicep, and the tight compact knee which gives way to the full, fantastically shaped calf are all things to be seen visually in order to be appreciated. Simply fabulous! No photographs of Schemansky has ever, even remotely, done justice to the physique he now possesses.
>
> I have had the opportunity of seeing this man of men fairly close at hand and I can honestly state that I never before was so impressed with such fullness, shape, density and circumference of forearms. These wonderful forearms connect to the thickest upper arms imaginable. They appear to be almost as thick as they are deep; very impressive. And if you ever care to see a deltoid developed as it was meant to be, gaze upon the fullness from front and rear. There is no parallel. The lateral sweep, especially, has yet to be approached.
>
> I am attempting to give the reader a view of the Schemansky physique through the eyes of one who is critically interested in physique development. I, as a Mr. Universe title winner, feel that it is almost ironic that a weightlifter's weightlifter, without the innuendo practice of bodybuilding, has capped such a high pinnacle.

"Schemansky's physique is a complete statement unto itself, the type of which the Greeks imaginatively dreamed yet never approached," wrote Randall. "Photographs cannot catch movement and his movements are catlike in their smoothness and fluidity. Shape, massiveness, strength, experience and grace add up to the mature man of Graecian Ideals."

A look at Norb's measurements from selected years gives a sense of his physical development.

	1951	**1952**	**1964**
Body weight	198 lbs.	215 lbs.	270 lbs.
Height	71½ in.	71½ in.	71½ in.
Chest (normal)	46 in.	48 in.	52 in.
Waist	32 in.	34 in.	40 in.
Hips	40 in.	41 in.	44 in.
Thighs	25 in.	26½ in.	30 in.
Calves	16¾ in.	17 in.	18½ in.
Neck	N/A	N/A	18½ in.
Arm	17 in.	18 in.	19½ in.
Forearm	N/A	N/A	15½ in.
Wrist	N/A	N/A	8½ in.

Bodybuilder Harry Johnson, Mr. America in 1959, recalled the stir Norb's appearance once caused at an event in Cleveland. "Believe me, Norb was the talk of the gym before he arrived," said Johnson. "I told everybody he looked like a bodybuilder, that his legs were incredible. I think he could have won any competition he entered if he wanted to. He was so solid—he didn't fit the image of the typical heavyweight lifter back then." Said Clyde Emrich: "Norb looked terrific physically. He could've been mistaken for Apollo on the statue."

There was a continuing problem with this Olympian vision of Norb. The Greek God with the thinning hair and horn-rimmed eyeglasses was still damn near always broke. And to the consternation of one privileged fifteen-year-old fan, there was no modern equivalent of a golden chariot to whisk him to and from the arena.

Doug Stalker and two of his friends took a bus from Rochester, New York to Harrisburg, Pennsylvania for the 1963 Senior Nationals. Stalker, today a retired philosophy professor living in South Carolina, confessed his first ride on a Greyhound was a jolt to his system. "I was a prep school boy and used to the suburban niceties of living in a house on a private drive, going to a country club, and all that *fol de rol.* When my parents took the family on trips, it was always first-class arrangements."

Stalker checked into a first-class hotel in town and then watched as his idol was edged out by the Texas heavyweight, Sid Henry. "Norb took 435 in the clean and jerk for his last attempt, a new personal record for him, and lost to Henry by five pounds in the total lifted. Norb had a light knee touch in the clean and that nixed his lift as a legal one."

After that it was time for Stalker and his friends to return home to upstate New York.

"We left to go back on the bus with the wailing babies, the old ladies yelling 'Is this Wilkes Barre, are we in Wilkes Barre now?' and the occasional smell of cheap wine coming from some seat or other. As we waited—half-awake and a little bit nervous—at the noisy and poorly lit bus station in a seedy part of Harrisburg, we decided to walk around a little bit. As we turned a corner, we almost walked right into Norbert Schemansky, standing there in a white t-shirt, jeans or work pants, and carrying a gym bag. He was taking the bus back to Dearborn.

"The more extroverted of our trio said, 'Tough luck, Norb.' But I just stood there in disbelief. Here was the champion lifter, bigger than life, a foot or two away from me, and he was here to travel on…well, on a *bus*. This couldn't be. Champion lifters, and especially those of Norb's stature, didn't travel on some damn bus, rocking back and forth as it slowly made its way from town to town in the night with its unimpressive passenger list. I was struck dumb and dared not say a thing. I was seeing the champion, but not in the setting I would put him or wanted, at my naïve age, to have him in. I would've had him in first class on a direct flight to Detroit. Nothing less for Mr. Schemansky. Here was excellence incarnate in the sport of Olympic weightlifting. But taking a bus home?"

Norb was happy enough to have had money for bus fare. His financial woes continued even as he followed up his Olympic performance with wins at the North American Championships in December 1964 and the National Y.M.C.A. Championships and the Senior Nationals the following spring. "Oh, I've had job offers," he said at the time. "But they're all the same. They're really not interested in me. They just want to capitalize on my size, and after a while they're not interested in that any more."

An unflattering write-up in a 1966 issue of *Sports Illustrated* called "Looking for a Lift" painted Norb and Jack Katchmar, denizens of the Astro Gym, as desperate beings. At times, Norb admitted, they were. "Jack and I were doing all sorts of flaky jobs, trying to make a few bucks here and there. Got twenty-five bucks a day unloading boxcars, which was an OK job until the first hot day. Ever work in a paper mill? A real hell-hole. Loud, stinky, dirty. I had to clean the mulch. Christ, I'd come home and take a shower and the stuff would turn to glue. Seems like every time a friend got me a job, it was the worst kind of job possible. I'd tell them, 'What kind of friend are you?'"

Skee wasn't interested in pulling tree stumps out of the ground or bending iron bars across his back, like some act in a carnival sideshow. He'd had enough of people daring him to pull apart the plastic that holds a six-pack together or asking him to move a piano up three flights of stairs. A more dignified and natural calling would have been to put his vast experience to work as a coach on the national team. "But they never give those jobs to guys like me," he said of the A.A.U. hierarchy. "They give 'em to the ones who hang around them and butter them up. Well, I'm not made that way." Norb approached one of Detroit's professional sports teams about creating a weight-training program but was rebuffed. By now Clyde Emrich was the strength coach of his hometown Chicago Bears. Emrich, who worked out with Norb at the Astro Gym whenever he was in town, was an accomplished middle heavyweight, but his credentials in international lifting paled alongside Norb's.

If certain parties held Skee's outspokenness against him, fellow lifters appreciated his candor. "He was not afraid to express himself about some things," said Joe Pitman. "It was refreshing that he was willing to speak out and tell the truth when it needed telling."

Lifters elected Norb to represent their interests at the annual A.A.U. conventions. One day in 1966, sitting inside a hotel room in York during the Senior Nationals (he would finish third with a three-lift total of 1,085 pounds), Norb unloaded onto a reporter years of frustration over what he viewed as an absurd and antiquated system of amateur athletics in America. "I'm 42 and I've been lifting for 26 years," he told Jim Murphy. "That makes me ready for an A.A.U.

pension—exactly nothing. That's what the A.A.U. is doing for the athletes of this country. Nothing. The first time you ever see anybody from the organization is when you're going overseas. A guy comes along and pins a little button on your lapel, and from then on, they take credit for what you do."

Norb was just warming up. "They met for five hours again today, and probably did nothing as usual. They only make rules, the kind of rules that hinder the athlete, rather then help them. Don't eat—and go out there and see what you can do—that's their philosophy. I don't know how they think we can continue to compete with all the athletes from other countries who are subsidized, like the Russians. We have fellows here today that worked on their regular jobs yesterday, then rushed out here to try to do their best. They can't take two weeks off to get in shape because they can't afford it. That's true in all amateur sports in this country, the richest country in the world."

Norb had in mind one especially galling incident. In 1960, some friends had organized a benefit dancing and weightlifting exhibition to raise money to send Bernice to Rome for the Olympics. Detroit A.A.U. officials got wind of the benefit and forced the goodwill sponsors of the program to cancel, saying it could affect Norb's amateur standing. "It is against the Olympic code for any athlete to receive funds to help his family," the A.A.U. official told the press. Decisions over such matters typically were made on the local level, meaning rule interpretation was uneven and personal politics often got in the way. At the same time the A.A.U. was slamming the door on the Schemanskys, it permitted a collection to send the parents of an Olympic swimmer from Royal Oak.

Recalling the episode today, Norb practically breathed fire. "An amateur back then was considered a bum, an athletic bum. There wasn't any money, so most of it had to come out of your own pocket if you wanted to compete, even at the highest levels. I'd lose a job because I wanted to compete, or I'd have to take unpaid time off in order to train or travel." The rules would not allow an amateur to be paid for coaching or for managing a gym, although those were natural outlets for an athlete's expertise. The result was a world-class performer unloading boxcars for a few bucks under the table in order to muddle through until the next big competition.

"The A.A.U. never did anything for anybody," continued Norb. "One

Norb warms up in preparation for some serious training. Amazingly, he developed his incredible physique as the "Heavyweight Champion of the World" without the use of anabolic steroids, amphetamines or any kind of special nutritional supplements that are so common in sports today.

Fédération Internationale
Haltérophile et Culturiste

Record du Monde

NORBERT SCHEMANSKY de U.S.A.

ayant réussi avec

TWO HANDS SNATCH 164 kg. (361½ lb.)

le 28 April 1962 à Detroit, U.S.A.

au poids du corps de 115,6 kg. a établi

Un Nouveau Record du Monde

dans la catégorie de Poids Lourd

Signé Oscar State

Secrétaire-général F.I.H.C.

World record certificate presented to Norb after establishing one of his remarkable 26 world records.

Bernice and Norb at the dinner where Norb was inducted into the Michigan Amateur Sports Hall of Fame. Norb never turned professional.

Bernice was always Norb's biggest supporter.

After nearly fifty years, Norb still lives in the same home in Dearborn, Michigan. By contrast, in the country of Turkey, their weightlifting champion owns 26 homes.

Norb, along with children Paula, Laura, Larry and Pam.

Norb's daughter Paula, her husband Bob, their daughter Karen and her boyfriend.

Norb's daughter, Pam, with her husband Steve, their daughter Nori, and their son Steve, with son-in law Garrett and Norb's great-granddaughters Autumn and Claire.

Norb's son Larry with his daughters Vanea, Tara, Kristin, Karrie, and Norb's great-granddaughter Lauren.

Norb's daughter Laura, her husband Bill, their son Chris, and their daughters Eydie and Julie with Norb's great granddaughter Audre.

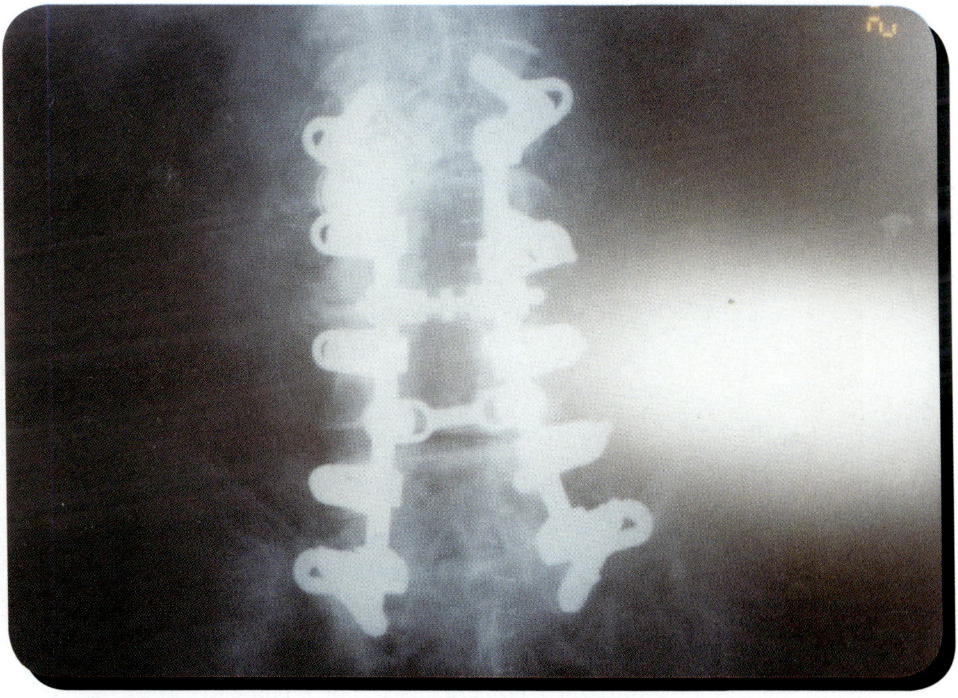

X-ray showing the metal screws in Norb's back. He still became an international champion after 2 major back surgeries in the 1950s.

Norb, along with Detroit Tiger's great Mark Fidrych and fellow inductee Bill Mazeroski, enjoy the presentation of their National Polish Sports Hall of Fame awards before the baseball game at Tiger Stadium in 1976.

Norb displays his National Polish Sports Hall of Fame plaque.

Norb was inducted into The Helms Athletic Hall of Fame in California in 1965. Besides receiving this very prestigious honor, he is also a member of seven other halls of fame.

After many years, America's greatest weightlifting champion was honored by the city of Dearborn with a park bearing his name and a stone marker listing his remarkable accomplishments.

Norb, along with city officials and family members dedicate the Norbert Schemansky Park in 1996.

The first United States Olympic athlete to ever medal in four separate Olympic Games proudly carries the Olympic torch as it traveled through Dearborn in 1996.

Although Norb garnered little publicity in America for his world famous accomplishments, he appeared on a number of European and Russian weightlifting periodicals in his time.

Norb and friend Bob Suchyta discuss current affairs with Russian Super Heavyweight champ Sultan Rachmanov.

Norb with Russian Super Heavyweight legend Anatoly Pisarenko.

Weightlifting superstar Stanley Stanczyk, Dr. Bob Suchyta, and Norb attend an out-of-town weightlifting meet.

Norb and Tommy Kono are considered the two greatest American weightlifters of all time.

With Clarence Johnson at the Olympic Games in Atlanta, Georgia. (1996)

Norb and Gottfried Schodl, the former President of The International Weightlifting Federation.

Vic Boff, the founder of the Association of Old-Time Barbell & Strongmen, called the athletes pictured above the two greatest world champions in history. For bodybuilding and agility John “The King” Grimek was his top choice. For the sport of Olympic weightlifting, Nobert Schemansky received the nod as the greatest.

Dr. Terry Todd, Phil Grippaldi, and the two greatest heavyweight champions of all time, Vasily Alexiev and “Mr. Weightlifting” Norbert Schemansky, visit a local diner after attending The World Weightlifting Championships in Columbus, Ohio. (1970)

Norb's four Olympic medals.

Silver medal London, England 1948; gold medal Helsinki, Finland 1952; bronze medal Rome, Italy 1960; bronze medal Tokyo, Japan 1964.

For 36 years Norb was listed in the *Guinness Book of World Records* for earning four Olympic medals in four separate Olympic Games. Today, he is still immortalized in the famous record book for achieving the distinction of being the oldest weightlifter to ever set a world record.

Former Wate Man gym owner John Reddy, admires Norb's four Olympic medals. Reddy, a fitness historian, believes that, pound for pound, Norb is the greatest Olympic heavyweight lifter in history.

Dr. Bob Suchyta hosted Norb's 80th birthday celebration in Farmington Hills, Michigan. Attending were Norb's closest friends John Haskett, Mike Anderzak, Steve Mansour, Manuel Mansour and Del Reddy. Also pictured are Norb's son Larry and his daughter, Tara Schemansky.

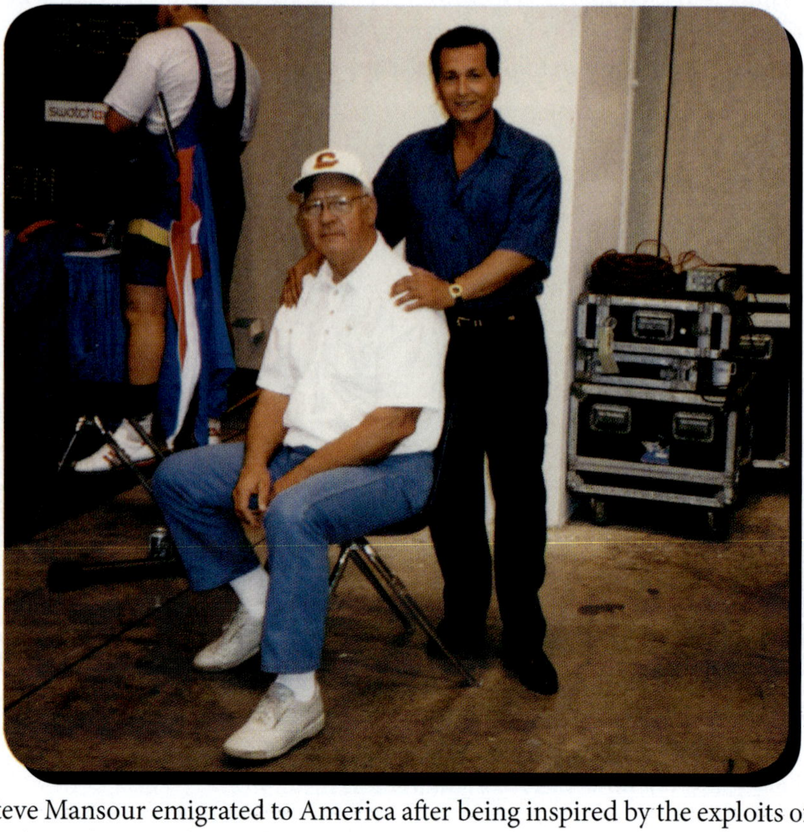

Steve Mansour emigrated to America after being inspired by the exploits of the legendary Norbert Schemansky.

The Kings of Their Sport™: Mr. Hockey® Gordie Howe® and "Mr. Weightlifting" Norbert Schemansky are immortalized in a classic portrait.

Photo by Matt Howard

Entrepreneur Aaron Howard, Gordie Howe, and Immortal Investments Publisher Del Reddy admire some of the many trophies and medals earned by Norb in his unprecedented career.

Some of the breathtaking medals Norbert Schemansky earned as "Heavyweight Champion of the World."

time they gave me $27 expense money for a meet out in Los Angeles. This was for the Senior Nationals. Big deal, huh? Twenty-seven bucks. If I'd decided to walk out there it wouldn't have paid for the shoes."

The worst part of any competition was coming home.

"Our house payment was $87 a month, including taxes and insurance, and we still almost lost it to the bank. Can you imagine that?"

As Norb got older, he found the injuries came more frequently—a not unusual development for even the best-conditioned athletes. In September 1965, he tore his elbow and shoulder trying to snatch 335 pounds at the North American Championships in Montreal, causing him to miss several months of competition including the World Championships. Hampered by a variety of strains and pulls, he still managed to win the Milwaukee Open and the National Y.M.C.A. Championships in April 1966. But that year and the next, "I never got in good shape," he said. "I broke a toe in 1967 and tried out for the World Championships, but I couldn't lift too well with a couple of toes taped together. It kind of hurts when you get 400 pounds on it." That year he also failed to gain a spot on the U.S. squad for the Pan-Am Games. Younger heavyweights like Gary Gubner, Joe Dube, Bob Bednarski and Ernie Pickett were the future of American lifting, though this battered blast from the past was not conceding anything to anyone.

As 1967 wound down, Norb worked himself into rock-solid shape. In December he lifted at an invitational in Monticello, New York. Now tipping the scales at 277 pounds, he set a personal high in the press with a 415, snatched 345, but then hit himself in the chin while jerking 400. Still, his 1,160—good for third place behind Dube and Gubner—indicated the old warhorse of international lifting was preparing yet another comeback. In early 1968, his eyes set on the Nationals and then the Olympics in Mexico City, Skee took first in a couple of tune-ups in Monroe, Iowa and Kittanning, Pennsylvania. He felt good, his form was fine. Then disaster struck during a spring meet in Milwaukee. He'd easily pressed 400 and snatched 350 when, attempting to clean 425, he ruptured the quadriceps tendon in his right knee. The injury is not a common one. But when it does occur, it almost always happens to a person over the age of forty.

He continued to train with his knee on the mend, his thoughts on a fifth Olympics. Then, one day, he decided he'd had enough—or rather, his body decided for him. His desire was still strong, his mind was still clicking on all eight cylinders, but his sinews stubbornly refused to cooperate as they had in the past. After winning four Olympic medals, nine national championships, three world championships, and some three hundred other medals and prizes during twenty-six years of competitive lifting, Norb Schemansky retired. There was no fanfare, no formal announcement, not even a specific date to point to on the calendar so historians of the iron game could later say, "*This* is the day an era ended." No, it was just the culmination of a gradual awareness that to continue was to risk embarrassment, and Skee was too proud a man to be embarrassed.

Perhaps the most wondrous aspect of Schemansky's competitive career between 1942 and 1968, beyond its sheer breadth, was that he accomplished all he did without the aid of a basement chemist.

During his lifting days Norb uncomplainingly took what few urine tests were asked of him. And why not? He had nothing to hide. Officials typically were looking for signs of "speed"—amphetamines—which affect the central nervous system and can deliver a short-term boost to athletic performance. Once in the early 1960s an A.A.U. official "offered to pee in the cup for me," said Norb, who was mildly insulted by the gesture. However, the widespread use of "pep pills" paled alongside the abuse of the male sex hormone testosterone and its artificially produced derivatives.

The use of natural testosterone stretches back centuries, with testis tissue being touted in some cultures as an aphrodisiac. In 1889, a French physiologist used the testicles of dogs and guinea pigs to create a "rejuvenating therapy for the body and mind" that he claimed not only increased his physical strength and sharpened his mental acuity, but relieved his constipated bowels and improved the arc of his urine stream. Obviously, *liquide testiculair* was a potent concoction. In 1935 a pair of European chemists created an artificial form of testosterone (sharing a Nobel Prize for their work) and by the 1940s it was being used experimentally on both the battlefield and the athletic field. In 1953 the first anabolic steroid, called 19-nortestosterone, was synthesized. ("Anabolic" refers to muscle-building and "steroid" signifies the class of drugs.) The effects of this man-made substance were up to five times more powerful than that of testosterone. At the 1954 World Championships in Vienna, an inebriated Russian coach let slip to an American team doctor that Soviet lifters were using drugs. Russia's overall performance at the '52 Olympics already had many observers speculating that there was more to that country's success than just refined training techniques and a state-sponsored emphasis on everyday exercise and organized sport. Russia was not the only Eastern Bloc nation working overtime on developing more potent "strength pills." East Germany, in particular, was well on its way to becoming notorious in international circles for the systemic integration of drugs into its highly secretive sporting program.

Anabolic steroids, which allow muscles to recover faster and stronger than nature otherwise would permit, have legitimate medical applications—helping to speed up the recovery of cancer patients, for example, or to facilitate the repair of tissue and muscles torn in accidents or combat. Steroids can be taken orally or injected. To achieve the best results, they should be used in cycles rather than continuously. Long-term use can produce serious, even fatal, side effects, such as hypertension, heart palpitations, cardiovascular disease, impotence, liver disease, and aggression (known as "roid rage"). "Bodybuilders were among the first to use steroids," noted Norb. One renowned bodybuilder publicly admitted he used them. "But he said only a couple weeks before a contest, which is B.S.—you can't blow up like he did that quick."

By the 1960s steroids had made serious inroads into the sport of weightlifting on both sides of the Iron Curtain. The incremental gains that had once been the result of long hours of hard work and perfected technique were blown away by sizable pharmaceutical-assisted leaps. "Before steroids," said Norb, "if you had a fifteen-pound lead on the guy behind you, you were safe. I remember gaining seventeen pounds in one year and people were questioning *me*.

"I think for a while officials kind of looked the other way. They wanted to see records being broken. You could almost tell by the totals in the World Championships. For years 450, 460 pounds in the clean and jerk was tops. Within a couple of years it was 520 pounds.

"Some guy would come out of nowhere and do 500. The guy would weigh 190, maybe total 900 pounds. The next year he was weighing 240 and doing 1,100. It took me ten years to go from 220 to 260, to pack on forty pounds of muscle. Now guys were gaining forty pounds bodyweight in one summer. Something had to have happened, and that something wasn't natural. In the mid-1960s there was an influx of lifters doing amazing lifts, guys who'd have big spurts. I don't have to mention names. Just track the progress and see for yourself the big spurts."

In 1970, Vasili Alexeyev, the mammoth Russian who had just become the first man ever to total 600 kilograms (1,323 pounds) in the three Olympic lifts, was deemed "the most spectacular example of strength building with the aid of pharmaceuticals" by the West German magazine *Der Spiegel*. When shown the article by a Russian reporter, the super-heavyweight merely laughed and suggested Western athletes should also take them. They already were. According to the same article, the 1968 Games in Mexico City had been an "International Pill Fair" with an estimated 90 percent of weightlifters, shot putters and discus throwers owing their performances to the "enchanted pills."

The International Olympic Committee finally banned steroid use in 1975, but mandatory drug testing of athletes did not begin until the 1988 Summer Games in Seoul, South Korea. That same year the sale of anabolic steroids for non-medical purposes was banned by the U.S. Food and Drug Administration. About this time Yuri Vlasov—who had become a writer and political agitator after leaving competitive lifting—rattled the Soviet sports establishment by charging the country's athletic officials with tolerating the use of steroids, amphetamines, and other drugs. "Sport is about strength, fortitude and beauty, not chemicals," he declared. His anti-drugs crusading annoyed international weightlifting officials who had turned a blind eye to the problem both inside and outside Russia.

To this day Norb doesn't believe Vlasov took performance-enhancing drugs, not even after what happened at the '62 World Championships in Budapest. He points to the Russian's progress, which was steady and consistent throughout his career. There was a popular refrain among lifters grunting away inside Soviet gyms during the 1950s: "If you want to press more, press more." As far as Norb is concerned, Vlasov's success was the result of hard work and a more comprehensive and scientific approach to amateur sports under the hammer and sickle. That *all* Russian athletes were considered amateurs by their government, even as it was obvious to the Western world that sport was their only profession, was beside the point. Skee figures A.A.U. officials could have picked up a few pointers from their Communist counterparts.

When he was competing, Norb occasionally would spot drugs in an open gym bag or overhear fragments of a whispered conversation about what drugs worked best. One American he would only describe as "a good international lifter" flat out told Norb he used steroids.

Norb was curious. "What happened when you used them?" he asked.

"My lifts went up."

"What happened when you quit?"

"My lifts went down," the lifter replied. "I've been on them ever since."

That lifter's attitude continues to poison competition today, Norb moaned. The lure of fame and wealth, coupled with the confidence that the newest designer drug will go undetected in blood and urine tests, ensure that many performers in all sports will continue to cheat and bet on not getting caught. Like any old-school athlete, Norb deplores the fact that many records today are made in labs, not gyms, while those that are not chemically assisted still fall under the same umbrella of suspicion. "It used to be that a lifter in his late twenties was in his prime. Now it's the early twenties. They're hyped up like cattle. It was just another reason I quit competing. I couldn't go on forever."

In September 1972, Norb visited the Astro Gym for the final time, picking up some loose weights and personal items before Jack Katchmer shut the place down for good. That spring Norb had been certified as an associate engineering technician. He had already been working since 1970 for Wade Trim & Associates, a local engineering firm. The certification, followed five years later by one that made him a full-fledged engineering technician, gave him a chance to make a decent and steady income as an inspector in the construction trades.

Norb joined other major figures from America's golden age of weightlifting who had already left the arena. Tommy Kono, often mentioned in the same breath as Norb when the topic of America's greatest all-time lifter comes up, retired from competition in 1965 having officially established thirty-seven U.S. and twenty-six world records in four separate weight classifications. Afterwards he served as the national weightlifting coach for Mexico, West Germany, and the U.S. while also working as a recreational specialist for the city of Honolulu. Also in Hawaii was Pete George, who had finished dental school and set up practice there. Stan Stancyzk operated a successful bowling alley in Florida, John Davis worked fulltime as a corrections officer in New York, and Jim Bradford was the most intimidating librarian at the Library of Congress. "Jim told me he could have done more in his lifting career but he was 'owe' so tired," recalled Norb. "He said he was tired of owing at the grocery store, of owing at the gas station…."

Bernice, who in the 1960s had started accompanying Norb to some out-of-town meets for the first time (ear problems often made flying a painful experience for her), was happy to see her husband stick closer to home. But Norb understandably found it hard to completely douse his competitive fire. He even maintained that he could have qualified for the 1972 Olympic Games in Munich, Germany. However, professional pride got in the way. "I had a slow period at work and I started training," said Norb, who recalled pressing 380, snatching 310, and clean and jerking 410 for an 1,100-pound total.

"My weights were good enough to make the United States team, but compared to what the Russians, the Poles and Bulgarians were lifting, I would've been about tenth.

"I didn't want to go over there and make a bad show."

CHAPTER ELEVEN

The Old Master

When we discuss the great champions of the past, Norb Schemansky's name always comes up. He's the Gordie Howe and Jimmy Brown of our sport. You talk to any weightlifting expert on the international level and he is right there at the top.

U.S. Olympic Lifting Coach Jim Schmitz

Bob Hoffman, Peary Rader, George Kirkley, and other chroniclers of the iron game foisted a variety of nicknames upon Norb during his lifting days, the most popular in the twilight of his career being "The Old Master." That particular honorific not only recognized Schemansky's longevity and his impact on the record book, it paid tribute to the many physical and financial obstacles he had overcome through the years. His stirring tale of resolve and hard-purchased success helped set him apart from most other barbell legends. "He was an inspiration to three generations of American stars," observed Joe Weider. "He overcame so much to thrill so many. He can never be forgotten." Certainly not by wrestling great Bruce Baumgartner, who, like Norb, won medals in four different Olympics. "What Norb did was phenomenal," he said. "Earning four medals is no easy task in any era in any sport."

"Everybody loved and respected him," said Joe Pitman, Norb's teammate at the 1948 Olympics. "He should be admired just for coming back from the surgeries, let alone anything else."

Don Bragg is perhaps best known for letting loose a Tarzan yell on the victors' podium after he won the gold medal in the pole vault at the 1960 Summer Games. Five years later he underwent major back surgery, an ordeal he managed to get through using Norb as his inspiration.

"I had a spinal operation, and at that time I kept reflecting on how Norb had experienced major back surgery and still came back and performed so well," said Bragg. "How can you have two back operations—your back is the trunk of your power—and still do what he did? His example was an incentive for me. So hell, I said, I can handle this back operation."

It's not often that one's name becomes an inspirational synonym, but early on that was the case with Schemansky.

"Norb was on top when I was coming up," remarked fitness guru Clarence Bass, who started lifting exercises to build his storied "ripped" abdominals as a youngster in 1952, "and for about the next fifteen years or so he was still pretty much on top." Bass recalled an Olympic lifting contest that he and Steve Klisanin, the 1955 Mr. America, attended together in El Paso, Texas. Bass, still only a high school student at the time, became one of the youngest lifters ever to clean and jerk 300 pounds. "That set my hopes soaring. I must have been popping off about the great things I was going to do, because I remember that Klisanin brought me abruptly back to earth. He said, 'You're no Norbert Schemansky.'"

No, he wasn't. Then again, who was? He was an original. There was an aura of quiet strength about the intimidating guy in the Clark Kent glasses. Maybe he wasn't wearing a Superman costume underneath his shirt. But one admirer suggested Norb was kind of like Gary Cooper—that is, if Gary Cooper could have clean and jerked 400 pounds. "People didn't pull any stuff on him," recalled Joe Pitman. "One time we were in the food line. Everybody was lined up, waiting their turn, and somebody kept trying to break into the line. People were saying, 'What's that guy doing, breaking into line?' You know, kind of just watching and grumbling but not doing anything. Norb was the only one who had the guts to do something about it. He said, 'You better stand aside or somebody is going to dump you.' The guy took one look at Norb, did an about-face and took off."

Norb preferred the no-nonsense approach whenever possible. "He wasn't exactly forthcoming with the how-to's," observed Doug Stalker, a split-style heavyweight like Norb. "I'd ask, 'Why did I miss the lift?' Norb would answer, 'You're not strong enough.' Tommy Kono would give you a lecture on the fine points of lifting; he was more of an instructional guy. Norb was more like, 'Lift the damn thing, will ya.' There is a place for that, too, let me tell you."

Stalker, like most young lifters in the 1960s, revered Skee. Norb had been a staple of the fitness magazines they had devoured as they were growing up and now here he was, lifting alongside them at tournaments. "Norb is weightlifting and weightlifting is Norb," said Stalker, who fell back on his prep-school manners and always referred to the living, breathing legend as "Mr. Schemansky."

"I was always very polite," said Stalker. "One time I saw him and I said, 'Hello, Mr. Schemansky. I would like to be heavyweight champ like you.' He just shook his head and said, 'Kid, you don't want to do this.'

"He tried to discourage me because he is sensible. This is not exactly a sport where you are going to be popular in America and get untold riches unless you're a freak show. Norb was never a freak show. He wasn't going to do any of those silly things like some big guys do to make money. He wasn't some softie caving into money. The Olympic lifts and that was it. That's what made Norb so impressive—his persona, his defiance, his posture, the way he carried himself. He just kept going. He never wavered."

While being true to himself, the Old Master could often come across as the original grumpy old man. But his abrupt manner and bulldog countenance hid one aspect of his personality that comes up in almost every discussion of the man: his dry wit. Said Tommy Kono: "In 1954 I won the Mr. World contest and Norb came over to congratulate me. As he was shaking my hand he was weaving his head around and around, as if to say, 'It's a small world.'" Kono laughed hard at the memory. "That's the kind of humor he had."

"He had a heck of a sense of humor," agreed Harry Johnson, the 1959 Mr. America winner. Johnson maintained that at a bodybuilding competition in Atlanta, Norb gave him the finest compliment he ever received. After several contestants had finished grimacing and flexing on stage, Schemansky delivered what amounted to high praise. "You were the only one out there," he told Johnson, "who didn't look like he was taking a crap."

Norb didn't save his best shots for bodybuilders. He was an equal-opportunity jokester. Lou Riecke remembered when he and Norb checked into a Los Angeles Y.M.C.A. during a tournament sometime in the middle '60s.

"This was at the time when they were having a lot of racial problems, the Black Panthers were in the news, all that. Anyway, the clerk at the counter handed us some forms to fill out. So we fill them out and the clerk looks at Schemansky and says, 'You didn't fill in your religion. What's your religion?' Norb's got the blonde hair and blue eyes. He looks back at him as deadpanned as can be and says, 'Black Muslim.' This threw the clerk off. It took him a few seconds to realize Norb was kidding."

Riecke was with Norb and Bill March in Tokyo for the '64 Olympics when the trio decided to go get a beer. "A little Japanese guy comes up to us with some postcards," recalled Riecke. "Schemansky didn't want to buy any but he asked how much. The guy says, 'Six dollars each.' Schemansky says, 'I'll give you two dollars.' The guy says, 'Oh no, six dollars.' So Norb throws up his hands and starts yelling, 'Police! Police!' The guy goes, 'Okay, okay, two dollars.' Norb didn't want them. He was just pulling the guy's leg."

Among the most steadfast of Norb's many admirers is longtime collegiate powerlifting coach Charles Fraser. During a car ride one evening in Detroit in the spring of 1958, recalled Fraser, he was sandwiched in the back seat between Schemansky and big Jim Bradford as Bob Hoffman and a group of lifters returned from a U.S.-Soviet exhibition. Fraser, then a student at Michigan State University, had been backstage putting his Russian language skills to good use. As they sped down Michigan Avenue in pursuit of some Oriental cuisine, they passed Briggs Stadium, where the Detroit Tigers and St. Louis Cardinals were staging an exhibition of their own.

Looking to make conversation, Fraser brought up the name of Cardinals star Stan Musial. Norb, slightly grumpy over his convalescing back, threadbare finances, and lack of renown, was in no mood to discuss one of the most beloved and well-paid athletes in the country. "Yeah?" he grunted. "So what?"

"Well, uh," Fraser carefully responded, "he's a great ballplayer. You know, a great athlete."

"Yeah?" Norb shot back. "How much can he press?"

There was a moment of silence, followed by an explosion of laughter.

Everybody in the car was howling, except Norb, whom Fraser noted always made his wisecracks funnier by maintaining a stony face.

"Good old Norb," Fraser reflected. "He made you proud to be a weightlifter in three ways. By how he looked, by how he lifted a barbell—and by his outspoken pride in his chosen sport."

Gruffly Great

by Sid Henry

Sid Henry was an asthmatic teenager when he first started lifting in the mid-1950s. The young Texan's role model was the champion he read about for years in various fitness publications, Norb Schemansky. In 1963 Henry won the heavyweight title at the Senior Nationals and the Pan American Games.

Schemansky liked to go to the bar and have a couple of beers. I didn't drink so it would never happen in my case. He was always civil to me, though, and kind of blunt. He impressed me as a rough, tough stevedore kind of guy. He was kind of a gruff character, but every time I think of him I also think of how comical he could be. To me he was really a character. He was so unassuming, but then he'd make a comment that would make me double over laughing. He said what he wanted, he really didn't care. I am one of his greatest admirers, no doubt about it.

I was so much in awe of his capabilities. I outweighed him and yet he had such terrific form, scale, and technique. He was a hard man to compete against. My opinion is that Norb is equivalent to the elite athletes in other sports, guys like Johnny Unitas or Joe Montana in football. He was amazing in his prime. If he wasn't in such an obscure sport he would be rich as hell like all the rest of them are now.

I couldn't work out with him, though. He would get on the platform, make a lift, then I would make a lift, then he'd make a lift, and then I wouldn't be ready so he'd say, "If you're not ready to go then I'm going to jump in." That's what he would do with everybody. He'd say, "If you're not ready I'm gonna lift. I'm not gonna sit around like you guys." He was that kind of guy, so I would work out somewhere else. It really tickled me.

One thing that really impressed me was when we went to Stockholm in '63 for the World Championships. We were competitors in the same class but we were on the same team. He was pulling for me like everybody else. When I went out to the platform he would give words of encouragement. I thought that was great and I felt really complimented by that because here I am, I'm basically a nobody. I came in fourth in that meet and he came in second. We pulled for each other.

One year, when we were getting set for the Pan American Games, there was some kind of confusion over the heavyweight rankings, who they were going to select to go. While talking with the people at York, they said Schemansky was going to be the heavyweight representative. I said, "Wait a minute, I made a better total than he did." So a few other people got involved and this went on for several days. Meanwhile, Norb sent me a telegram. It simply read: "You won. You go." That is exactly the kind of comment I expected from him. He knew it was fair.

CHAPTER TWELVE

Winning and Losing

I think I had 300 trophies at one time but we had a dog with a big tail and he kept knocking them over and they dwindled down. I guess I've got about 50 left.

Norb Schemansky in a 1976 interview

With the closing of the Astro Gym, Norb finally ended his obsession with lifting and channeled his energy into making a living. Now in his late forties, an age at which many of his contemporaries were already several rungs up the conventional career ladder, he started fulltime work as a project inspector for a series of civil engineering firms.

The job required Norb to attend ongoing educational seminars and successfully pass tests along the way. Working directly under the direction of a registered professional engineer, he inspected roads, sewers, bridges, and pump stations. He also did some estimating and contract administration work. The jobs kept him outside, which he preferred to being holed up all day in some cramped cubicle. "Some guy told me when I started off, 'You turn your timecard in on Monday, you pick up your check on Thursday, and you always keep your mouth shut.' I thought that was pretty good advice," said Norb.

Since he wasn't the type to bring up his athletic feats, many people meeting the solidly built middle-aged guy in the hard hat and safety glasses for the first time didn't realize he was something special. Some who did, however, trotted out the inevitable "dumb strong-guy" stereotypes that weightlifters have always suffered from in the workplace. "Thought the face looked familiar," was one society columnist's stab at humor. "That is former Olympic weightlifter Norbert Schemansky overseeing the Grosse Ile water line project across the river for his engineering firm employer Chuck Raines. Schemansky probably could just toss the pipeline in from the bridge and save [the construction company] all those giant crane costs."

"He had the demeanor of a typical working-class Polish-American," Paul Paruk, the current president of the National Polish-American Sports Hall of Fame, said of Norb's unassuming manner. "Only his muscular physique gave any clue that he competed on an international stage. His four Olympic medals garnered world-wide acclaim and established Norb as America's greatest strength athlete!" (Norb was inducted into the hall in 1979.)

Norb had always had more than a passing interest in local politics, dating back to his experiences as a clerk and election supervisor for union elections while working for Clarence Johnson in the 1950s. Some remembered his quip from the Olympic medal winners' traditional visit to the White House, shortly after returning from the Tokyo in 1964. "Just think," Norb remarked while being introduced to President Lyndon Johnson, "the two strongest Democrats in the country finally meeting face too face."

A few years later Norb served as a minor elected official on the commission that revised the city of Dearborn's charter, an experience that reinforced his belief that he could do as well or better than many of the people who were steering civic affairs. "A couple of friends said I had some name recognition, so I took a stab at it," Norb said of his unsuccessful runs for public office. At various times he was a candidate for the state legislature, Dearborn City Council, and Wayne County Commissioner. Exhibiting a champion's pride, he's never cared to talk much about these rare occasions in life when he failed to take the podium. Suffice it to say that he and his small band of loyal supporters probably miscalculated the name recognition value of a politically inexperienced Olympic weightlifter (though it wouldn't be too many more years before a professional wrestler and an Austrian-born bodybuilder were elected governors of Minnesota and California, respectively).

The back-slapping, money-grubbing, double-tongued nature of politics didn't really suit Norb's nature, anyway. "I want no endorsements from political, fraternal, or any other groups," he declared to a local weekly in that paper's roundup of candidates for the county commissioner's seat. "I do not want to be obligated to anyone but the people who elect me. A real man cannot serve too many masters." Norb went on to blast career politicians, saying, "The other candidates have been around the political scene for years. What possibly do they think they can do now, if they haven't done anything for the last 30 or 40 years?" That was a logical question, but elections on any level usually have far less to do with logic than with organization, connections, and deep pockets. Norb had none of them. It also didn't help his chances that as a public speaker, the lifelong Democrat made a fine weightlifter. He preferred lawn signs and bumper stickers to giving speeches. "Some guys kill themselves talking," he said. "I got to the point quick, no B.S. But, yeah, that probably hurt me."

All the while he stayed close to the arena he was most comfortable in, weightlifting. He attended scores of local contests and major meets in other cities whenever possible, serving in whatever capacity was needed, be it awarding medals or working as a back-room scorekeeper. "He was always available for any job," said one friend. "He'd give an exhibition at any school or church or college that asked. He never got paid, not even his expenses." Norb didn't participate in the masters' tournaments for lifters over 40, deciding they weren't for him. "Some of those guys are taking more steroids than the young kids," he once complained to an interviewer. "Some are also falling over with bad hearts and everything else. To walk out there with big varicose veins, huffing and puffing, is kind of silly. I can see guys staying in shape, but forget the competition." When asked, Skee lent advice through the mail, providing brief but thoughtful responses to correspondents from as far away as Argentina, Australia, and all over Europe. For ten years he served as chairman and advisor to the handicapped lifters in the Wheelchair Olympics.

He continued to work out regularly, though not with huge poundage. "I figured if you've got an old car, you don't push it too hard,' he explained. "Just enough to keep toned." Occasionally he'd see if he could get up to 300 or so pounds in a couple of months, just for the hell of it. Old habits die hard.

Throughout, Norb never hid his distaste for what he viewed as the ineptness, cronyism, and lack of vision that helped lead to America's decline as a lifting power. In his mind amateur associations at all levels had failed to properly promote Olympic lifting, had ignored suggestions like regional coaches (after all, not everybody could go to York to train), and had demonstrated an unwillingness or inability to assist athletes when they were injured or otherwise in need. "The bad part is that officials who know little about lifting become important figures in the sport and ride to the top on the muscles of the athletes," he complained to a visitor to the Astro Gym in 1972.

One of the "important figures" Norb was referring to was Clarence Johnson, who had risen to become national chairman of the A.A.U. and president of the International Weightlifting Federation. At the Astro Gym, a picture of Johnson dozing in a rocking chair was taped to the wall. Someone had added a caption: "Our glorious president, hard at work." Part of Norb's animus stemmed from the feeling that Johnson had abandoned him after he injured his back, deciding the ailing lifter was of little further use to his ambitions. "I learned a lot of lessons in my career," Norb said. "One is to not trust some people. They're the ones who pat you on the back when you're doing good, but you can't find 'em when you're on the way down."

Ironically, he and Johnson were inducted into the International Weightlifting Hall of Fame together in 1974, with Johnson presenting Norb his plaque. "I used to tell him, 'You're proof that the good die young,'" teased Norb. Indeed, Johnson did seem to go on forever, even being named the I.W.F.'s "president for life" in 1992. He continued to lift weights, play handball and fly his private plane right up to the end, finally succumbing to a heart attack six years later at age 92.

Although construction can be a fickle trade, Norb's regular paychecks were a welcome supplement to Bernice's salary as a secretary for a downtown brokerage firm. Household finances improved to the point that they could finally say goodbye to the succession of clunkers Norb had been driving his entire life. Meanwhile, they watched with mixed emotions as the kids grew up and, one by one, left the nest.

Pamela was the first to move out, graduating from high school in 1967 and getting married three years later. Paula, the oldest, graduated in 1965 and waited until 1973 before tying the knot with a young auto worker who had grown up near Norb's old eastside neighborhood. Larry enlisted in the army and parlayed his experience as a military policeman into a job with the Michigan State Police, where he became a sergeant on the governor's detail, while Laura got married and became a homemaker. Between them, Norb's kids have produced ten grandchildren, eight great-grandchildren, and an uncounted number of crayon drawings and Father's Day cards.

All of Norb's children retain positive memories of growing up. None ever felt that they were somehow "going without" because of their father's frequent absences. Said Pamela: "Whenever Dad was around he took us places: out to the park or to the pool or just a Sunday drive. We'd go up north on vacation, all the way up to the Upper Peninsula. My mom and dad loved it up there. I remember staying at a cottage and going biking, fishing, swimming." Added Paula: "Of the two, Dad was a little bit stricter, but he'd usually be the one helping us with sports while Mom was the one who helped us with our homework. To me it was a completely ordinary upbringing." Although family finances were tight in the '50s and '60s, Norb somehow found the money to buy a movie camera and pay for the processing of hundreds of feet of 16-mm. color film. Maybe the Schemanskys didn't enjoy the overpowering familial bliss of an episode of *The Donna Reed Show* or *Father Knows Best*—but then again, who did? To judge by the decades-old footage of birthdays, holidays, vacations, and other standard family fare that survives in several dusty tins, Norb, Bernice and the kids were a close-knit and absolutely normal bunch. "We didn't have many vacations," said Pamela, "but every holiday we'd go to my Uncle Dennis's place in Utica. So we were close to our cousins." Going to the farm that Norb's brother owned north of Detroit was always a good time. The rural property was flanked by a gun range and a quarry. These attractions, coupled with the slides and swings Dennis built, meant there were plenty of diversions for all ages. "We kids would have a play day," she said.

According to Larry, growing up as the son of Norb Schemansky was a unique experience. "I did have the strongest dad on the block!" he said. "As far as I knew, I was the only kid with a makeshift gym in his garage." Larry sometimes accompanied his father to the Astro Gym, where he learned the "true meaning of a workout." Thanks to his dad (and Bob Hoffman), he also grew up "eating protein bars before they were popular or tasted good."

Laura remembered always having the support of both parents. "When I came home for lunch from elementary school, my dad would have a meal waiting for me," she said. "He and my mom split the care of raising us because he was there during the day and my mom was there in the evenings while he worked out at the gym. Throughout my school years they gave me support in my schoolwork and my outside activities.

"Even as I grew older we have remained close. During the ups and downs of my first marriage, my dad took my son, Christopher, under his wing to teach him responsibility while still rewarding him for his hard work."

Over the years Norb has wrestled with what to do with his four Olympic medals, going so far as to have somebody float their value with collectors. Four medals, four kids—the math is temptingly simple. But for the time being, at least, he has been dissuaded from selling them and distributing a four-way split of the proceeds. Tucked inside one oversize Father's Day card was a note from Pamela: "The medals are yours to do with what you want—but we think they should not be sold—no money is worth their value. They mean too much to us. Just my sentiments."

There's no arguing that Norb felt his accomplishments were not honored in his time as widely as those of other world-class athletes. Sometimes he gave off mixed signals, one minute implying recognition was not that important to him, then a couple of breaths later mildly bemoaning his anonymity.

After years of unaccountably being passed over for the Michigan Sports Hall of Fame, Norb was officially inducted on May 20, 1976, at a Thursday night banquet before 1,500 people at Cobo Hall. Also ushered in that evening were former Detroit Lions coach Raymond "Buddy" Parker, Hudson High School football coach Tom Saylor, and five others. "It's nice to get this in the Bicentennial year," said Norb, accepting his plaque from local sportscaster

Al Ackerman, who had long championed the lifter's cause. "It seems like I've waited 200 years."

Those familiar with Schemansky's sardonic wit and deadpan delivery knew he was joking. To some people, however, that remark, like many others he had made over the years, came across as slightly bitter.

On the morning of Norb's induction, Joe Falls of the *Detroit Free Press* paid him a visit on the job. Falls seemed determined to write a certain kind of story, one that had become practically boilerplate over the years. In a column that ran the following day, he wrote, "I did not expect to find a happy man working with the construction crew two blocks in off Telegraph Road, near Goddard, and I didn't."

> Norbert, who was supervising the project, came walking down the street and when I saw him, I said: "Hey, lift that cement truck for me."
>
> I didn't expect him to smile and he didn't. Too many years of brooding have left a deep mark on this man. I only wish there was something I could do for him—some way I could make him feel better—but this is impossible.
>
> Norbert Schemansky was the very best at what he did—a four-time Olympic medal winner (one gold, one silver, two bronzes). He's also been the world champion heavyweight weightlifter, which in effect made him the "strongest man on earth."
>
> You've heard Al Ackerman fighting Schemansky's cause for years now, and rightly so. The man did deserve a spot in our Hall of Fame. How many athletes from our state ever competed in as many as four Olympics and brought home a medal every time? Terry McDermott got in with one medal. So did Lorenzo Wright. Hayes Jones made it with two.
>
> But these were popular heroes. Schemansky was a man who wanted more than medals and let everyone know it. So he was left on the outside looking in, brooding almost every day of his life.
>
> You see, Norbert Schemansky, who is 51 years old, has never been able to figure out his place in life. He was great at something but it was something which did not bring any monetary rewards. The rewards were of a much more aesthetic nature—the pride of being a champion and the knowledge that you were the very best.
>
> As we sat over coffee in a greasy spoon on Telegraph Road, I asked

> Schemansky about his medals—where they were and did he plan to bring them to the banquet with him.
>
> "Why should I?" he said. I knew I could not give him an answer that would placate him. All I said was: "Maybe somebody would like to see them."
>
> Schemansky shrugged. "They're so small you could put all four of them on this napkin," he said.
>
> I had hoped that in this moment—this long-awaited moment—Schemansky would change. I hoped he would display a sense of appreciation for what was happening to him. He was receiving one of the greatest honors any athlete in Michigan could receive. I hoped for too much.
>
> The bitterness kept coming through in his conversation. He talked about all the rule changes which made weightlifting easier today than it was in his day. He talked about the drugs that are now being taken to make a man stronger so that he can lift more than he is really capable of lifting.
>
> Most of all he kept talking about how the amateur athletes were more appreciated in other countries than they are in the United States, especially in the ways they are subsidized. "I got a friend who went to Russia and they asked him for his autograph just because he knows me," said Schemansky.
>
> I kept hoping he would say, "I'm really happy about this moment."
>
> He never did.

It was just like Falls, a baseball writer with a reputation for having a major-league ego, to think he could plumb the depths of one of history's most honored weightlifters in a twenty-minute conversation over coffee. Norb, as dour a champion as ever walked the earth, wasn't bound to say, "I'm really happy about this moment" for *any* reason. He just wasn't an emotive type looking to inject drama into a situation. After all, by now Norb was a member of several halls of fame. While appreciated, those honors paled alongside the many international titles and medals he had earned, the records he had set, the respect his name commanded in even the most far-flung corners of the iron game. And Norb didn't want sympathy, just a fair shake. What most reporters came away with from their first—and usually only—encounter with Norb was an impression of acrid resentment. Like Falls, they didn't know their man. In his typically matter-of-fact, straight-shooting style, Norb simply called them as he saw them. Rule changes *had* made it easier for lifters to compete. Drugs *were* being used to help lifters obliterate records that old-school types like Norb had spent years systematically building. And amateur athletes *were* better appreciated in other countries. These weren't sour grapes, just immutable facts. If Schemansky was growing bitter about anything, it was about always being portrayed as being bitter.

Those around the iron game knew better. "When pressed or asked, Norb has comments and opinions," Vernon Hollister wrote in a perceptive profile for *Strength & Health*. "They are often witty, always precise, full of candor, and often satiric; yet honest beneath it all. Everything he says can't be taken literally, which may be why he has been so often misunderstood and maligned."

One of Norb's opinions has no chance of being misunderstood. "There aren't any more Olympics," he has said on many occasions since the U.S. Olympic Committee first allowed corporate sponsorship and the participation of professional athletes. "They're the money games now."

Time invariably removes important figures from each person's life, and so it was with Norb. His father, Joseph Schemansky, died in 1962, having attended only a couple of Norb's meets over the years—both local—and never once congratulating his son on his iron-game accomplishments. Norb insisted he was okay with that. "He wasn't the kind of guy to say something like that to me in person. Maybe he bragged on it a little to someone at work, but he never mentioned anything about it to me."

A heart attack claimed Joseph Schemansky, just as it later claimed all three of Norb's brothers. Ralph, the only one of the four Schemansky boys not to get into lifting, was the first to go, in 1981. He was followed a few years later by Jerome and Dennis. Jerome died in New Hampshire, where he was living with his daughter, while Dennis passed away one strange winter day in Rogers City, Michigan, where he had bought a 40-acre property upon retirement. "He was plowing a road on his tractor," said Norb, "and about eleven that morning he stopped to talk with a neighbor. A couple of hours later they found him sitting on his tractor, dead in his seat."

On Sunday, January 21, 1996, Bernice Schemansky died of heart failure at Botsford General Hospital in Farmington Hills. She was seventy-one years old and had been suffering from complications following her treatment for ovarian cancer. She was buried at Michigan Memorial Park in Flat Rock. For the first year Norb visited her grave every Saturday and Sunday, a routine he scaled back to the weekly sojourn he continues to this day, despite his difficulty in getting around. "It's the least I can do for her," said Norb, who still finds it hard to talk about his wife of forty-nine years. "He's a private person," said Pamela. "But I would say he went through a lot. It was devastating."

Bernice also went through a lot. She sacrificed a lot, missed out on a lot, while encouraging Norb during his stubborn pursuit of goals and dreams. She was the one who knew him best, the one person a strong, quiet guy could really open up to when needed. That hole in the heart will never be healed, though Norb, of course, would never express that sentiment in such flowery terms. He has said, however, that Bernice deserved the title, "Olympic wife."

Not long after Bernice's passing, Norb was enlisted to be a ceremonial torch-bearer as the Olympic torch made its way to Atlanta, Georgia, which was hosting the upcoming Summer Games. A few weeks later, on July 17, 1996, Elmhurst Park—a leafy public field at Outer Drive and Penn Street in Dearborn—was formally renamed Norbert Schemansky Park. "When the Olympic torch visited Dearborn in June," Mayor Michael Guido told the assembled crowd, "it not only rekindled the Olympic spirit, it made us aware that an unsung hero of our community had not received proper recognition for his outstanding accomplishments. That hero is Norbert Schemansky." The honoree's feat of medaling in four different Olympics, continued Guido, "still stands as one of the most awesome achievements in Olympic history."

That said, it still wasn't enough to get Norb named one of the "100 Greatest Living Olympians" in a publicity stunt sponsored by Xerox Corporation to help celebrate the Olympics' centennial. Honorees were flown to Atlanta for the Games, given first-class accommodations and free tickets to events, introduced at the opening ceremonies and feted at a gala banquet. That Schemansky was not among the "golden hundred" was astonishing, given that media darling and basketball star Earvin "Magic" Johnson—one of the many multimillionaire sports figures who had benefited from the U.S. Olympic Committee's decision to open the door to professionals and major corporate sponsorships—had appeared in just one Olympics. Dozens of other participants who had lesser credentials than Norb also were included on the list.To those familiar with Norb's history, it was a galling oversight. After all, at the time he was one of only two athletes in history to win four individual medals in four Olympics. (Discus thrower Al Oerter was the other. Two other Olympians won more medals, but in team events.) He also was the oldest person ever to medal in weightlifting, and one of the oldest to medal in *any* sport.

Two weightlifters made the list: Tommy Kono, who had won gold medals at Helsinki and Melbourne, and Pete George, who captured a gold in 1952 and silvers in 1948 and 1956. One of Norb's friends, Bob "Doc" Suchyta, was irked enough by the slight to fly Schemansky to Atlanta on his own dime. "I'd just like to see Norb get some credit for what he did," said Suchyta, a local physician and amateur lifter. "It bothers me that people with lesser credentials are going, and Norb is not."

Although Norb was not part of the official hoopla, he was not entirely overlooked. He received a nice hand from the crowd at the George World Congress Center when he was recognized by the public address announcer between rounds of the super-heavyweight competition. "They lift a lot more weight now," observed the seventy-two-year-old legend.

Norb's youngest child, Laura, never knew her dad was a big deal until she was in junior high and saw his name in a history book. By then he was in the twilight of his career. She never attended one of his competitions. "I wish I knew then what I know now," she told a reporter writing a story about her father's omission.

"Now, if he came home, would things be different for him?" she continued. "I don't know. But he never had the recognition. Now, when I read things, I know he was really, really something. But the only thing I can do is share that with my kids. I can tell them that their grandfather was someone special. They can go to school and know he was really something."

♦ ♦ ♦

In 1997 Norb retired from the city of Dearborn, for whom he had been working as a construction inspector since leaving a similar job in the private sector a decade earlier. Late in life he had finally caught a break, qualifying for an increased pension thanks to the credit he received for time served in the army. "I could've stayed there a few more years, I had it easy," said Norb. "But my legs were starting to bother me."

The pension, coupled with his social security benefits and the fact that his home mortgage has long been paid off, have given Norb a measure of financial stability, something he never enjoyed in his prime. "I'm sure the hell not rich," he said, "but I'm getting by okay." There's enough to regularly eat out at a favorite Polish restaurant, in any case. The house he has lived in for nearly a half-century is tidy, snug, and basically unadorned. The main floor is bare of plaques and proclamations. His trophies—at least those very few that haven't already been lost, broken, discarded or given away—are packed away somewhere. There is a smattering of minor miscellaneous awards nailed to a paneled wall in the basement, but nothing on the smudged bronze plaques cries out that the man of the house is arguably the greatest American weightlifter, pound for pound, that ever hoisted a barbell in competition. This air of quiet calm and apple-pie order perfectly fits Norb's personality. A daughter comes over every Saturday to clean and dust a little, and every once in a while a visitor will drop by, but mostly it's just Norb, his television, and whatever memories might float through his head during the course of a day.

On this particular morning the large man sat at an angle in his easy chair, trying to find the best position for his chronically ailing back. The living room TV was turned to ESPN. A kitchen radio blasted news-talk in the background. Normally on such a nice day Norb would be putzing around in the garden, doing his best to maintain his late wife's flower beds, but his old nemesis has given him a lot of trouble of late. X-rays are produced. The milky images of metal rods, screws, and links are more suggestive of the hardware aisle at Home Depot than a human spine. Three surgeries in the 1990s and numerous visits to specialists and chiropractors have done little to remedy the degenerative condition of his back.

The four Olympic medals are "in a box, somewhere," said Norb. A safety box? "No, just a box—in the bedroom, I think." A blue velvet bag that once held a bottle of Chivas Regal whiskey now functions as a handy carrying case for what remains of the scores of decorations he received in national and world competition. He loosened the drawstring and spilled the contents onto the living room floor. The names of Old World cities—Milan, Budapest, Stockholm, Vienna—poked out of the jumbled, jagged pile of tarnished metal and soiled silk. Many of the medals are handsomely crafted, a reflection of the higher value European countries have historically placed on the sport and its stars.

In a way Norb's entire life is in that bag. A little bit of fame, even less fortune, and in the end the good scotch is gone. And why keep the symbols of a lifetime of hard work and achievement jammed inside a Chivas Regal bag, anyway? Displaying a perfect sense of timing, Norb waited a beat before replying, "Because I don't drink Seagrams."

His large hand like a steam shovel, he scooped up some medals and dumped them back into the sack. "Why did I keep on lifting?" he mused. "I guess I always thought something good would come out of it, but nothing ever did. I was born thirty years too soon. I stayed at the top for what—fifteen or sixteen years? But it doesn't really mean anything."

Many would disagree with that assessment. Once an Australian visiting the area wanted to meet him so badly he went to the Dearborn police station, asked where Norb Schemansky the great weightlifter lived, then trudged several miles on foot through a rainstorm to his house. Letters from strangers continue to occasionally arrive in the mailbox. Some are from overseas dealers disguised as fans, who enclose a flattering stock greeting ("Dear Sportfriend," is a typical salutation) along with several blank cards or small photos to be autographed and returned in the self-addressed stamped envelope. Other writers are more sincere and ask Norb for nothing more in return than the time needed to read a heartfelt sentiment. One such letter, hand written and undated, came from Herb Glossbrenner, a powerlifting historian on the West Coast who was struggling to make a go of it with a new publication. *Olympic International Lifter* was intended in part to make up for the failings of *Strength & Health*, whose decline mirrored that of American lifting in the 1970s and '80s. (*Strength & Health* was put to rest in 1986, then brought back to life as an online quarterly fifteen years later.) "Hello Norb," the letter began.

> I'm enclosing our latest + last issue of *International Olympic Lifter* magazine. Since S & H folded we're the only one in existence—S &H hasn't really been a good W/L mag since the 60's and early 70's.
>
> No I'm not hitting you up for a subscription—I decided that you deserve to receive the magazine for nothing. I do the whole thing single-handedly—our latest issue cost $5000 more than we take in, in subscriptions in 2 yrs....Our magazine is a labor of love—We'll still keep pumping our time + energies into the magazine despite the fact that American W/L has gone down the tubes—Whether or not it will ever be good in USA again who knows –
>
> Your 15-20 years of competition will never be forgotten—an Olympic medal in 4 Olympics will never again be equaled!—The world will never again see a World Record at age 38!
>
> You gave Vlasov cardiac arrest in Budapest and got the typical Communist screwing with that controversial double-dip jerk by Vlasov—A bronze medal at age 40 in Tokyo.
>
> Few athletes had your will and determination—few in the history of the sport—few in any sport.
>
> You lived with pain—you trained with the guts few men possessed –
>
> Nobody would break Anderson's records—they claimed—You DID! At age almost 40!
>
> Of course you never got the recognition you deserved. It will probably take another half century for it to soak in.
>
> I don't need to tell you that you were the greatest heavyweight in USA History—you know that and so does everybody else....

Glossbrenner signed off with "You are the Greatest"—a sentiment that the many devotees of "Mr. Weightlifting," both past and present, would have no trouble echoing.

Afterword

In Praise of a True Champion

by Mike Kuhne

One measure of a champion's greatness is how many lives he managed to touch, often without his even knowing it. In this concluding chapter to the Norb Schemansky story, Mike Kuhne—a native Detroiter and a competitive weightlifter from 1955 to 1960—describes in his own words Norb's impact on his life and on the wider world of weightlifting.

♦ ♦ ♦

When asked about the most memorable aspects of my youth, particularly my high school years, it's not high school that comes to mind. Good fortune granted me some unique extra-curricular sources for growth of both mind and body. One old friend recently remarked, "You once knew and trained with a great American Olympic champion. How many people can say that?" True, indeed, and at least I had sense enough to know it, even at that time. I sometimes do reflect back on how remarkable it was that this came to be, and how I came to meet one of the greatest Olympians, Norbert Schemansky.

Like many youngsters, I had a desire to be stronger and more athletic. At fourteen I was weaker than average for my age, not being able to do a single chin-up and being capable of only two or three push-ups. At this time, a top-notch athlete from school invited me and a close friend to join him for weight training sessions in his basement. He had many photographs of famous bodybuilding champions and Olympic weightlifting champions adorning his basement walls. Among these were action photos of Norbert Schemansky, the reigning middle-heavyweight Olympic weightlifting gold-medal winner and the world champion. He had become the heaviest man in history to lift double his bodyweight overhead in a record-breaking clean and jerk lift. Our new friend also had a collection of sports magazines that emphasized competitive weightlifting and bodybuilding. He acquired the latest issues every month. In this way we soon became familiar with the great national and world champions who were regularly featured, along with their records and achievements.

Schemansky was often referred to as "The Professor" because he wore glasses and possessed remarkable speed and technical skill, which allowed him to outperform even the most powerful of his opponents. We knew which champions, like Schemansky, were from the United States, but generally not which cities they called home. We knew that many often visited famous places such as Muscle Beach in California, and York, Pennsylvania, where some legendary men worked for Bob Hoffman's York Barbell Company.

I made some progress from my training and after a few months, I purchased my own weight-training equipment with my paper-route money, and set up my own basement gym. Although my athlete friend showed us the exercises and various competitive lifts as best he could, none of us had ever actually seen them done—only still photos.

One day in early 1954 I bought the latest issue of *Strength & Health,* which featured Norb Schemansky on the cover. The story inside revealed that he had decided to become a heavyweight and compete in that class. This was amazing because our great U.S. heavyweight, many times world and Olympic champion John Davis, had been dealt a stunning defeat by Canada's massive, ultra-powerful Doug Hepburn at the 1953 World Championships. Davis weighed 235 pounds, but Hepburn weighed a solid 290 pounds of supreme massive power at 5-foot-9! Hepburn had established a sensational new world record in the press, which was way beyond the old record. This was remarkable because most new records exceed the old ones by just a couple of pounds. No one could come close to this new record. Schemansky, less than six feet in height, had made his incredible records as a middle-heavyweight, at a very muscular 198 pounds bodyweight, even defeating Russia's great Grigori Novak. Novak was very powerful in the press, yet no match for "The Professor's" speed and technique in his record-setting snatch and clean and jerk lifts. But Schemansky's bulk and pressing power was nowhere near that of Hepburn, even though he had increased his muscle mass to just over 220 pounds.

Then I came to the part where the article mentioned that Schemansky lived in Detroit! My jaw dropped in astonishment as I stared into the magazine. Right away, I phoned my friends. They could not believe it. My neighborhood training buddy came right over to see the article. We looked in the phone book and found that he was listed, and that he was an East Sider like ourselves, living only about one mile from us! We were beside ourselves with excitement. After some discussion, we decided to call his number and speak with him. It took quite some time for us to work up our nerve to actually do it. We flipped a coin to determine who would make the call. I was it.

I nervously dialed the phone. It was Norb himself who answered. In my young mind, with all I had read about "The Professor" and all the pictures I had seen, I rather expected that he would sound like a professor! I was a little surprised to hear the great athlete's husky voice over the phone line.

I explained that we were just a couple of teenagers who trained in my basement and had no idea whether we were executing movements correctly, since we'd never had the opportunity to actually see them performed, only still pictures in magazines and training courses. We really did not know what to expect at this point, other than having the pleasure of actually speaking with him, and maybe getting a tip on an event to which we might travel. Or maybe he wouldn't want to bother with us at all. Much to my surprise, he asked if we knew where the Northeastern Y.M.C.A. was located. Indeed we did! I was a member for several years as a small kid and learned to swim there! He asked if we could meet him there the following Monday night. We eagerly said we'd be there.

On Monday, we rushed home after school, had our customary snack, but instead of heading for the basement, we hopped on a bus to get to the "Y" early. We waited, sitting on a sofa just inside the large TV lounge, where we could keep an eye on the entrance door. As Schemansky walked in, we immediately recognized him and hurried over to introduce ourselves. He shook our hands and simply said, "Come along with me." We went along with him, past the check-in desk, no questions asked, looking at each other thinking, "Is this for real?"

But this was just the beginning. After changing into his training attire, we were awed at his spectacular musculature as we followed him up to the club weight-room. Upon entering, he had us sit on the side to watch. There were some other very impressive athletes already training, but none to compare with him. He began effortless warm-ups with poundage we had yet to dream of mastering. As his workout progressed, the poundage kept increasing, but his power was amazing. The bar was loaded to incredible amounts, yet his movement remained fluid, his speed actually increased, getting lower under the weight quick as a cat, and his balance was always perfect!

This was far beyond anything we could have hoped for. We had never seen Olympic weightlifting actually done. Now we were seeing it live for the first time, and by the best in the world!

After a time, we were startled to see a very impressive blonde man come in. We soon recognized him as a bodybuilding champion and Mr. America contender from the cover of one of our magazines, Vic Seipke. While still gawking at that discovery, in came yet another big champion who had graced a magazine cover, powerful Don Van Fleteren. These champions were training here, as were numerous Michigan lifting and bodybuilding competitors, alongside the great Norbert Schemansky, at our local YMCA, right here in Detroit! To us two kids, this was beyond belief. Only our obvious excitement prevented our friends from thinking we had concocted some wild story!

Schemansky evidently gave the word to the "Y" staff that we could come in once per week to watch, and we did so without any questions. We learned from what we saw, and taught our friends back in our basement gyms. Progress was greatly enhanced for all of us. After a couple of months, being big for our age, we joined the men's section of the "Y," telling them we were eighteen when we were actually fifteen, and once again putting our paper-route money to good use. Of course, we also joined the lifting club, where we were welcomed aboard. We thus trained in this incredible club, alongside Schemansky, and watched as he prepared for some very history-making events.

We were all aware that the next challenge Schemansky faced was a very formidable one—to successfully compete against top American heavyweights Jim Bradford and John Davis at the forthcoming 1954 U. S. Senior National Championships in Los Angeles. Norb was truly a major contender, as he had been within their range even as a middle-heavyweight, and they were well aware of that fact. Norb was doing some power movements for further improvement in basic strength, but his main emphasis was on the three Olympic lifts themselves. As the weeks went by, he gradually increased not only the poundage used, but also the number of sets done, resulting in workouts of greater duration, and more total pounds lifted during each session. Of course, he continuously honed his unsurpassed technical skills. He worked hard to improve his power in the press, eventually coming close to that of Davis. Jim Bradford was one of the world's best in that lift, capable of even more than Davis. Norb trained a great deal on snatches and cleans. Interestingly, although he was a world record holder and the greatest performer on the planet when it came to the jerk, he did relatively few jerks in training.

We continued to progress and to learn, surrounded by seasoned veterans as we were. We also learned gym etiquette. For instance, you did not walk in front of a champion when he was preparing to make a lift or do a heavy exercise. But we discovered that the same courtesy was extended to the least of us. My training partner's name was also Mike, but we both went by the nickname of "Mickey." The club members liked that nickname, as it was that of a popular Mr. Universe winner, Mickey Hargitay. Many of our club members were Detroit firemen, including Vic Seipke, Don Van Fleteren, and our club founder, Captain Eldon Dreher. Eldon was older, yet still very strong. He was also a good coach. He was a very pleasant person, as were Vic, Don, and the others. The focus in our club was on serious training, but there was a great deal of camaraderie and good humor. Our clubroom was rather small, and when it became crowded, we could open the large sliding doors at the rear to expand into a smaller adjacent gym that was used for basketball. After his workout, Norb was fond of shooting baskets with a one-handed straight-arm toss all the way across this gym. He was quite accomplished at this feat, and was delighted when he could sucker some unknowing individual into betting him a case of beer, giving him three tries at such a seemingly unlikely possibility. He would often make it on the first try.

Although basically a man of few words, we found Norb to have an excellent sense of humor. He often dropped a quip or two into whatever conversation was going on, which would make everyone laugh. Sometimes in the shower room one of us would feel a stinging smack on the butt, in the form of a piece of soap turned missile. Norb would be under his shower, looking nonchalant. After catching him in the act out of the corner of the eye, we'd return fire. Soon, the others would join in, causing the shower room to come alive with laughter and flying pieces of soap! Afterwards "the two Mickeys" would catch the bus across the street, and we'd arrive back home in good spirits and with a ravenous appetite. Finally, the time was at hand for Norb to depart for the senior nationals, and we all wished him luck. As my partner and I came in for our workouts over the next several days, we'd check with Eldon, or with club president Frank DeMatteis, for news. Finally, it came. Norb had prevailed! He was now the new U.S. heavyweight champion!

Of course, Norb then took a little time off, and when he did reappear, he received congratulations from all. But there was barely a footnote buried in the sports section of the local press. There was more coverage of a high-school basketball game! Unbelievable! We heard that Norb's previous Olympic victories resulted in similar disinterest. He'd even faced conflicts with employers over his participation. There apparently was little appreciation for Norb's dedication to representing his country in top-level international sports competition, which he did just because he was capable of doing so, and of bringing honor to the U.S. But subsequent weightlifting magazines were all buzzing with Norb's success, complete with photographs. Norb's workouts consisted of relatively light (for him) training for a while. Then, once again, he gradually resumed his efforts to increase his power, as he would be facing very stiff competition at the upcoming World Championships, to be held in Vienna, Austria, in just a few months. Among his adversaries was the mighty heavyweight world champ, Doug Hepburn of Canada.

My own progress was going very well. I was still coaching a number of neighborhood boys in my basement gym, using what I was learning to help them. Some were as young as twelve. My progress was so pronounced that I was approached by a coach at school about going out for football. But the athletic experience I was enjoying at our club was far, far above anything school had to offer. Besides, I actually had little interest in that sport. The other Mickey, however, did go out for baseball. I might have gone for wrestling, if they'd had it. But both of us did take a judo class at the "Y" once a week, right after our workout in the clubroom. What energy teenagers have! We also helped out when our club hosted competitive lifting events.

As Norb's training neared its peak, if a major event was being held locally, he would give an exhibition as sort of a "tune-up" for his own forthcoming competition. Knowing this in advance, it was always seen to that internationally accredited judges were present to officiate, in case he felt like going for a new American or world record. Word that he would appear got around, and quite a large crowd would turn out, wall-to-wall beyond the seating capacity of the large gym. Photographers and reporters would show up. In these lifting events, which featured each of the three Olympic lifts, the bar was first loaded to the lightest amount that the lowest ranked lifter indicated he would start with. Then it was loaded upwards as the various lifters announced their next attempted poundage. So, the heaviest loaded bar, indeed a considerable amount, would usually be for a big state champion trying his best clean and jerk. This effort would end the event, to great applause from the admiring audience. But then, soon after that, considerably more weight would be added, as was indicated by Norb Schemansky, which would be his starting weight for his exhibition! The enormous barbell would sit there on the platform by itself for a brief period, as a hush would fall over the crowd. Then Norb would emerge from the warm-up room, his musculature an awesome sight as he checked the loading and approached the bar. He would then, with ridiculous ease, proceed to execute a perfect lift with this huge weight, which was far above that just barely managed by the big state champion while straining every shaking fiber during his third attempt! Flashbulbs would go off, and the crowd, of course, would go crazy.

The "Y" was not without its odd characters. One oddball I remember was a basketball player and fitness buff, who also concentrated on chin-ups and other calisthenics, but had a disdain for weight training. He would actually pop his head into our clubroom door and poke fun at our members as they trained. He'd mock the lifters as slow, moronic sloths who couldn't run a single block. He was saying these things in a snide way, not just joking. He was also being disruptive. The other Mickey and I considered him to be a total nutcase. We'd look at each other: *Didn't he know who he was talking to?*

One day, when he popped his head in and started his yammer, who happened to be inside? Indeed, it was Schemansky. I just shook my head. At first Norb said nothing, but I could tell he was getting ticked off. Soon, words flew between them. Beyond the doorway, in the big gym, the two climbing ropes had been let down and were dangling from the ceiling. As Mr. Nutcase yammered on, he pointed out towards them and said contemptuously, looking directly at Norb, "Why, you can't even haul your big, slow ass up one of those ropes, which I can climb with ease!" He may have known that there is a physical law making it more difficult for a larger individual to lift his own weight, compared to a smaller individual. Certainly, Norb knew it. But Goofy did not know with whom he was dealing, and this was too much crap for Norb to put up with. Norb pointed a finger in the guy's face and said, "I haven't climbed a rope in years—since I was in the army—but I'll bet (I've forgotten what) that I can beat you to the top!" Light, wiry, and well-practiced on the ropes and on chins, the wise-cracker's face lit up with a gleeful smile of anticipated victory. "Now I've really got this big weight-lifting oaf who thinks he's so hot" was written all over his face.

All who were present filed out into the big gym to see the action. The YMCA physical director, as an impartial party, agreed to act as referee and judge. He had a stopwatch and whistle. Each man took hold of a rope and got ready. The whistle blew. The loudmouth had evidently attained expertise in securing a grip on the rope with both his hands and his legs, using both to propel himself rapidly upward. Even with his far greater bodyweight, Schemansky decided to grasp the rope with just his hands alone, allowing his legs to swing free as he pulled himself up the rope hand-over-hand. But he was doing so at a much greater speed than his competitor. Our goofy intruder had gotten somewhat past the halfway mark when he found himself looking up at Schemansky, who had reached the ceiling far above. Never again did he stick his face inside our door, or even stop to look in. We were never again bothered by him in any manner.

The date of the 1954 World Championships was approaching. Norb's workouts were incredible. My partner got the idea that we would bring a tape measure to the next training session and measure the arms of Seipke, Van Fleteren, and Schemansky. We got there early to catch them as they arrived, to get a "cold" measurement; that is, before any exercise could pump blood into the muscles. Seipke was first to come in, and he flexed his great arms for us. They were 17¾ inches. Very impressive in size and shape, although arms were not among Seipke's best accomplishments. Then came Van Fleteren, who flexed his powerful arms, which were amazing at a shade under 19 inches, with huge peaked biceps that nearly reached up against his thumbs! They were among the most impressive in the United States. We were betting on him.

When Schemansky came in and flexed his arms for us, we could see that they did not quite have the kind of high-peaked shape Van Fleteren's had, but Norb did not often do bodybuilding exercises like curls. He put his energy into Olympic lifting. Nevertheless, his arms were huge- massively thick, and solid muscle. To our surprise, they proved to be even larger than Van Fleteren's at 19¼ inches! Norb had put on several more pounds of solid muscle and had attained greater power than ever before. But his pressing capability was still not in the same league as that of Jim Bradford or Doug Hepburn's world record of the year before.

There is a lot of strategy between competitors as to the starting weight of their first attempts and how much increase each will decide for his following attempts. The question here was going to be whether Schemansky would succeed in improving his own press enough to narrow the gap between him and Hepburn, where he could more than compensate for Hepburn's superior pressing power with his unsurpassed skills in the snatch and clean and jerk. It now seemed that he at least had a good shot at the formidable Hepburn. When we acquired the latest magazine issues, we were dumbfounded to discover from the latest photos and coverage regarding Hepburn that he had become even more massive, and his untouchable pressing power had improved to an unimaginably substantial degree! It was said he was capable of pressing 385 pounds, if he could clean it, far above his great world's record set the previous year. Hepburn had some problems with snatches and cleans, two of Schemansky's specialties. A congenital club foot condition was blamed, but we felt that since he was extremely powerful in the squat exercise, he should have been able to do well as a squat-lifter in the clean and snatch, like our great light-heavyweight champion, Tommy Kono. Hepburn now weighed around 290 pounds, while Schemansky, even though having gained muscle, was still a couple of pounds short of 225! He would face the daunting prospect of going up against a world champion and supreme world-record setter, who was more than 60 pounds heavier than himself. Normally, a five-pound advantage could make a difference. Schemansky, though, had often succeeded against opponents larger than himself, but none even close to having the mass and power of Hepburn.

Norb's training had been very focused and methodical. He seemed unperturbed at the odds he faced. His mood and spirits were good. The time was finally at hand, and we club members wished him all the best as he finished his final workout and would soon be packing for his trip to Europe. All we could do was wait and speculate.

As the days passed, there was frequent discussion and speculation among our club members as to Norb's chances. We'd recently read that Hepburn now weighed around 290 pounds, was in top training condition and had greater strength than ever. He may have mastered the squat style, improving his snatches and cleans. There was no telling what unreachable records this superman could be capable of! Big Jim Bradford had been making improvements as well and would be in top contention. Sometimes at school I would look up from my assignment to ponder the outcome. Even the great light-heavyweight, Tommy Kono, was not a sure winner in world competition. Who else, though, but Norb Schemansky was facing super record-setting powerhouse lifters, who outweighed him by considerable margins? Finally the first reports came.

Communications came through the office of A.A.U. weightlifting chairman, Clarence Johnson, who was a businessman in the Detroit area, and via club president Frank DeMatteis. But everyone seemed to know the news. My mouth hung open as I listened. New world records had indeed been set in the heavyweight class...by Norbert Schemansky! He had won! He was now the heavyweight champion of the world! Sure, Schemansky was out-pressed, but then it was lesson-time from "The Professor." The lighter Schemansky out-lifted the field of competition in the snatch and the clean and jerk, setting new world records, including a new world record total of 1,074 pounds! It was an astounding triumph.

The next time we came in, there was yet more news. Schemansky's outstanding success was big press in Europe. The Russians had also specifically assigned film crews to cover him right from the beginning, so they might better study his exceptional skills for their training camps. There was a post-competition tour of the champions with exhibition lifting. It was also revealed that during this time, Schemansky had broken his own new world record with a phenomenal clean and jerk of 425 pounds! Unbelievable!

Upon our next visit, we were again surprised with more news. Schemansky's name repeatedly made headlines in the sports sections of foreign press. His feats were being featured on TV news in Europe. He had performed a "continental style" clean (two-step pull to the shoulders) and jerk with 440 pounds, the most ever done, and subsequently attempted 450, narrowly missing the jerk! He had been a heavyweight competitor for just one year. Clearly, we could safely say, he would become the first heavyweight in history to clean and jerk double his bodyweight. This was astonishing, but there was even more. Schemansky made yet more European sports headlines. After his phenomenal lifting feats, and the tour having included a trip to France, the French authorities agreed that Schemansky should be given a try at the famous Apollon railway car wheels, the first since John Davis a few years earlier. Unlike the questionable success of Davis, Schemansky succeeded with a spectacular display, to great acclaim by the French and other European observers. The report stated that he cleaned the wheels to the shoulders with ease, using a standard grip, and jerked the ponderous weight overhead three times! The bend in the bar was still there from Davis having dropped the wheels. Schemansky's performance with the wheels was so impressive and historic, no further attempts with them have been permitted by the French authorities to this day.

I can still clearly remember the day Norb finally reappeared at our "Y" club. Soon after the other Mickey and I began our workout, we heard some yelling and general commotion coming from members just outside the door. Along with others, I stepped over where I could see through the doorway. I can still see Norb coming towards us down the long corridor running alongside the big gym. The cheers increased with much patting-on-the-back as he entered. Once again, though, the frequent European press articles were reduced to a scant paragraph or so on the third page of the sports section in his hometown newspapers. We had expected front-page headlines with the mayor of Detroit shown handing Norb the key to the city!

That same year, Hepburn did indeed establish yet another world record in the clean and press during the British Commonwealth Games. But even so, his new total of 1,037 pounds in the three Olympic lifts remained well below Schemansky's world record of 1,074.

Eventually, the latest issues of various magazines featured coverage of the European events. There were photos and articles covering Norb's sensational accomplishments, much to our delight. Norb, who seemed rather unaffected by these accolades, was generally relaxed and in a good mood, as he resumed activity with some light (for him) training. About the same time, we saw increasingly more published reports about an amazing, huge young strongman from Georgia, whose name was Paul Anderson. He had previously created a stir with his raw power. Could Anderson be developing into an American version of Doug Hepburn? Anderson, who at 5-foot-9 weighed even more than Hepburn, would then be yet another huge powerhouse for Norb to face. As 1954 faded into 1955, much to the amazement of expert commentators in the sport, and everyone else, this young man, who had a very limited training background, was rapidly overtaking Hepburn in pressing power! Hepburn was such a phenomenon, how could a young fledgling come out of nowhere and overtake him? Anderson had already achieved incredible leg strength, superceding all in the squat lift! He outweighed Norb by over 100 pounds! He had not yet, however, developed good technique in the snatch or clean & jerk, not close to equaling Norb's world records, and not even snatching his own bodyweight. He was a perfect example of how it is harder for a larger individual to lift his own bodyweight. But he was progressing very rapidly.

Norb would have to upgrade his training to a greater level than ever to compete against Anderson, Bradford, Davis, *et al* in the 1955 Senior Nationals to be held in Cleveland. Vic Seipke and Don Van Fleteren were training for the Mr. America bodybuilding competition, to be held in conjunction with the Senior Nationals, as it had been since its inception. Vic had won major national titles just below the Mr. America event, and was the leading contender. His training was very intense—doing sets of 10 repetitions in the full squat, for instance, with well over 300 pounds. Don's exceptional power was manifest in his training, such as strict seated dumbbell curls with 80-pound dumbbells! Norb knew that he would have to be ready to break his own world records at the Senior Nationals, if necessary, then break them again at the World Championships later in the year. Thus it would be possible for us to have both the great Norb Schemansky, national and world champion, and a Mr. America training at our club as well! What excitement!

Then a great catastrophe: Norb injured his back. At first we thought it to be a pulled muscle, a training setback that could possibly jeopardize his chances to succeed at the Senior Nationals. But as time went on, it became apparent that he was not recovering well at all. Time was getting to the point where we did not see how he could make it, even with the best therapy. This was a terrible disappointment. Norb was found to have damaged a disc in his spine. It was decided that corrective surgery was needed. But the road to recovery would be long, and doctors were saying he would not compete again. He eventually did reappear at the club, but he only did some bodybuilding exercises to keep his muscles in tone. It was disheartening. Life was now a struggle in many respects for Norb.

Of course, Norb finally did return, and in true championship style. By 1960 he was back in the Olympics, winning a bronze medal. Aside from our own Jim Bradford, who had also become bigger and stronger, his main competitors were now from the Soviet Union. Although Norb had gained so much muscular weight, these competitors were still even heavier than he. Most weighed around 300 pounds. Once again he found himself competing against top athletes who not only outweighed him by a considerable margin, but were younger. Much to their shock, the older and lighter Schemansky broke more records! A new U.S. record in the clean and jerk. Another new world record snatch! In the 1964 Olympic Games, Norb was the oldest lifter and may have been the oldest competitor in the entire games! Yet he still brought home a bronze medal, pushing the best, larger Soviet lifters to their limit, nearly beating them. They looked upon him with awe. As in 1960, in terms of pound-for-pound bodyweight, he was the best lifter of the three on the winners' podium. And they knew it.

In the decades since Norb retired, Olympic lifters—some helped by performance-enhancing drugs—have hoisted amounts unimaginable during his era. Nevertheless, Norbert Schemansky became the first weightlifter in history to win medals in four Olympic Games! No one can take that away. This record stood for thirty-six years. Only a handful from any sport have now done that. He is truly one of the greatest Olympians. Only in recent years have three other weightlifters joined Schemansky in that select club. It must be remembered that "Skee" had to miss the 1956 Games. He is widely regarded as the greatest American Olympic weightlifter. Certainly, he is regarded as one of the greatest from any country. Furthermore, as my friends and I speculated back in 1955 as to what might have occurred if he had been at his best competing against Paul Anderson, there is no doubt in my mind what would have happened in 1956—another Olympic medal for Norb. Therefore, it is safe to say that had he not injured his back, he would have won medals in five Olympic Games.

When I get to thinking about those marvelous times, the golden years of American weightlifting and a golden period for America in general, there is so much that comes to mind. But no memory is sweeter or has greater meaning for me than how very nice a great Olympic champion was to two aspiring young teenagers.

Acknowledgments

I'd like to extend my thanks to the father-son team of Mike Reddy and Del Reddy at Immortal Investments Publishing, who thought Norb Schemansky's life story was worth writing about and insisted that I was the fellow to write it. Del was especially helpful in tracking down scores of obscure weightlifting publications and conducting many of the interviews.

I'd also like to acknowledge the contributions of a number of Norb's family members, friends, and weightlifting contemporaries. Their reminiscences helped make this a richer book than it otherwise would have been. Thanks to: Clarence Bass, Bruce Baumgartner, Ike Berger, Jim Bradford, Don Bragg, Frank Cwik, Artie Dreschler, Clyde Emrich, Mary Beth Fox, Charles Fraser, Dr. Pete George, Sid Henry, Don Howard, Emerick Ishikawa, Harry Johnson, Mike Karchut, Al Koernke, Tommy Kono, Phil Levine, Helen Mamalakis, Steve Mansour, Paul Paruk, Pam Petro, Joe Pitman, Joe Puleo, John Reddy, Louis Riecke, Joe Roark, Laura Rowe, Larry Schemansky, Jim Schmitz, Vic Seipke, Frank Spellman, Paula Sperka, Doug Stalker, Dr. Bob Suchyta, Richard Tom, Frank Zane, and Esther Zoran. Special thanks to Al Oerter for writing the foreword and to Mike Kuhne for providing the afterword.

Finally, thanks to Norb himself, with whom I was pleased to discover some common ground. Both of us were born and raised in Detroit and, outside of military service, have spent our entire adult lives in Dearborn, buying houses, paying taxes, and sending our kids to school there. Both of us are third-generation working-class Polish-American Catholics with mixed memories of the confessional and the shop floor. And both of us heartily endorse the health benefits of fresh kielbasa and cold beer. However, Norb has always had a reputation for taking on all interviewers, so such built-in rapport was probably superfluous. He patiently sat through hours of questioning (not always an easy task considering his chronic back troubles) and answered every query in the methodical and honest way he's known for. Although there was an occasional fly on the *golombki* en route to getting this manuscript finished, all in all

I found it a rewarding experience revisiting a more innocent era in sport with one of the true unsung heroes in Olympic history.

Hopefully, this book will resurrect the memory of Norb's many achievements, and the subject of this biography will stick around long enough to enjoy any renaissance of recognition it may inspire. To that end I offer Norbert Schemansky, the exemplar of what it used to mean to be an athlete playing purely for the love of competition and country, the traditional Polish salutation: *Sto lat, sto lat, niech zyje, zyje nam!* That is: "A hundred years, a hundred years, may he live for us!"

Richard Bak
Dearborn, Michigan
October 6, 2006

Appendix A

The Three Olympic Lifts

During Norb Schemansky's career, weightlifting competitions involved the three "Olympic lifts": the two-hand military press, the two-hand snatch, and the two-hand clean-and-jerk. (The press was eliminated after the 1972 Olympics because of the growing difficulty in judging it.) The rulebook of the Amateur Athletic Union of the United States, the national organization that began sanctioning nonprofessional lifting competitions in 1927, spelled out the proper movements for each of the lifts:

Two Hands Military Press

First Movement

The bar must be laid horizontally in front of the lifter's feet, gripped with both hands and brought with one single distinct motion up to the shoulders while either lunging or springing on bent legs. The bar is then rested on the chest or on the arms closely flexed. The feet must be brought back on the same line not more than 16 inches apart.

Second Movement

When in this position, hold the bar motionless for 2 seconds standing still. The time will be indicated by the clap of the judge's hands. The bar is then lifted up vertically until the arms are completely extended without any jerking or sudden starting. When the motion is completed, another stop of at least 2 seconds is required, the arms and legs stiffened. During the entire lift, the lifter's body, as well as his head, must constantly remain in the vertical position.

Important Remarks

As a rule, the bar must touch the chest before performing the second motion, which must not commence until the judge gives the signal by clapping his hands. Lifters who are unable to rest the bar on their chests must inform the judges of this fact before commencing the test. For this class of competitors the starting position of the press, as far as the uplifting proper is concerned, shall be indicated by the meeting point of the collarbone with the sternum.

Cause of Disqualification
Any departure of the body or head from the vertical position; any foot work (heel lift or toe raise, etc.); any bending of the legs; any uneven raising of the arms during the uplifting, will be cause for disqualifying the lifter on that attempt.

Two Hands Snatch

The bar is laid horizontally in front of the athlete's feet, gripped with both hands and pulled with one continuous motion from the ground to arms' length raised vertically above the head, while either lunging or springing on bent legs.

The bar is passed with a continuous, non-stop motion along the body. No other part of the body except the feet may touch or graze the ground while the lift is being performed.

The uplifted weight must be held for 2 seconds motionless in the final position with the arms and legs stiff and the feet in the same line not more than 16 inches apart. This motion must be done while the hands are extended direct from the shoulders. The hands may not move or slide along the bar once the grip has been taken.

Important
In this lift the fundamental principle is a single motion. No slowing of movement shall be permitted until the wrists turn over, which shall not take place until the bar has reached higher than the top of the lifter's head.

Two Hands Clean and Jerk

The bar is laid horizontally in front of the athlete's feet, gripped with both hands and brought with a single distinct motion from the ground to the shoulders while either lunging or springing on bent legs.

The bar must not touch the chest before reaching its final position at the shoulders, there to rest on the chest or on the closely flexed arms.

The feet are brought back to the original position; that is, on the same line. Then the legs are bent and both legs and arms are then stiffened suddenly with a jerk so as to lift the bar to the end of the vertically raised arms.

The weight is held motionless in this final position for 2 seconds, the feet on the same line and not more than 16 inches apart with the knees and arms stiffened. It is illegal to repeat the uplifting.

Incorrect Motions

Leaning with a knee on the ground or any shouldering in the course of which the bar may touch any part of the body before finally reaching the shoulders; elbows coming in contact with the thighs in the Two-Hand Clean Movement, shall be cause for disqualification.

General Particulars

Each participant has the privilege of three trials for each scheduled event and not for each weight. The increase of weights between each trial must not be less than 10 pounds, except the last one, when it may be 5 pounds. A premature increase of 5 pounds denotes the last try. The judges will count as a trial all exercises during the course of which the athlete steps off the platform. When a lifter fails to complete an exercise, the judges shall accord him a rest of not more than 3 minutes before the next attempt, but in no case may the weight be removed from the platform until the lifter completes the exercise, unless it is to be replaced by a heavier weight.

In case of a tie in a weight division, the lighter of the two contestants shall be declared the winner. No lifter shall be permitted to compete in a heavier class than that in which he weighs on the scales. In all lifts the judge shall register as a trial any attempt not completed in which strain was evidently exerted, especially attempts in which the implement reaches the height of the knees. In the event of a new record, both the competitor and the bell shall be weighed immediately after the lift. Existing records must be exceeded by one full pound in order for one to qualify for a new standard.

The participant shall hold the bell at arm's length directly above the head, the feet parallel, until the referee instructs him to lower the bell, which shall be done by a downward motion of the arm. At each trial, the name of the competitor, club, class and weight to be lifted shall be announced.

Appendix B

Norb Schemansky's Career Highlights

(Note: Schemansky never finished lower than third in any international tournament.)

Olympic Games

Year	Classification	Finish	Venue
1948	Heavyweight	Silver medal	London, England
1952	Middle-heavyweight	Gold medal	Helsinki, Finland
1960	Heavyweight	Bronze medal	Rome, Italy
1964	Heavyweight	Bronze medal	Tokyo, Japan

World Championships

Year	Classification	Finish	Venue
1947	Heavyweight	Second place	Philadelphia, PA
1951	Middle-heavyweight	First place	Milan, Italy
1953	Middle-heavyweight	First place	Stockholm, Sweden
1954	Heavyweight	First place	Vienna, Austria
1962	Heavyweight	Second place	Budapest, Hungary
1963	Heavyweight	Second place	Stockholm, Sweden

Pan-American Games

Year	Classification	Finish	Venue
1955	Heavyweight	Gold medal	Mexico City, Mexico

A.A.U. Senior Nationals

Year	Classification	Finish	Venue
1947	Heavyweight	Second place	Chicago, IL
1948	Heavyweight	Second place	New York, NY
1949	Heavyweight	First place	Cleveland, OH
1950	Heavyweight	Second place	Philadelphia, PA
1951	Middle-heavyweight	First place	Los Angeles, CA
1952	Middle-heavyweight	First place	New York, NY
1953	Middle-heavyweight	First place	Indianapolis, IN
1954	Heavyweight	First place	Los Angeles, CA
1957	Heavyweight	First place	Daytona Beach, FL
1959	Heavyweight	Third place	York, PA
1960	Heavyweight	Second place	Cleveland, OH
1962	Heavyweight	First place	Highland Park, MI
1963	Heavyweight	Second place	Harrisburg, PA
1964	Heavyweight	First place	Chicago, IL
1965	Heavyweight	First place	Los Angeles, CA
1966	Heavyweight	Third place	York, PA

North American Championships

Year	Classification	Finish	Venue
1949	Heavyweight	First place	Montreal, Canada
1950	Heavyweight	First place	Montreal, Canada
1952	Heavyweight	First place	Montreal, Canada
1957	Heavyweight	First place	Montreal, Canada
1959	Heavyweight	First place	Quebec City, Quebec
1963	Heavyweight	First place	Trenton, Ontario
1964	Heavyweight	First place	York, PA

National Y.M.C.A. Championships

Year	Classification	Finish	Venue
1950	Heavyweight	First place	Baltimore, MD
1951	Heavyweight	First place	Detroit, MI
1952	Heavyweight	First place	Cincinnati, OH
1954	Heavyweight	First place	Providence, RI
1955	Heavyweight	First place	Washington, DC
1964	Heavyweight	First place	Los Angeles, CA
1965	Heavyweight	First place	Wilmington, DE
1966	Heavyweight	First place	Detroit, MI

A.A.U. Junior Nationals

Year	Classification	Finish	Venue
1946	Heavyweight	First place	Akron, OH

I.W.F. World Records (Middle-Heavyweight Class)

Snatch

Date	Weight (Lbs.)	Venue
June 15, 1951	295	Los Angeles, CA
July 27, 1952	297½	Helsinki, Finland
July 27, 1952	308½	Helsinki, Finland

Clean and Jerk

Date	Weight (Lbs.)	Venue
June 16, 1951	370¾	Los Angeles, CA
October 28, 1951	374¾	Milan, Italy
October 28, 1951	385¾	Milan, Italy
July 27, 1952	391¼	Helsinki, Finland
August 30, 1953	398¾	Stockholm, Sweden

Three-Lift Total

Date	Weight (Lbs.)	Venue
October 28, 1951	942¼	Milan, Italy
July 27, 1952	980¾	Helsinki, Finland

I. W. F. World Records (Heavyweight Class)

Snatch

Date	**Weight (Lbs.)**	**Venue**
October 10, 1954	330½	Vienna, Austria
March 16, 1955	*333	Mexico City, Mexico
January 14, 1961	343½	Detroit, MI
February 25, 1961	351	Baltimore, MD
April 28, 1962	362	Detroit, MI

Clean and Jerk

Date	**Weight (Lbs.)**	**Venue**
October 25, 1952	408	Philadelphia, PA
January 17, 1953	412½	York, PA
June 25, 1954	416½	Los Angeles, CA
October 4, 1954	418¾	Copenhagen, Denmark
October 17, 1954	424¼	Lille, France

Three-Lift Total

Date	**Weight (Lbs.)**	**Venue**
October 4, 1954	*1,068¾	Copenhagen, Denmark
October 10, 1954	1,074¼	Vienna, Austria

U.S. National Records (Middle-Heavyweight Class)

Press

Date	Weight (Lbs.)	Venue
June 15, 1951	270	Los Angeles, CA
October 28, 1951	275½	Milan, Italy
July 27, 1952	281	Helsinki, Finland

Snatch

Date	Weight (Lbs.)	Venue
June 15, 1951	295	Los Angeles, CA
July 27, 1952	297½	Helsinki, Finland
July 27, 1952	308½	Helsinki, Finland

Clean and Jerk

Date	Weight (Lbs.)	Venue
June 15, 1951	350	Los Angeles, CA
June 16, 1951	370¾	Los Angeles, CA
October 28, 1951	374¾	Milan, Italy
October 28, 1951	385¾	Milan, Italy
July 27, 1952	391¼	Helsinki, Finland
August 30, 1953	398¾	Stockholm, Sweden

Three-Lift Total

Date	Weight (Lbs.)	Venue
June 15, 1951	915	Los Angeles, CA
October 28, 1951	920¼	Milan, Italy
October 28, 1951	931¼	Milan, Italy
October 28, 1951	942¼	Milan, Italy
July 27, 1952	953¼	Helsinki, Finland
July 27, 1952	963¾	Helsinki, Finland
July 27, 1952	980¾	Helsinki, Finland

U.S. National Records (Heavyweight Class)

Snatch

Date	Weight (Lbs.)	Venue
October 10, 1954	330½	Vienna, Austria
March 16, 1955	333	Mexico City, Mexico
January 14, 1961	343½	Detroit, MI
February 25, 1961	351	Baltimore, MD
April 28, 1962	362	Detroit, MI
October 18, 1964	363¾	Tokyo, Japan

Clean & Jerk

Date	Weight (Lbs.)	Venue
October 25, 1952	408	Philadelphia, PA
January 17, 1953	412½	York, PA
June 25, 1954	416½	Los Angeles, CA
October 4, 1954	418¾	Copenhagen, Denmark
October 17, 1954	424¼	Lille, France
February 2, 1964	*445	Detroit, MI

Three-Lift Total

Date	Weight (Lbs.)	Venue
October 4, 1954	1,068¾	Copenhagen, Denmark
October 10, 1954	1,074¼	Vienna, Austria
September 22, 1962	1,184¾	Budapest, Hungary

* Unofficial record

Bibliography

"American A.-A. Guns In Action During An Enemy Raid On London." *The Illustrated London News*, February 12, 1944.

"Anderson Raises 3 Weight Records." *New York Times*, June 2, 1956.

"Anderson Winner in Weight Lifting." *New York Times*, October 17, 1955.

"Area 'Lift' Champ Denied Red Trip." *Detroit World*, March 21-27, 1962.

"Ashman, U. S., Loses to Russian, Then Sets World Lifting Record." *New York Times*, September 22, 1958.

Baker, Chris. "John Davis: Not Even Strongman Can Win Battle Against Cancer." *Los Angeles Times*, January 27, 1984.

Barnas, Jo-Ann. "The Forgotten Olympian." *Detroit Free Press*, July 1, 1996.

Barnes, Ronnie J. "Paul Anderson & I." *Iron Man*, May, 1969.

Bennett, Bob, and Bob Carroll. "The Uplifting Story of Paul Anderson." *Saturday Evening Post*, November 1, 1988.

Berry, Jack. "Schemansky remains proud of medal feats." *Detroit News*, March 7, 1976.

Bloch, James F. *Sam Karres: Urban Expressionist*. Royal Oak, Mich.: Centaur Books, 2002.

Bowen, Ezra. "Think and Lift." *Sports Illustrated*, December 20, 1954.

"Bradford Competes in Olympics Today." *The Washington Post*, September 10, 1960.

Brown, Clifton. "Weight lifter who was ahead of his time." *Detroit Free Press*, June 9, 1983.

Carlson, Lewis H., and John J. Fogarty. *Tales of Gold: An Oral History of the Summer Olympic Games Told by America's Gold Medal Winners*. Chicago: Contemporary Books, 1987.

Conley, John. "Norbert Schemansky Holds World Title." *East Side Shopper*, December 27, 1951.

Coster, Charles. "Norbert Schemansky: Greatest Middle Heavyweight Lifter of All Time." *Muscle Power*, November, 1952.

Cotsonika, Nicholas J. *Century of Champions*. Detroit: Detroit Free Press, 1999.

Dann, Marshall. "Lifter Has a Problem." *Detroit Free Press*, February 1, 1954.

"Davis, Schemansky Excel." *New York Times*, July 28, 1952.

Desbonnet, Edmond. *The Kings of Strength*. France, 1911.

Drechsler, Arthur J. "Norbert Schemansky: A Comeback of Comebacks." *The Association of Oldetime Barbell & Strongmen Newsletter*, August, 2003.

Drechsler, Arthur J. *The Weightlifting Encyclopedia*. Flushing, N. Y.: A Is A Communications, 1998.

Epstein, Edward. "Schwarzenegger linked to contest with steroids." *San Francisco Chronicle*, October 1, 2003.

Fair, John D. *Muscletown USA: Bob Hoffman and the Manly Culture of York Barbell.* University Park, Pa.: Pennsylvania State University Press, 1999.

Fair, John D. "Olympic Weightlifting and the Introduction of Steroids: A Statistical Analysis of World Championship Results, 1948-1972." *The International Journal on the History of Sport*, Spring, 1988.

Falls, Joe. "He's King Without a Kingdom." *Detroit Free Press*, December 6, 1964.

Falls, Joe. "Schemansky's Day Came Too Late." *Detroit Free Press*, May 21, 1976.

"Final Trials Slated for Weight Lifters." *New York Times*, August 23, 1964.

Fischer, David. *The Encyclopedia of the Summer Olympics.* Danbury, Conn.: Watts Reference, 2004.

Forgeron, Henry V. "Davis' Talent Covers Barbells and Bel Canto." *New York Times*, October 10, 1955.

Fraser, Charles. "Training at Olympic Lifting." East Lansing, Mich.: M.S.U. Olympic Lifting Club, n.d.

Frommer, Harvey. *Olympic Controversies*. New York: Franklin Watts, 1987.

Gay, Arthur. "TERRIFIC is the Word for Stanczyk." *Your Physique*, December, 1947.

"George Lifts 885 Lbs." *New York Times*, June 24, 1957.

Glick, Shavenau. "But Schemansky, 41, Goes on and on—His Goal: Another Olympics." *Los Angeles Times*, June 14, 1965.

Gorgon, Dave. "Miffed. Local Olympic hero Schemansky—despite 26 world records in weightlifting—remains a forgotten man." *Dearborn Times-Herald*, July 12, 1979.

Green, Jerry. "Renowned lifter recalls life as true amateur." *Detroit News*, January 21, 2002.

Greenspan, Bud. "Flowers For An Olympian." *Sports Illustrated*, April 14, 1986.

"Gubner the Weight-Lifter Hopes to Equal Gubner the Shot-Putter." *New York Times*, April 16, 1962.

Guttmann, Allen. *The Olympics: A History of the Modern Games*. Chicago: University of Illinois Press, 1992.

Halls, Bill. "Sports greats feted." *Detroit News*, May 21, 1976.

Hoffman, Bob. "Budapest World Championships." *Strength & Health*, January, 1963.

Hoffman, Bob. "Moscow Revisited." *Strength & Health*, July, 1963.

Hoffman, Bob. "1962 Senior National A.A.U. Championships." *Strength & Health*, September, 1962.

Hoffman, Bob. "The Apollon Bell Meets Its Master." *Strength & Health*, February, 1955.

Hoffman, Bob. "The Russian Pressing Style." *Strength & Health*, March, 1963.

Hoffman, Bob. "Wise Words From A Great Champion." *Strength & Health*, August, 1963.

"Hold Lifting Trials Today For Olympics." *Chicago Daily Tribune*, June 20, 1948.

Hollister, Vernon. "Norbert Schemansky. . . the 'Old Master.'" *Strength & Health*, July and August, 1973.

"How Russia became sports power." *Detroit News*, May 3, 1970.

Ivanov, Dmitry. *The Strongest Man in the World: Vasili Alexeyev*. New York: Sphinx Press, 1979.

Johnson, William O. "The Best At Everything." *Sports Illustrated*, April 14, 1975.

Keller, Bill. "Olympic Star, in Passionate Talk, Attacks K.G.B. in Soviet Congress." *New York Times*, May 31, 1989.

Kennedy, Robert. "Mr. Strength—Paul Anderson." *Iron Man*, May, 1969.

Kiiha, Osmo. "Dave Sheppard." *The Iron Master*, April, 1994.

Kiiha, Osmo. "John Henry Davis." *The Iron Master*, April, 1993.

Kiiha, Osmo. "Joseph R. Puleo." *The Iron Master*, January, 1993.

Kiiha, Osmo. "Norbert Schemansky." *The Iron Master*, October, 1992.

Kiiha, Osmo. "Stanley Anthony Stanczyk." www.naturalstrength.com.

Killanin, Lord, and John Rodda (eds.). *The Olympic Games 1984*. Salem, N.H.: Michael Joseph, 1984.

Kirkley, George. "Controversial decision helps Vlasov to survive." *The Strength Athlete*, June, 1975.

Kirkley, George. "The 1951 World's Weightlifting Championships." *The Weightlifter & Bodybuilder*, January, 1952.

Kirkley, George. "The Weightlifting World in 1955." In *Health & Strength Annual 1956*. York, Pa.: Health & Strength Publishing Co., 1956.

Korsgaard, Robert. "A History of the Amateur Athletic Union of the United States." Ed.d thesis, Columbia University, 1952.

Kram, Mark. "Looking for a Lift." *Sports Illustrated*, September 12, 1966.

Kuhne, Michael. "My Personal Recollections of Norbert Schemansky." Unpublished manuscript.

Lawson, Larry. "Paul Anderson Modern Superman—And How He Trains." *Iron Man*, March, 1956.

Lechenperg, Harald (ed.). *Olympic Games 1960*. New York: A. S. Barnes & Co., 1960.

"Leonid Zhabotinsky—honored master of acting." *Strength & Health*, February, 1965.

"Leonid Zhabotinsky Talks About Himself, His Friends, His Lifting." *Iron Man Lifting News*, May, 1967.

"Lifter Gains Fourth Trip To Olympics." *Washington Post*, August 24, 1964.

Litsky, Frank. "Vote-Seeker Makes a Representative Showing Here." *New York Times*, August 23, 1964.

"Major Lee Named for Sullivan Trophy as Exemplar of Good Sportsmanship." *New York Times*, December 31, 1953.

Mamalakis, Helen K. "Norbert Schemansky: A Champion Among Dearbornites." *Dearborn Historian*, Summer, 1996.

Marsh, Richard. "Elmhurst Park name changed to honor local Olympic champion." *Dearborn Press & Guide*, August 8, 1996.

Marsh, Richard. "Norbert Schemansky; Won four medals in weight lifting in four Olympics." *Dearborn Press & Guide*, September 28, 2000.

"Mel Whitfield Given Sullivan Award for '54." *Los Angeles Times*, December 31, 1954.

Moss, Charles. "Why the American Team Won!" *Strength & Health*, January, 1951.

Moyset, Rene. "A Tribute to Charles Rigoulot." *Strength & Health*, January, 1963.

Murphy, Jim. "Exclusive!" *Harrisburg Patriot-News*, June 19, 1966.

Murray, Jim. "John Davis: Iron Game Immortal." *Strength & Health*, June, 1954.

Murray, Jim. "Training Programs and Best Lifts of the Fabulous 'Skee.'" *Strength & Health*, February, 1954.

O'Brien, Alan. "1957 Sr. National Championships." *Iron Man Lifting News*, June, 1957.

"Olympian Breaks Mark in AAU Lifting Meet." *Los Angeles Times*, June 12, 1965.

"Olympians' flames still burn." *Detroit Free Press*, October 14, 1984.

Park, Reg. "My Tour of America." *Iron Man*, October, 1956.

Paschall, Harry B. "Strongest Man Who Ever Lived." *Iron Man*, January, 1956.

Peale, Norman Vincent. "Positive Thoughts Elevate Barbell." *The Washington Post*, March 5, 1955.

Preibus, Fred. "Never Worse Than Third." *Sports Fans' Journal*, June, 1989.

Puscas, George. "Big Norbert Finally Makes Michigan Hall." *Detroit Free Press*, March 7, 1976.

Pyle, Ernie. "American Ack-Ack." In Ernie Pyle, *Brave Men*. New York, Henry Holt, 1944.

Rader, Peary. "Heavyweights Sensation Of Senior Nationals." *Iron Man*, August, 1962.

Rader, Peary. "World Weight Lifting Championships 1947." *Iron Man*, November, 1947.

Randall, Bruce. "Norbert Schemansky: A Marvelous Physical Speciman." *Iron Man*, December, 1964.

Rinehart, Mary Ann. "Mr. President." *Weightlifting U.S.A.*, March, 1993.

Robinson, Stewart. "Muscles By Mail." *The Family Circle*, January 20, 1939.

"Russia's Vlasov Keeps Weightlifting Title." *The Washington Post*, September 23, 1962.

"Russian is First in Weight Lifting; Vlasov Breaks World Mark 3 Times in Olympics—Americans 2d and 3d." *New York Times*, September 11, 1960.

"Russians Triumph in Weight-Lifting." *New York Times*, August 31, 1953.

Schemansky, Norb (as told by Bob Hasse). "Norbert Schemansky's Tips on Training—the Clean." *Strength & Health*, December, 1959.

"Schemansky Betters Weightlifting Record." *New York Times*, April 30, 1962.

"Schemansky on Top in Olympic Weight Trials." *Los Angeles Times*, August 23, 1964.

"Schemansky Wins Title." *Los Angeles Times*, June 24, 1957.

Silver, Bernie. "The Sporting Life." *Dearborn Press*, July 28, 1966.

"Soft Jobs For Lifters." *Detroit Times*, August 23, 1960.

"Soviet Athlete First in Lifting; Vlasov Beats Schemansky in World Competition." *New York Times*, September 23, 1962.

"Soviet Lifters Set Four World Records." *New York Times*, December 23, 1961.

State, Oscar. "Behind the Scenes at Milan." *The Weightlifter & Bodybuilder*, January, 1952.

Stephens, Hal. "Sr. National Championships And Mr. America Contest." *Iron Man*, September, 1954.

Symon, Charles A. *We Can Do It! A History of the CCC in Michigan, 1933-1942*. Gladstone, Mich.: RonJon Press, 1983.

Talluto, Pete. "Impressions From Russia." *Strength & Health*, July, 1973.

Tarapacki, Thomas M. *Chasing the American Dream: Polish Americans in Sports*. New York: Hippocrene, 1995.

"The 50 Greatest Sports Figures From Michigan." *Sports Illustrated*, December 27, 1999.

Tuckner, Howard M. "N. Y. U. Athlete Does 401 in the Last Phase of Event; Gubner Beats Schemansky." *New York Times*, April 8, 1962.

United States Army in World War II. The War Against Germany: Europe and Adjacent Areas. Washington, D. C.: Center of Military History, U. S. Army, 1951.

U. S. Army. *184th AAA Gun Bn*. Fulda, Germany, 1945.

U. S. Army. *The Story of Antwerp X*. Germany, 1945.

"U. S. Stars Score in Weight-Lifting; Schemansky, Kono Set World Records as Russia Retains Title in Vienna Meet." *New York Times*, October 11, 1954.

"U. S. Team Heavy Favorite." *New York Times*, August 26, 1953.

Van, George E. "Weight Champ's Return Dismal." *Detroit Times*, February 22, 1956.

Waldmeir, Pete. "World's Strongest Man Also Is World Traveler." *Detroit News*, November 16, 1954.

"Wayne County Commission line-up." *Dearborn Press*, July 29, 1976.

Webster, David. *Bodybuilding: An Illustrated History*. New York: Arco, 1982.

"Weight Mark to Schemansky." *New York Times*, April 16, 1951.

"Weight Men in AAU Meet." *Los Angeles Times*, June 23, 1961.

"Weight-Lift Title Goes to Stanczyk." *New York Times*, May 23, 1949.

"Weightlift Mark Set; Schemansky Hoists 416½ Pounds for National Mark." *New York Times*, June 22, 1954.

"Weight-Lifters of U. S. and Soviet Get Together; Result: Ping-Pong." *New York Times*, August 23, 1953.

"Weight-Lifting Meet Ends." *New York Times*, August 12, 1948.

Wilhelm, Bruce. "Norbert Schemansky: Sweet Performances, Bitter Memories." *Milo*, April, 1995.

Willoughby, David P. "Early American Strongmen." *Iron Man*, April, 1960.

Willoughby, David P. "Famous American Strongmen Of The Nineties." *Iron Man*, February, 1960.

Willoughby, David P. "How Strong Was Charles Rigoulot?" *Muscle Power*, July, 1953.

Willoughby, David P. *The Super Athletes*. Cranbury, N.J.: A. S. Barnes & Co., 1970.

"Wilson Laments Amateurs' Status." *New York Times*, November 29, 1954.

"Winter Olympics 2002." www.usnews.com, January 28, 2002.

Wolf, Al. "Gary Gubner Enters Times Games." *Los Angeles Times*, January 27, 1963.

"World's strongest man, the conqueror of the Russians." *Detroit News*, January 15, 1955.

Yablokova, Oksana. "Gymnast Recalls 1952 Olympics." *St. Petersburg Times*, August 17, 2004.

Yesalis, Charles E., and Virginia S. Cowart. *The Steroids Game*. Champaign, Ill.: Human Kinetics, 1998.

Yorobyov, Arkady. "Paul Anderson's Moscow Triumph." *Iron Game History*, October, 1995.

Index